A Complete Guide to
Brass

A Complete Guide to

Brass

Instruments and Technique

SECOND EDITION

SCOTT WHITENER

Rutgers University

Illustrations by

CATHY L. WHITENER

SCHIRMER BOOKS

NEW YORK

Schirmer Books

1633 Broadway
New York, NY 10019

Library of Congress Catalog Number: 96–9849

Printed in the United States of America

Printing number:

3 4 5 6 7 8 9 10

Library of Congress Cataloging-in-Publication Data

Whitener, Scott.
    A complete guide to brass : instruments and technique / Scott
Whitener ; illustrations by Cathy L. Whitener. — 2nd ed.
      p. cm.
    Includes discography (p.), bibliographical references (p.),
and index.
    ISBN 0–02–864597–9 (alk. paper)
    1. Brass instruments. 2. Brass instruments—Instruction and
study.   I. Whitener, Cathy L.   II. Title.
ML933.W52   1997
788.9'19—dc20   96–9849
                                                    CIP
                                                    MN

To the memory of my parents,
E. DeWitt and Irma M. Whitener

Contents

APPENDICES

Preface

It is gratifying to any author to be invited to prepare a second edition of a book. I am thus grateful for the interest shown in this work and for the acceptance it has received. This new edition contains many revisions to reflect the current state of my research as well as a full presentation of my method of teaching. As before, the book has three purposes: to serve as a text for college brass techniques courses; to serve as a reference book for brass players, composers, conductors, or anyone interested in the world of brass; and, most importantly, to set forth a method of playing.

The book is divided into two parts. Chapters 1 through 9 contain discussions of the instruments and an outline of their historical development. Chapters 10 through 13 are concerned with the techniques of playing. Chapter 14 is directed to conductors.

In bringing forth this edition, I would like to acknowledge my debt to the work of the great tubist Arnold Jacobs. Mr. Jacobs has made an enormous contribution to modern brass playing. I would also like to express my deep appreciation to Scott Mendoker for bringing me into contact with Mr. Jacobs and his ideas.

Many people have contributed to this book, and without their assistance it could not have been written. In particular, I am indebted to Lawrence Benz, Scott Mendoker, Ann Teehan-Mendoker, Dr. B. P. Leonard, Vernon Post, Matthew Paterno, and Col. Gilbert Mitchell for their comments and suggestions for this edition; and to Paul Hlebowitsh, Dr. Richard Plano, Dr. John Bewley, Kenneth Kemmerer, Dr. Robert Grechesky, Dr. Jonathan Korzun, Ralph Acquaro, and Dr. William Trusheim for their help with the original edition.

An important aspect of this book has been to include photographs of leading brass players to illustrate some of the points emphasized in the text. I would therefore like to express my appreciation to Arnold Jacobs, Dale Clevenger, Jay Friedman, Charles Schlueter, Philip Jones, George Coble, Peter Bond, Frøydis Ree Wekre, Barry Tuckwell, Peter Sullivan, Steven Kellner, and Dr. Brian Bowman. Thanks are also due to my friend Steven DeSee, who collected many of the photographs that appeared in the original edition and are continued here, and Brooke McEldowney (the Brooke of *9 Chickweed Lane* of the comic strips) for the gift of one of his musical cartoons.

In addition, I am grateful to Vincent Cichowicz, trumpet maker Joseph Hetman, Prof. Roland Berger of the Vienna Philharmonic, Margaret Fletcher, Philip and Ursula Jones, Prof. William Fielder, Scott Woska, Peter Del Vecchio, Alan Charlesworth, Keith Clark, my editor, Jonathan Wiener of Schirmer Books, production editor James Hatch, and copyeditor Carol Anne Peschke.

Most of all, I am grateful to my wife, Cathy, who painstakingly prepared all of the line drawings and contributed in incalculable ways to the completion of this work; and to my daughters, Alexandra and Diana, for their forbearance during this process.

Scott Whitener

PART ONE

INSTRUMENTS

CHAPTER 1

How Brass Instruments Work

Brass instruments are among the oldest of all instruments. In antiquity, simple instruments such as the Scandinavian *lur* and the Roman *buccina* admirably fulfilled their ceremonial and musical functions. As each epoch unfolded, instruments were modified to serve the musical requirements of the new era. The line of development from ancient to modern is a process of refinement of a basic idea: the sounding of a flared tube through the vibration of the lips. Although the outward appearance of the instruments has changed, their internal operation has not changed over the last millennium.

In years past, brass instrument makers working with leading players evolved some excellent instruments by trial and error without really understanding the acoustical processes that were taking place. Speculative theories, sometimes inaccurate, surrounded discussions of how the instruments actually functioned. Now, due to the research of acousticians such as Arthur H. Benade,[1] the basic principles at work within the tubing of a brass instrument have been established objectively.

The sound of a brass instrument is made by the vibration of the lips initiating and maintaining a longitudinal standing wave in the air enclosed within the instrument's tubing. The tapered bell flare, which is of great importance, is designed to contain acoustical energy within the instrument in order to set up standing waves at specific frequencies. The player's embouchure may be seen as a flow-control valve acting on the steady air flow coming from the lungs. The closed lips are blown apart, setting them into vibration. Puffs of air are thereby emitted into the mouthpiece, setting in motion a sound wave that eventually reaches the instrument's expanding bell. As the bell flare widens, the wave encounters a drop in impedance (resistance) that, perhaps surprisingly, causes it to reflect back toward the mouthpiece (Figure 1.1). It is then reflected at the mouthpiece, where it is modified by the motion of the lips, encouraging a specific frequency dependent on the effective length of the vibrating air column. The oscillation of the lips (vibration) is itself modified by the reflecting wave so that its pattern of vibration corresponds to the instrument's timbre and the desired pitch. As the wave bounces back and forth while interacting with the instrument and the vibrating lips, the standing wave characteristic of brass instrument sound is formed. In reality, the process takes only a few hundredths of a second.

Although some acoustical energy leaks through the "barrier" in the expanding bell flare, most is reflected in the middle and low frequencies. As frequencies rise,

[1] See Arthur H. Benade, *Fundamentals of Musical Acoustics* (New York: Oxford University Press, 1976), pp. 391–429; also see Benade's article "The Physics of Brasses," *Scientific American* (July 1973), pp. 24–35. Another source is John Backus, *The Acoustical Foundations of Music,* 2nd ed. (New York: W.W. Norton, 1977), pp. 259–280. I am grateful to Dr. Richard J. Plano, Professor of Physics at Rutgers University, for enlightening discussions on this subject.

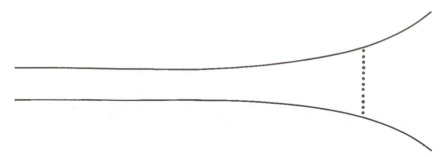

Figure 1.1 **Approximate point of wave reflection in a horn bell.**

the reflective threshold moves ever closer to the mouth of the bell and less energy is reflected. At this point the bell flare begins to operate more like an old-fashioned megaphone. This is why high notes are more difficult to play than pitches in the middle register.

In the production of a sustained tone, the fluctuations in pressure within the mouthpiece brought about by the standing wave help the embouchure to open and close in its vibrational pattern.[2] The player adjusts the embouchure and force of the air stream so that vibration at a specific frequency is favored. The changes in pressure within the mouthpiece act on the adjusted embouchure to produce a steady tone. The embouchure's vibrations per second correspond to the cycles per second of a specific pitch (for example, the tuning note A is 440 cycles per second). The pressure variations have been measured inside the mouthpiece and the peaks that occur at specific frequencies (indicating greater input impedance) recorded on a graph.[3] The resonance peaks—points at which the standing wave's amplitude is greatest—closely approximate the harmonic series in a well-designed brass instrument (these are the notes that can be played without using the valves). The length and shape of the instrument govern the pitches produced at the resonance peaks, but in each brass instrument the peaks always appear in the same pattern.

The Harmonic Series

Notes of the harmonic series are familiar to all brass players because a considerable amount of practice time is usually devoted to exercises based on them. Before the invention of valves, these were the only notes available to the natural trumpet and horn, although a technique of handstopping (used after 1750) allowed hornists to fill in the gaps between harmonics. What is not often recognized is the importance of the bell flare in deriving a usable harmonic series. If one attempts to play a harmonic series by inserting a mouthpiece into an appropriate length of cylindrical pipe, such as a garden hose, the following musically unusable series (approximating the odd numbered harmonics) results:[4]

[2] The opening and closing motion of the lips in vibration can be clearly seen in a videotape made by Ellis Wean (tubist of the Vancouver Symphony Orchestra) using TRU-VU transparent mouthpieces. Both the tape and TRU-VU mouthpieces are available from Ellis Music, 510–1333 Hornby St., Vancouver, B.C. V6Z 2C1, Canada.

[3] See Benade, *Fundamentals.*

[4] See Richard Merewether, *The Horn, The Horn* . . . (London: Paxman Musical Instruments Ltd., 1978), p. 36. The mouthpiece applied to a cylindrical tube also has an influence on the harmonic series; see Backus, *The Acoustical Foundations of Music*, pp. 260–268.

If a well-designed flared bell is attached, the harmonics are raised to form the standard harmonic series shown below:[5]

Although different fundamental pitches can be used, depending on the length of the instrument, the structure of the harmonic series is always the same. For example, the series for the horn in F (written in concert pitch) is

8va⌐

During the seventeenth and eighteenth centuries, trumpets were made with sufficient length to enable the player to use the area of the harmonic series that more or less resembles a diatonic scale. In modern trumpets, which are of shorter overall length, the fundamental is placed proportionally an octave higher, since the spaces between harmonics can be filled by notes played with the valves. The fundamental is positioned similarly in the other brass instruments, with the exception of the horn, which retains the octave-lower fundamental of the natural horn.

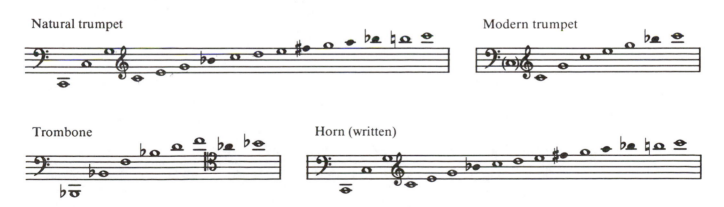

Natural trumpet

Modern trumpet

Trombone

Horn (written)

---

[5] Pitches are approximate for the two series shown. Certain harmonics do not agree with the equal-tempered scale (the most obvious of these are shown as quarter notes).

Another important aspect of the harmonic series is that partials of the series also sound in greater or lesser degree when a note is played. This is what defines the characteristic tone quality of an instrument. Also, notes with less sharply defined resonance peaks (making these notes more difficult to produce) are made more stable by the participation of other harmonically related peaks when the instrument is played at medium and loud dynamic levels.

Valves

The valve is an ingenious device that opens an additional section of tubing for the air column to pass through, thus lengthening the wind-path within the instrument and making available notes of the harmonic series of a different fundamental (this is accomplished on the trombone by extending the slide). The segments of tubing that can be added by the valves lower the fundamental by a tone (first valve), a semitone (second valve), and a tone-and-a-half (third valve).[6] The valves can also be used in combination by depressing valves simultaneously. The air column is then directed through the tubing of each valve that has been opened, making accessible up to three additional harmonic series (2–3, 1–3, 1–2–3).

Trumpet (fundamentals not shown)

By use of the various overtones of the seven harmonic series, the instrument is made fully chromatic.

Trumpet

Because the 7th, 11th, 13th, 14th, and 15th overtones of the harmonic series are not in tune in the equal temperament system in use today, they are replaced by valve notes. In the interest of finger dexterity, the 1–2 combination, which also low-

---

[6] This is true of a descending valve system. In France and parts of Belgium, a valve system was in use on the horn in which the third valve raised the pitch by one tone. In this system, the third valve is set to direct the air column through its tubing; when the valve is depressed, the third valve tubing is bypassed, raising the overall pitch of the instrument one tone (F to G; B♭ to C). Ascending horns began to fall out of fashion during the 1970s and were largely replaced by instruments constructed with the usual descending system. Players are still sometimes seen using ascending horns, and the idea (which offers some genuine advantages) may be revived in the future. The *cor ascendant* is discussed in Chapter 4. A fourth ascending valve was a feature of the Merri Franquin system trumpets, dating from the early twentieth century. When the fourth valve is depressed, the pitch of the trumpet is raised from C to D.

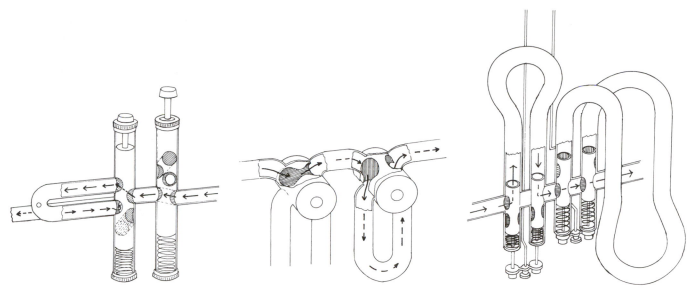

Figure 1.2 **Piston valve.**   Figure 1.3 **Rotary valve.**   Figure 1.4 **Vienna valve.**

ers the fundamental a tone-and-a-half, is normally used in place of the third valve alone. A basic problem of the valve system is inadequate tube length when the valves are used in combination, causing sharpness. Various approaches are used to correct this deficiency.[7]

There are three principal valve types in use today. All function similarly, but they differ in their method of opening and closing the ports between the main tube and the tubing that can be added by the valve. In each, the vibrating air column runs down the valve section from one end or the other (depending on the construction of the instrument) and, with the valves closed, continues directly into the bell flare. If a valve is depressed, the air column is sent through the valve tubing before it proceeds to the bell. The operation of the principal valve types can be seen in Figures 1.2, 1.3, and 1.4.

Piston valves offer a light, quick action but have less direct and accurate windways than the other two types. A shorter finger stroke may be used on rotary valves, but their action is not quite as immediate as that of piston valves. An advantage of the rotary type is that the diameter of the windway is maintained with somewhat greater consistency (although there is still some constriction), providing less resistance. Vienna valves (now found only on Vienna horns) cause the least disturbance to the air column, enabling the Vienna horn to play and sound more like the natural instrument. With the valves closed, the air column goes straight through the valve section, avoiding the angles and inconsistent windways inherent in rotary and piston designs. Although their action is not quite as fast as that of other valve types, Vienna valves contribute greater fluency and smoothness to slurred passages.[8]

In recent years, attention has been directed toward improving the response and timbre of the trombone's F attachment (and attachments in other keys). Previously, it was somewhat difficult to match the timbre of notes played on the attachment and those played in B♭. This led to the development of new types of change-valves with better windways. The first and best-known of these is the Thayer Axial-Flow valve,

---

[7] This problem is discussed in depth under "Intonation" in Chapter 6; related discussions appear under the same heading in Chapters 3 and 7.

[8] The Vienna valve is discussed further in Chapter 4.

which has received wide acceptance among trombonists. In this valve design, the diameter of the windway remains constant as it rotates from port to port. This offers improved response and tone quality. So far, the Thayer design has only found use as a change-valve for the trombone, although it was originally conceived for the horn. In addition to the Thayer valve, several instrument manufacturers have developed improved rotary change-valves.

In using any type of valve, it is important to recognize that there are only two positions: open and closed. Therefore, valves should always be depressed as quickly as possible to avoid an audible discontinuity between notes. In slow passages, students often tend to move their valves sluggishly. This produces an unattractive sound, particularly on slurs. Sometimes placing the finger tips slightly above the valve caps or levers encourages a quicker motion.

Design Considerations

Every brass instrument consists of four basic parts: the mouthpiece with its tapered backbore, a conical leadpipe, a section of cylindrical tubing containing the valves or slide, and the gradually expanding bell flare. The diameter of the bore, the shape and size of the tapered sections, the thickness and type of material, and overall mass are variables that cause instruments of the same type to play and sound differently.

Bore size is determined by the diameter of the tubing of the instrument's cylindrical section, although the bell throat and leadpipe taper usually conform to the main bore. Instruments of smaller bore generally respond with less effort and have a lighter tone. Their timbre tends to be brilliant and clear, but they can be overblown at high dynamic levels, causing an overlay of edge on the sound. Large-bore instruments typically have a darker, weightier tone that remains more consistent from soft to loud.

Along with the leadpipe taper, the shape of the bell taper and how it is made are of primary importance in determining both the quality of an instrument and the character of its timbre. The size of the bell, how sharply it is flared, and especially the diameter and taper of the bell throat strongly influence tone, intonation, and response. The rate of expansion of the bell section from the valves onward also has a significant effect on timbre. (Bell tapers are discussed in relation to the horn in Chapter 4). The method of construction of the bell governs the overall quality of the instrument. The finest bells are formed from sheet brass, which is beaten on a mandrel and then spun and brought to final shape on a lathe by hand. This work requires the skill of a master instrument maker and must be reflected in the instrument's price. Bells of this type have a strong, resonant tone that carries well. Brass instruments are made primarily from yellow brass, gold (red) brass, and nickel–silver alloys.[9] Each of these materials contributes certain qualities to the timbre, and players usually have definite opinions as to their respective merits. The Physikalisch-technische Bundesanstalt of Braunschweig, Germany, has investigated the influence of different alloys on horn timbre. The findings tend to confirm the views expressed in Chapter 4, but more research is needed to arrive at firm conclusions.[10] Other alloys, such as beryllium and sterling silver, are sometimes used as trumpet bell materials, and ambronze has been used in the construction of horns.

[9] The relative contents of the alloys are as follows: yellow brass, 70 percent copper and 30 percent zinc; gold (red) brass, 85 percent copper and 15 percent zinc; nickel–silver, 63 percent copper, 27 percent zinc and 10 to 12 percent nickel.

[10] The effect of different materials on timbre is considered in Chapters 4 and 5.

The finish that is applied to the metal is another issue of personal preference. Some feel that any type of finish degrades an instrument's tone and response; others find no important difference, or welcome the effect that lacquer or silver plating contributes. Plating and lacquer do serve as protective coatings and resist deterioration of the metal. Gold plating is more rarely used because of its cost.

An instrument's mass also affects its playing and tonal qualities. A heavier instrument normally has a darker and more solid timbre, but requires somewhat more exertion to play than a lighter one. Lighter instruments often feel more responsive and flexible to the player, but exhibit tonal differences from those of greater mass. Whether the difference is positive or negative is a subjective question that must be determined by the player in consideration of the music being performed or the performance situation. In general, instrument designers seek a careful balance between lightness and sufficient weight to produce a full, resonant tone. The thickness of the walls of the cylindrical tubing and bell flare also has a significant effect on both timbre and playing qualities.

Another area where the question of mass has come to the forefront is in the design of mouthpieces. The use of heavy-mass or heavy-wall mouthpieces has increased recently among trumpet, trombone, and tuba players. Some players find definite advantages to this type of mouthpiece, whereas others still prefer mouthpieces of traditional shape and weight.[11]

Recently, attention has been focused on the effects of stress reduction both in the construction of the instrument and in the metal itself. Stress is often built into an instrument through misalignment of parts and the soldering process when it is assembled. These can be relieved to a certain extent by taking the instrument apart and meticulously reassembling it with minimal stress. Another approach (which is also directed to the alloy) is by either heavy annealing, which softens the metal, or bringing the instrument to a subfreezing temperature. Opinion is divided on the merit of these procedures; some players find that these methods improve the instruments, but many reaffirm the importance of traditional "work hardening" in the making of brass instruments. "Work hardening," which makes the metal harder through the process of forming and reforming, is traditionally believed to contribute resonance and carrying power to the timbre.

The bends in the tubing and its arrangement within the overall pattern of the instrument are other design factors now being given much consideration. Open-wrap designs emphasize broad, gentle bends in the tubing. This is believed to create lessened resistance and contribute greater flexibility in changing notes. In trombone F and other attachments, the open-wrap configuration is considered to improve the sound. Although it is generally agreed that sharp, tight bends are best avoided, some designers feel that more squared-off bends in the tubing give the timbre a more solid, ringing tone that projects well in a concert hall (as in earlier Vincent Bach trumpets, for example).

---

[11] The variables of mouthpiece design are discussed in Chapter 2.

Anatomy of the Mouthpiece

As discussed in Chapter 1, the mouthpiece forms a chamber in which the movement of air coming from the lungs is converted to acoustical energy to create sound within the flared and cylindrical tubing of the instrument. (See Figure 2.1). This is why the mouthpiece plays so crucial a role in influencing tone quality, response, and intonation. It is also the interface between player and instrument. Therefore, the selection of a mouthpiece is not only an important consideration, but a highly individual and personal matter. Not only must a particular mouthpiece enable the player to produce a good tone quality (and one that is appropriate to the music being performed), but it must offer a quick response in all ranges without undue effort, as well as clear tonguing, reliable intonation, and good endurance. There is considerable variation between individuals in embouchure formation due to differences in facial musculature, lips, and teeth. Consequently, a mouthpiece that works very well for one player will not necessarily produce comparable results with another. The important thing is that along with being of effective design, the mouthpiece must *suit the player*. Choosing the right mouthpiece can make an important difference in the player's advancement; a wrong choice can hold the player back. The best way to select a mouthpiece is to first consider the variables of mouthpiece design and their effects.

The five basic components of a mouthpiece are shown in Figure 2.2.

The main points to consider are the following:

- Rim: inner diameter, width, contour, and edge (bite)
- Cup: depth and shape; air volume
- Throat: diameter, length, and shape of opening
- Backbore: rate and shape of taper
- Shank: length in relation to the instrument and accuracy of fit into receiver

Each of these factors significantly influences the playing qualities of a mouthpiece and the timbre it produces.

Carefully study Figures 2.3 through 2.6; these are side views of actual high-quality mouthpieces (not drawings) that have been cut in half to reveal their inner contours.

Inner Rim Diameter (Cup Diameter)

Although it is often identified as the diameter of the mouthpiece cup, this measure is the distance between the inner edges of the rim and thus is considered with other

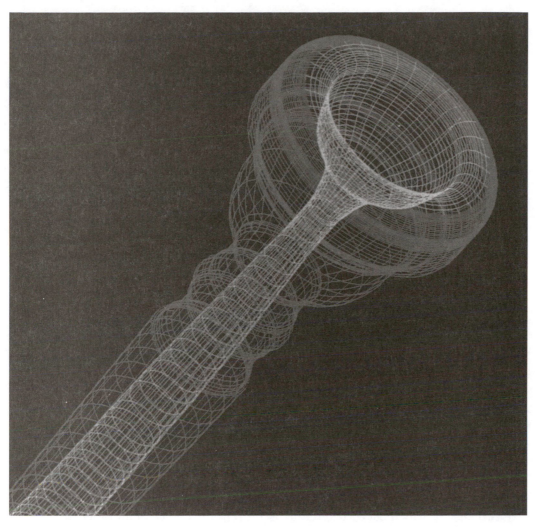

Figure 2.1 **Courtesy Yamaha Corporation of America.**

aspects of rim design. This distance defines the area in which the lips vibrate and, in conjunction with the depth of the cup and its shape, determines the air volume of the cup. Consequently, the inner rim diameter is a key factor in influencing the size of sound (breadth and fullness), although the throat and backbore are also important factors. The opening and closing motion of the embouchure in vibration is affected by the inner rim diameter. A larger diameter encourages the embouchure to open more in its oscillation for a given pitch. This creates a greater range of vibrational motion (at the same *frequency* of vibration) than a smaller diameter, thereby contributing a fuller, more resonant tone.

Brass players, especially trumpet and horn players, are extraordinarily sensitive to differences in inner rim diameter. The ability to detect differences of two tenths of a millimeter is not uncommon. The very broad range of inner rim diameters in use on mouthpieces of each brass instrument is, among other things, an indication of the significant individual variability in the dental arch. This can best be understood by visualizing the arch-shaped line of the upper teeth as if viewed from above. In some players, the arch is flatter at the center, where the mouthpiece rests. Individuals with this type of arch can use a wider inner rim diameter without compromising the seal at each side of the rim. Players with a more pronounced arch usually require

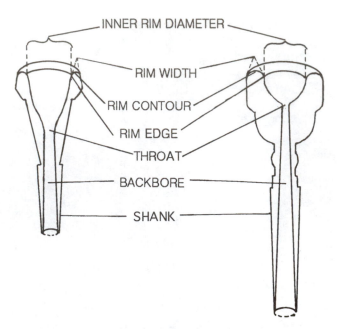

INNER RIM DIAMETER

RIM WIDTH

RIM CONTOUR

RIM EDGE

THROAT

BACKBONE

SHANK

Figure 2.2 **The parts of a mouthpiece.**

mouthpieces within a slightly narrower range of inner diameter in order to maintain a balanced seal at the sides without increased mouthpiece pressure. (The circumference of the mouthpiece rim is symmetrical; if the area of seal at each side of the rim is significantly rearward of the central seal area due to the shape of the dental arch, more pressure must be applied to create a stable seal.) Any decrease in inner rim diameter can be compensated for by increasing the depth (or altering the shape) of the cup, increasing the throat diameter, or enlarging the backbore.

There is also variability in the thickness of the lip tissue itself and the size of the teeth. These factors must be taken into account in the choice of an inner rim diameter. Players with fuller lip tissue and larger teeth usually require a wider inner rim diameter to allow sufficient space for unrestricted vibration. An inner diameter that is too narrow inhibits free vibration and can cause the mouthpiece placement to shift, creating problems in tone production (mouthpiece placement is discussed in Chapter 10). An inner rim diameter that is too wide for a player will cause a feeling of loss of control and the high range will suffer. It should be recognized, however, that in changing from a more narrow inner diameter to a larger one, there will be a period of adjustment in which these same effects are present to some degree until the muscles at the sides (where the rim contacts the lips) and just inside the rim adjust to the new diameter. The key is to determine whether this is a temporary condition or one that continues. Usually, this can be determined within a week or two. If the condition persists, it might be an indication that the inner rim diameter is too wide.

An experienced player will usually determine by trial and error a particular inner rim diameter that suits his or her embouchure, and one that offers sound and playing qualities consistent with what he or she is trying to achieve. In general, modern brass players try to use as large an inner diameter as possible, as long as the criteria described above are met. Aside from the fullness and resonance of tone that a wider diameter offers, greater comfort and flexibility are provided by having more room for the embouchure to make adjustments for higher and lower pitches. Wider diameters do require somewhat greater embouchure strength and more air than smaller diameters, which usually produce a lighter tone and require less effort. At one time, narrow diameters were thought to facilitate the high range, but this idea is largely discredited today. In fact, an overly narrow inner diameter can restrict the vibration of the embouchure and impede the airflow in the upper register. Most professional players use fairly large inner rim diameters for all of their playing, including the higher trumpets and descant horn, although cups of shallower depth are sometimes substituted on these instruments.

As important as the inner rim diameter is in the choice of a mouthpiece, it is surprising that the measurements presented by manufacturers in their catalogs are often approximations. This makes comparisons between mouthpieces of various manufacturers based on the stated measurements very different from comparisons made by actual testing. The reason for the lack of precision on this measurement is that there is no standardized depth (from the top of the rim into the cup) at which the measurement is taken. The problem is compounded by differences in rim contour (rim contour is discussed below). In some contours, the inside of the rim slopes inward and the inner diameter constantly changes (narrows), with no clearly defined point at which the rim ends and the cup begins. Consequently, measurements that are taken at a shallower depth will be wider than those taken further into the cup. Ideally, the inner diameter should be measured at the rim edge (bite); but again, in some designs, the edge is smoothly blended into the contour without a point of clear definition. In others, the edge is placed higher or lower along the inner rim face. The net effect of these variables is that manufacturers' inner rim measurements should be understood to be approximate, and only by playing a mouthpiece can one make a meaningful evaluation and comparison with other mouthpieces.

Ranges of Modern Inner Rim Diameters	*Most Common Range*
Trumpet 15.8 to 18.29 mm	16.2 to 17.2 mm
Cornet 16 to 17 mm	16 to 16.4 mm (conical cup type)
Horn 16.2 to 18.5 mm	16.8 to 17.5 mm[1]
Tenor trombone 24.3 to 26.4 mm	25.4 to 26 mm
Bass trombone 26.52 to 29.03 mm	26.4 to 28.52 mm
Euphonium 25.1 to 26 mm	25.4 to 26 mm
Tuba 30 to 32.76 mm	
	Bass tuba 30 to 32 mm
	Contrabass tuba 31.4 to 32.76 mm

[1] There is a current trend in the design of horn mouthpieces to produce inner rim diameters in increments of 0.5 millimeters (16.5 mm, 17 mm, 17.5 mm, 18 mm, etc.). Thus, there are too few sizes in the 17- to 17.5-mm range, where many horn players fall. A better approach is taken in the Stork Orval series. The basic mouthpiece is available in diameters of 17 mm, 17.25 mm, 17.5 mm, 17.75 mm, and 18 mm and with either an American shank or a larger European shank.

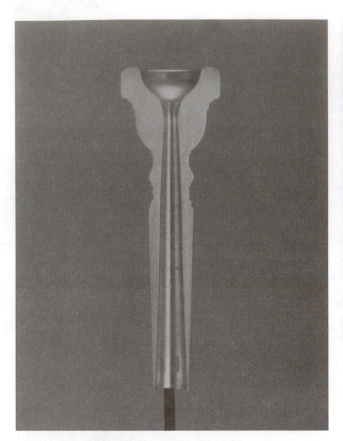

Figure 2.3 **Trumpet.**

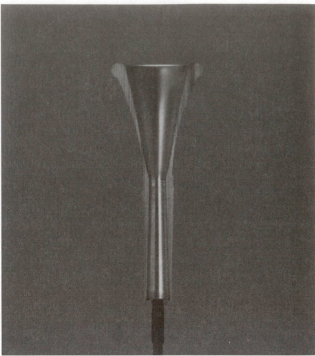

Figure 2.4 **Horn.**

Rim Width

The thickness of the mouthpiece rim is a prime factor in the interface between player and instrument. Rim width cannot be considered in a vacuum, however, because there is a subtle interplay between the shape of the rim (rim contour) and its thickness. A carefully designed contour can give a wider rim some of the qualities of a narrower rim, and make a narrow rim more comfortable to the embouchure. In general, wide rims (except those with sophisticated contours) tend to be less quick in response and limit flexibility somewhat. They are comfortable, however, and the added support contributes to endurance. Narrow rims offer excellent flexibility and faster response, but the smaller contact area does not provide the support of a wider rim. Usually, mouthpiece designers strive for a balance of these features by finding a compromise between wide and narrow in conjunction with an effective contour.

Most rims for trumpet, trombone, euphonium, and tuba are designated as medium or medium-wide rims. These offer a good balance of flexibility, comfort, and endurance. Somewhat narrower rims have been used recently on some of the larger bass trombone mouthpieces and a few tuba mouthpieces. The greatest diversity in rim width is among horn mouthpieces. Horn rims vary from around 3.5 to 5.7 mm! To interpret such a broad range of rim thicknesses, it would be fair to say that 3.9- to 4.0-mm rims could be considered conventional medium-narrow rims and 4.2- to 4.3-mm widths as medium-wide rims. Widths that are less than 3.9 mm should be regarded as quite narrow, and anything greater than 4.3 mm is a wide rim. The divergence in rim thicknesses in use on horn mouthpieces is an indication of the

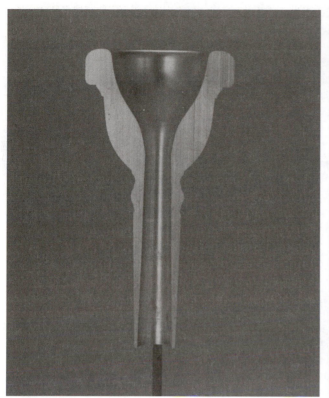

Figure 2.5 **Trombone.**

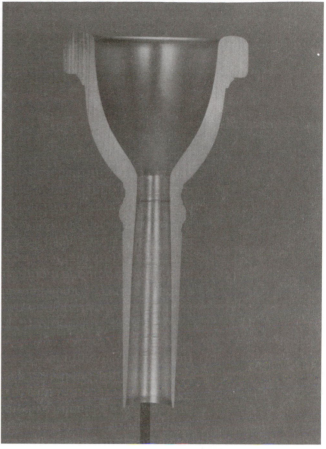

Figure 2.6 **Tuba.** *Figures 2.3 through 2.6 courtesy of the Yamaha Corporation of America.*

vastly different approaches designers have followed to balance the level of flexibility needed in horn playing with comfort and endurance.

The medium and medium-wide rim widths in use on the other brass instruments fall proportionally into smaller ranges:

Trumpet	5.05 to 5.50 mm
Cornet	5.17 to 5.30 mm
Tenor trombone	6.26 to 6.80 mm
Bass trombone	6.09 (narrow) to 6.73 mm
Euphonium	6.26 to 6.72 mm
Tuba	6.89 to 8.11 mm

Rim widths outside these parameters should be considered narrow or wide.

Rim Contour

The shape of the rim is known as the rim contour. Contours can be round, fairly flat, oval, or with the high point or peak shifted toward the inside or outside on the rim face. These variations affect individuals differently, so it is important that the player is aware of this variable in trying different mouthpieces. The only generalizations that can be made are that flatter rims tend to restrict the movement of the lips, impairing flexibility, and that round contours are often less responsive and limit endurance. Balanced-contour rims (oval-shaped) are probably the most widely used today.

The shape of the rim on the outside is also a consideration. On some trumpet mouthpieces the outer edge of the rim is rounded off to promote flexibility. Horn players who use the inset mouthpiece placement are particularly sensitive to the shape of the outer rim surface because some of the lower lip tissue is in contact with this part of the rim (this is also true of some players who use a conventional placement when they play in the low register).

Finding a suitable rim contour can be accomplished only by trial and error, but it should be recognized that this, along with the rim thickness and edge, is one of the most important factors in determining how a mouthpiece will work for an individual. This is the actual interface between the player's embouchure and the instrument.

RIM EDGE (BITE)

As part of the rim contour, an inner edge can be made so that its presence is clearly detected by the lips or reduced to imperceptibility. It can also be placed higher or lower on the inner face of the rim contour. Some performers believe that a slightly discernible edge improves response and attack; others find such a rim uncomfortable and tiring to play. There may be a relationship between rim width and the need for some definition in its edge. Medium rims probably require a subtle edge to feel responsive. Narrower rims, with their more direct response, cause discomfort if the edge is noticeable. Of course, rims can be altered to suit individual preferences. Often, the rim of one model is substituted on another cup, usually through the use of a screw-rim (component) mouthpiece.

Cup Depth and Shape

Of all the elements of mouthpiece design, the shape and depth of the cup have the greatest influence on tone quality. Deeper cups lend fullness to the sound and a somewhat darker character. Shallow cups produce a timbre that is both lighter in weight and brighter in color. Instrument designer Vincent Bach attributed these differences to the way in which partials are present in the sound. With deep cups, the fundamental tends to predominate with fewer of the highest partials present. A tone more endowed with upper partials results when a shallow cup is used. The goal is to find the right balance of these qualities to achieve a full and characteristic timbre, consistent with good intonation and response.

Quickness of response and ease of playing in different registers are additional factors influenced by the depth and shape of the cup (in combination with a well-designed backbore). Mouthpieces vary significantly in their ease and directness of response and how they center the production of sound in the middle, upper, and lower ranges. Some mouthpieces are superior in this respect, and this is an important criterion in the selection of a mouthpiece.

The two hypothetical cup shapes are the bowl and the cone; in actuality, most brass mouthpieces are carefully derived combinations of these two basic configurations. By comparing Figures 2.3 through 2.6, one can clearly see the differences in cup shape among brass instruments. The horn mouthpiece is the most conical. In earlier periods, horn mouthpieces were totally conical, but today most incorporate a slight cup while preserving the basic funnel shape. Cornet and euphonium mouthpieces are more conical than corresponding trumpet and trombone mouthpieces, giving these instruments their sweet, mellow tone. Although the trumpet cup is the most bowl-like, the bottom of the cup has a conical shape to contribute a characteristically clear, ringing sound. For much of their previous history, conical mouthpieces, more like those used on the horn, were favored by trombonists. These produced a pure, centered tone quality that was particularly effective on smaller-bore trombones.

As shown in Figures 2.3, 2.5, and 2.6, the trombone mouthpiece is proportionally more conical for its depth than the trumpet, and the tuba even more so. (The area at the bottom of the cup that opens into the throat and backbore is discussed below.) What this reveals is that the way in which the theoretical bowl and cone shapes have been combined for each instrument is different, and has evolved independently.

The depth of the cup also affects the high and low ranges to some extent. Very deep cups are normally used, for example, by fourth horn players and bass trombonists to facilitate the low register. Conversely, trumpeters often substitute a shallow cup when performing on the piccolo trumpet. Jazz and studio players usually prefer shallower cup depths to cope with high range demands in these fields and to produce an appropriately brilliant timbre. (Students sometimes use too-shallow cups, hoping to gain range quickly. Shallow cups are not conducive to good development in the formative stages, and wreak havoc in school bands and orchestras. A shallow mouthpiece should be viewed as a specialized tool for a specific performance situation.)

With the exceptions noted, most professional brass players use a cup depth that produces the fullest and most resonant tone, as long as the full range of the instrument can be played reliably, with good intonation, and without excessive effort. The shape of the cup for a given depth is a less obvious but important variable. There are many possibilities in cup shape within the limits of a specific depth, producing different effects. How the cup shape influences the tone and playing characteristics of a particular mouthpiece can be determined only by testing several mouthpieces and comparing their qualities.

Throat

The main consideration is the throat's diameter, although how the opening is shaped and its overall length are contributing factors. Large throats darken the tone and give it body. Smaller diameters have the opposite effect. The diameter can be measured by inserting numbered (or metric) drill bits into the throat until the correct size is found. Drill bits are numbered so that the higher the number, the smaller the diameter. For example, the standard throat bore of Bach trumpet mouthpieces is 27 (3.67 mm, or 0.144"). Symphony players typically use larger throats in the 25 to 23 range. There is less consistency among horn mouthpieces, with throats varying from 1 to 17 (5.79 to 4.39 mm, or 0.227 to 0.172"). Trombone and euphonium throats usually run from 6.4 to 7.4 mm (0.252 to 0.291") and tuba throats run from 7.4 to 8.85 mm (0.291 to 0.348"). Most professional brass players determine their preference in throat diameter through experimentation and either order their mouthpiece with the appropriate throat or have an existing mouthpiece drilled to that size.

How the opening of the throat is shaped also influences the sound and response. In the eighteenth century, trumpet mouthpieces were bowl-shaped, with sharp-edged throats drilled directly into the bottom of the cup. In modern trumpet mouthpieces, the cup's lower portion is fairly conical and any edge is smoothed out to blend with this shape. In some designs, more of a shoulder is left at the throat opening; in others, the opening itself takes on a conical shape. The latter lessens resistance and adds depth to the sound. The throat bore is cylindrical and its length must be carefully worked out in relation to the backbore and cup depth to ensure good intonation.

Backbore

Because it is impossible to gain any really useful information by visual observation, the backbore is the least understood aspect of the mouthpiece and all judgments must be made by trial and error. No system of measurements is in use to guide the player and allow for comparisons, so one must rely on catalog descriptions such as *large, medium, Schmidt, barrel,* and others, or on letter or number identifications (b, c, d; 10, 24, 87) that apply only to a particular manufacturer. However, response, intonation, flexibility, tone, and endurance are all greatly influenced by the backbore. To stress the importance and the variability inherent in this aspect of mouthpiece design, it should be noted that Vincent Bach developed 107 different backbores for trumpet, and the firm normally offers 1 standard and 7 other backbores to special-order.

It might be assumed that backbores are drilled to a constant rate of taper, but this is rarely the case. Larger backbores expand at a steeper rate during the first third, or less, of their length, and thereafter very gradually until the final diameter is reached. The final diameter should match the leadpipe taper. Smaller backbores have a much more gradual taper over approximately the first two-thirds of their length. So-called standard backbores represent a compromise between these extremes. The larger bores such as "symphony" or "Schmidt" models offer a fuller tone, but require more air and greater embouchure strength than standard models. Endurance is the critical factor. A player's embouchure can become exhausted quickly due to lack of resistance if the backbore is too large. Backbore experimentation should be undertaken only by experienced players who are well accustomed to a particular mouthpiece.

Shank

The purpose of the mouthpiece shank and instrument receiver is to bring the backbore into contact with the leadpipe without interruption so that a continuous taper is formed. If it were not so inconvenient, mouthpieces and leadpipes would probably be made in one piece to ensure the accuracy of this taper. Any inexactness at this point can influence the instrument's performance, so it is essential that the shank fit the receiver accurately.

American shanks are normally made with a Morse 0 or number 1 taper. This does not automatically ensure that the correct interface will be formed with the leadpipe. Sometimes a gap occurs between the end of the mouthpiece and the leadpipe. Designers of trumpet mouthpieces disagree as to the negative or positive effect of such a gap. Although no acoustical explanation has been forthcoming, it does appear that certain mouthpiece–instrument combinations produce far better results with a gap than without one. Horn mouthpieces sometimes go into the leadpipe too far, or not far enough, affecting the instrument's pitch center on certain notes.

No single standard similar to the Morse taper is used among European makers. On German and British horns, for example, American-made mouthpieces usually go too far into the mouthpipe. Similar complications arise with rotary valve trumpets and tubas. A mouthpiece maker can correct any problems of this sort by copying the mouthpiece with a larger or smaller shank, or by altering the cup, rim, and throat of a European mouthpiece to the player's requirements while leaving the original shank unchanged. Some enlightened firms offer mouthpieces with either American or larger European shanks.

Component Mouthpieces

Screw-rim mouthpieces have been available for many years. These allow different combinations of cup and rim to be used by the player, usually when switching between instruments (for example, C trumpet to piccolo trumpet or double horn to descant horn). This is accomplished by creating a threaded joint between the rim and cup so that the rim can be removed from one cup and attached to another. Normally, the player uses one rim with different cups (including the throat and backbore). In recent years, the possibilities inherent in this principle have been extended by creating three-piece component mouthpieces. These have threaded joints that subdivide the mouthpiece into rim, cup, and throat–backbore, permitting three-way combinations to be assembled.

Heavy Wall Mouthpieces

Mouthpieces purposely constructed with greater mass and weight have recently gained popularity. Players who favor these designs feel that they offer increased power, do not distort at high volume levels, and have better centers ("slots") for the notes of the upper and lower registers. Other players continue to prefer traditional designs and it is likely that both types of mouthpiece will coexist in the future.

Mouthpiece Materials and Finishes

Mouthpieces are usually made from brass, although nickel silver is widely used in Europe. Recently, mouthpieces made from sterling silver have become available. Silver or gold plating is used as a finish on brass mouthpieces. Nickel silver mouthpieces are normally left unplated, but these are also gold plated on occasion.

The finishes feel different to the player's embouchure. Many prefer the smooth contact offered by gold plating, but its cost probably has prevented it from being used more widely. Polished unplated nickel silver is probably next to gold plating in comfort, but it is not often used in the United States. Sometimes only the rim of the mouthpiece is gold plated, with silver plating applied to the cup and shank.

General Mouthpiece Suggestions

- Choose a mouthpiece from a recognized manufacturer.
- Remember that no single manufacturer produces the best mouthpieces for all brass instruments.

- Choose a mouthpiece that has a good sound, is comfortable, plays easily, and has good intonation.
- Keep in mind that although the upper range may suffer temporarily after a change to a larger mouthpiece, it should soon return.
- Avoid shallow mouthpieces.
- Different examples of the same mouthpiece may not be identical due to the way mouthpieces are made. It is important to test every mouthpiece individually.
- Mouthpiece makers do not use a consistent system of identification of different models. Therefore, the only way to determine the characteristics of a particular model is to study the catalog description and dimensions, if given.
- Although searching for the ideal mouthpiece is unwise, it is important to try different mouthpieces occasionally to see whether they offer any improvements.

Mouthpiece Recommendations

TRUMPET AND CORNET[2]

Some clarification of how models are identified by various manufacturers might be helpful. Bach, Denis Wick, and Giardinelli indicate progressively larger cup diameters as the numbers become smaller. Schilke and Yamaha use an opposite system. The system used by other firms should be determined by studying their catalogues. Cup depths on Bach mouthpieces are often misunderstood:

A = Very deep

Number without letter = medium-deep

B = medium

C = medium-shallow

D = shallow

E = extremely shallow

The medium-deep cups identified by number only were intended by Vincent Bach as a standard model for the B♭ and C trumpets. In recent years, they have tended to be overlooked in favor of the C cup. Both cups yield good results, but unlettered models offer a fuller, more resonant tone.

Cornet mouthpieces must be made with the smaller cornet shank; this should be specified when ordering if the mouthpiece is offered for both trumpet and cornet. The only cornet mouthpieces currently available having an authentic cup depth and shape are the Denis Wick models.

[2] For additional information, see Gerald Endsley, *Comparative Mouthpiece Guide for Trumpet* (Denver, Colo.: Tromba Publications, 1980).

Trumpet

Beginner	Intermediate	Advanced
Bach 7, 7C	Bach 6, 5, 5C	Bach 2, 1, X1, 1¼C, 1C
Schilke 9, 11	Schilke 14, 17	Schilke 18, 20, 20D2d
Denis Wick 4	Denis Wick 3	Denis Wick 2W, 1CW, 1W
Yamaha 11C4–7C	Yamaha 15B4	Yamaha 16C4, 17C4
Stork Vacchiano 7C	Stork Vacchiano 3C	Stork Vacchiano 1, 2B
Josef Klier 77C	Josef Klier 66B	Josef Klier 44C, 44B

Cornet

Beginner	Intermediate	Advanced
Denis Wick 5B	Denis Wick 5B	Denis Wick 5, 4
Yamaha 11E4		

Horn

Beginner	Intermediate	Advanced
Paxman 3B, 3C	Paxman 3B, 3C, 4B, 4C	Paxman 4B, 4C
		Paxman Halstead-Chidell 22A-AS, 23A-AS
Denis Wick 7, 7N	Denis Wick 7, 7N	Denis Wick 5, 5N
Stork Orval 4, 4½; C12	Stork Orval 4, 4½; C12	Stork Orval 4½, 5; C12
Josef Klier W33CK	Josef Klier W33CK	Josef Klier W22CK, W33CK
Giardinelli C12, S15, G17	Giardinelli C12, S15, G17	Giardinelli C12, C10, S15, G17
Yamaha 30C4	Yamaha 29D4, 30C4	Yamaha 31D4
Schilke 27	Schilke 27	Schilke 27, 31B

TROMBONE

Before purchasing a trombone mouthpiece, it is necessary to know whether the instrument's receiver has been designed to accept a large or small shank. Large-bore tenor trombones such as the Conn 88H and Bach 42B require large shanks, whereas medium- and small-bore tenors normally accept the smaller size. Bass trombones invariably take the large shank. Most mouthpieces for tenor trombone (with the exception of the largest models) are available with either shank, so the correct size must be specified in ordering.

Tenor Trombone

Beginner	Intermediate	Advanced
Denis Wick 12CS, 9BS	Denis Wick 6BS, 6BL	Denis Wick 5BS, 5BL, 4BL, 4AL
Bach 12C, 12, 11	Bach 7C, 7, $6\frac{1}{2}$ AL	Bach $6\frac{1}{2}$ AL, 5G, 4G
Schilke 46	Schilke 47, 50	Schilke 51B, 51
Josef Klier P89C	Josef Klier P77B	Josef Klier P66B, P55A

Bass Trombone

Beginner	Intermediate	Advanced
—	Denis Wick 5AL, 4AL, 3AL	Denis Wick 2AL, 1AL, 0AL
—	Schilke 57	Schilke 58, 59, 60
—	Bach 5G, 3G	Bach 2G, 1G, $1\frac{1}{2}$ G
—	—	Josef Klier P33AK, P22AK

BARITONE AND EUPHONIUM

Again, the question of shank sizes arises. American instrument manufacturers and Yamaha use a standard size equivalent to the small trombone shank. In the Denis Wick catalog, these are identified by the letter Y (the last letter of the mouthpiece's number indicates shank size). Boosey and Hawkes/Besson euphoniums made since 1974 accept the normal large trombone shank (L), but earlier models required a special shank size, which the Wick catalog designates as the letter M. When ordering Bach and Schilke mouthpieces, it is necessary to indicate the shank size or the instrument with which the mouthpiece is to be used.

Most trombone and euphonium mouthpieces are not interchangeable because an authentic euphonium tone can be achieved only with a deeper, more conical cup.

Euphonium[3]

Beginner	Intermediate	Advanced
Denis Wick 6BY, 6BM, 6BL	Denis Wick 6BY, 6BM, 6BL	Denis Wick 5AL, 4AY, 4AM, 4AL
Schilke 46D	Schilke 46D	Schilke 51D
Bach 7	Bach $6\frac{1}{2}$ A, $6\frac{1}{2}$ AL	Bach 5G, 4G

True baritones are used almost exclusively in brass bands. Because their bore is narrower, somewhat smaller mouthpieces such as the Denis Wick 6BS or 6BY are normally used.

---

[3] See David R. Werden, "Euphonium Mouthpieces—A Teacher's Guide," *The Instrumentalist* (May 1981), pp. 23–26.

TUBA

Considering the international range of tubas in use today, the safest procedure in ordering a mouthpiece is to indicate the manufacturer of the instrument it must fit because there is considerable variation in receivers. American tubas (such as Conn and King) and some imported instruments (such as Mirafone and Yamaha) take a standard shank.

Tuba

Beginner	Intermediate	Advanced
Bach 30E, 32E	Bach 22	Schilke S-H (Helleberg II)
Denis Wick 4L, 5L	Denis Wick 3L	Dillon M1C (Available from Dillon Music)
Yamaha 65	Schilke 66	Deck 3 (Available from Orfeo Products)
—	Yamaha 66	Monette
—	Conn 7B Helleberg	Perantucci 44, 48, 50
—	—	Josef Klier T55A, T44B
—	—	Denis Wick 2L, 1L
—	—	Bach 18, 12, 7
—	—	Yamaha 67C4
—	—	Conn Helleberg

CHAPTER 3

Trumpet and Cornet

Trumpeters have a wide assortment of specialized instruments available to help them to meet today's exacting performance standards. (See Figure 3.1.) This is in sharp contrast to earlier periods. The author recalls that his teacher, William Vacchiano, said that when he joined the New York Philharmonic in the 1930s, only one player in the section owned a C trumpet, and they were expected to play all of the standard repertoire on the B♭ trumpet. Today, there are trumpets pitched in the keys of every scale note of a full octave above the B♭ instrument. These fall into two basic categories: B♭ and C trumpets for general use and higher trumpets pitched in D, E♭, E, F, G, piccolo B♭/A, and C for orchestral and solo literature demanding a high tessitura.

It is fair to ask why so many trumpets are necessary. The answer can best be illustrated through a rather extreme example. Although a strong player might possibly be able to sustain the high range called for in Bach's *B-Minor Mass* on a B♭ trumpet, the notes would be produced fairly high on the harmonic series. By changing to a piccolo trumpet in A, the same notes may be played lower, in the most stable part of the harmonic series (where the harmonics are more widely separated). This facilitates making entrances and playing in the high register, and improves accuracy. Also, the undue effort required to maintain the high tessitura on the larger instrument would prove severely fatiguing. A smaller, higher-pitched trumpet brings such parts much more under the player's control.

Aside from these considerations, the larger and weightier tone of the B♭, though well suited to the works of later composers, would be incompatible with the transparent textures and light balances required in Bach's orchestration. The evolution of trumpets pitched in various keys has come about in response to the need for specialized instruments designed to enable trumpeters to adapt to the demands of the diverse repertoire performed by today's orchestras. Along with the need for these instruments in orchestras, the greatly expanded solo literature has provided a stimulus for their development. For example, the Haydn *Trumpet Concerto* is now usually played on the E♭ trumpet; the Hummel *Trumpet Concerto* is played on the E♭ trumpet, or on the E trumpet when it is performed in its original key. The Baroque solo literature written for the natural trumpet in D is invariably performed on the piccolo A trumpet (except in performances using historical instruments).

Although these instruments have come into wide use in recent years, the idea of trumpets in higher keys is not new. Teste, solo trumpeter of the Paris Opera, performed Bach's *Magnificat* on a G trumpet as early as 1885. The great Belgian trumpeter Théo Charlier gave the first modern performance of Bach's "Brandenburg" Concerto No. 2 in 1898 using a Mahillon G trumpet. French, Belgian, and German makers led the way in the development of the higher trumpets well into the twentieth century. In the last 35 years, however, high trumpets have undergone exten-

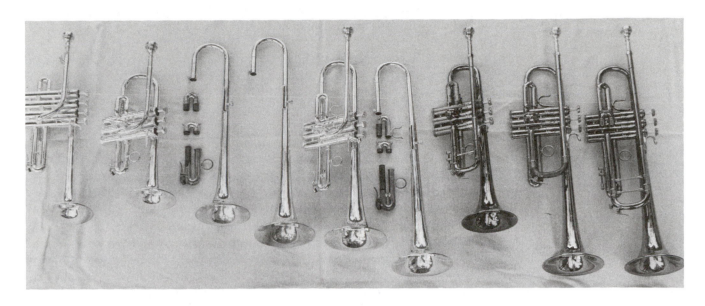

Figure 3.1. **The trumpets in use today (left to right):   Piccolo B♭/A; G; F bell and slides; E bell; E♭; D bell and slides (Schilke); E♭; C; and B♭ (Bach).** *Photo: Joseph Hetman.*

sive research and development everywhere in the quest for improved instruments to cope with the mounting demands placed on modern orchestral trumpeters.

Several factors have combined to create these pressures. The trend toward longer orchestral seasons, competition resulting from an oversupply of well-trained players, and the expectation by conductors and audiences of note-perfect accuracy in live performances (as they are accustomed to on recordings) have all had their effect. Most important, however, is that principal trumpeters are now regularly expected to perform the demanding Baroque literature with the flawless skill that was previously reserved for exceptional players and Baroque specialists.

Another important influence is the emergence of the trumpet as a major solo instrument. Just as Jean-Pierre Rampal popularized the solo flute and Dennis Brain the horn, Maurice André brought the trumpet into a new era of solo recordings and international concert appearances. The torch is being carried forward by today's generation of brilliant soloists who require responsive, reliable, and in-tune high trumpets.

The B♭ and C Trumpet

By the end of the nineteenth century, the modern B♭ trumpet had replaced the longer F trumpet as the standard orchestral instrument. Although the passing of the old F trumpet timbre was lamented by many,[1] trumpeters were confronted with parts of increasing difficulty from composers such as Strauss and Mahler, and the new instrument proved more effective in meeting these demands. The popularity of the B♭ cornet also contributed to the change because many orchestral players also played the cornet and were accustomed to the technical advantages of an instrument in B♭. Trumpets in C also made their appearance about this time and became

---

[1] See the discussion of the horn and trumpet by Ralph Vaughan Williams in *The Making of Music* (Ithaca, N.Y.: Cornell University Press, 1955), p. 29.

established as the standard orchestral instrument in France, Belgium (piston valve), and Austria (rotary valve).

The present widespread use of the C trumpet in American orchestras can be traced to the appointment in 1920 of Georges Mager as principal trumpet of the Boston Symphony Orchestra. A graduate of the Paris Conservatory in the class of Jean-Joseph Mellet (a student of Arban) and one of the greatest players of his time, Mager used the C trumpet as his primary instrument during his entire 30-year career in Boston. He led a section composed of his French colleagues Gustav Perret, Marcel LaFosse, and René Voisin playing C trumpets (this was unique in orchestras of the time) and established the pattern that has become standard in American orchestras today.

Among the first major figures beyond Boston to adopt the C trumpet was William Vacchiano, who joined the New York Philharmonic in 1935 and served as principal trumpet from 1942 to 1973. The use of the C trumpet has increased internationally (except in France, Belgium, and Austria, where the instrument has long been established) as a result of the influence of American brass playing, particularly that of Adolph Herseth, principal trumpet of the Chicago Symphony.[2]

The trend is not universal, however. British trumpeters, following in the great tradition of Ernest Hall, have maintained their allegiance to the B♭, preferring its rounder tone and blending qualities. The B♭ has to some extent retained its position in German and Eastern European orchestras as well. In bands, the B♭ remains the primary instrument due to its fuller timbre and greater ability to blend within an ensemble of wind instruments. The literature for band is almost entirely written for the B♭ instrument and would have to be transposed if C trumpets were used.

Another area where the C trumpet has failed to gain a foothold is in the jazz and studio fields. The C trumpet's timbre and playing characteristics do not seem to be particularly adaptable to the musical requirements of jazz performers.

Given the trend toward C trumpets in orchestral playing, it is important to emphasize that most trumpeters agree that students should begin and play through their formative years on the B♭ instrument. In this way, a good tonal concept and tone production are firmly established.

It would be well to consider what specific advantages the C trumpet has to offer the orchestral player. The primary factor underlying the trend to C trumpets is related to the nature of orchestral playing with its long periods of rest. The response of the C seems to be better suited to making "cold" entrances than the B♭, and it provides a greater feeling of security and control. This feeling is augmented by its being in the same key as the string section, particularly in the sharp keys in which orchestras often play. The C also seems to be more compatible with the range in which the first trumpet plays and the extreme dynamic contrasts required. The timbre of the C carries well and this allows the player to project the sound with slightly less effort than would be required by the B♭.

C trumpets are now available with a number of leadpipe and bell combinations and these have contributed to an improved instrument. American orchestral players generally prefer a large-bore C and a medium-large B♭. There is still an important role for the B♭, and the parallel use of B♭ and C trumpets is likely to continue indefinitely. By having two primary instruments available, the player is afforded maximum flexibility in adapting to the requirements of the part to be performed. There has been superb orchestral playing on the B♭ trumpet as well as the C; how the player uses these instruments to best advantage ultimately remains a matter of individual preference.

---

[2] Adolph Herseth is a former student of Georges Mager.

The D Trumpet

The high trumpet in D was developed in the late nineteenth century in response to the enthusiasm of the time for performing the choral works of Bach and Handel. It was often called a Bach trumpet, but this name is now discouraged to avoid confusion with the natural trumpet, which has enjoyed a revival in recent years. (The natural trumpet is the instrument of Bach's time. The fundamental of the natural trumpet in D is an octave below that of the valve trumpet.) The D trumpet offered an excellent solution to the problem of performing the difficult parts in Bach's *B Minor Mass,* Handel's *Messiah,* and other Baroque works. Modern composers, such as Ravel and Stravinsky, also used the instrument for colorful high-range effects in some of their compositions.

At present there are three types of D trumpet available: a medium-bore and bell model suitable as a Baroque instrument, a large-bore that can be used in place of the B♭ or C in regular orchestral passages, and a D–E♭ combination (actually an E♭ trumpet provided with a main tuning slide or bell to change the pitch to D, and a set of longer valve slides).

Students are sometimes under the impression that the higher trumpets provide "instant" range, as in the flute–piccolo relationship. Actually, trumpeters usually only add a note or two above what can be played on their regular instrument. What is gained is better control and consistency in performing high-register passages.

In recent years, the D trumpet has largely been replaced in the Baroque literature by the piccolo trumpet in A. The smaller instrument has brought the difficult Baroque trumpet parts within the capability of a greater number of performers. Although it offers greater security and ease of playing, the small bore and bell of the piccolo result in a timbre that is of lesser body and fullness than that of the D trumpet; it is also far removed from the tone of the natural trumpet of Bach's time. The D trumpet is a more effective substitute for the natural trumpet, combining the advantages of a valve instrument with a fuller tone quality that is closer to that of the Baroque instrument.[3] However, the use of the piccolo in A in place of the D trumpet is likely to continue because most players find that it offers more reliability in performance.

The E♭ Trumpet

E♭ trumpets are used today primarily in the performance of the Haydn and Hummel[4] concertos and for some orchestral passages. This raises an additional aspect of the use of high trumpets that is unrelated to tessitura: Some passages lie better (in regard to fingering and tone production) on one instrument than on another. For example, the above concertos can be played fluently on the B♭; however, they are much more oriented to the E♭, which places the player in the key of C. Many trumpeters feel that this facilitates fingering (especially on trills) and accuracy. Others find that the use of an E♭ trumpet creates a new set of problems, particularly in intonation and tone quality, and prefer to remain with the B♭. There have been equally fine performances using both instruments.

---

[3] The greatest trumpet performance of a Baroque work the author has ever heard was of Bach's *Christmas Oratorio* by Fritz Wesenigk, solo trumpet of the Berlin Philharmonic, on a Monke rotary valve trumpet in D. Some superb D trumpet playing on a Mahillon instrument by Charles Schlueter, now principal trumpet of the Boston Symphony, is also recalled by the author.

[4] The Hummel concerto was composed for a keyed trumpet pitched in E. It is most often performed in editions transposed to E♭ so that it may be played comfortably on the B♭ or E♭ trumpet.

The principle of substituting one trumpet for another applies to the entire range of trumpets and affords the performer a choice in matching the instrument to the part:

Professional orchestral trumpeters use both the D and the E♭ trumpets for passages ordinarily played on the C or B♭ when the tessitura tends to be high or when the part clearly lies better on the higher trumpet. The same practice is followed in brass quintets and large brass ensembles. The choice between D or E♭ trumpet depends on which instrument places the player in a more fluent key. In addition to the C and ·B♭, the D and E♭ trumpets are essential tools for the professional player.

Trumpets in E, F, and G

The E trumpet was developed specially for players who want to perform the Hummel trumpet concerto in its original key of E major. At present, models are available from Blackburn, Schilke (part of a bell-tuned G–F–E combination, consisting of a G trumpet with interchangeable bells and valve slides for G, F, and E), and Yamaha (a bell-tuned E–E♭ combination with corresponding bells and valve slides).[5]

---

[5] Bell tuning was developed by the late Renold Schilke. It allows bells in different keys to be used on the same basic instrument. Many players feel that this option offers improved playing qualities and intonation, particularly on the higher trumpets.

F trumpets were originally constructed for the difficult trumpet part in Bach's Second "Brandenburg" Concerto. The first recording of the work was made in 1935 by the great English trumpeter George Eskdale, using an F trumpet. The F trumpet has now been replaced by the piccolo B♭. The chief use of the F trumpet today is for occasional orchestral passages.

The G trumpet is preferred as a Baroque instrument by players who want the tone and feel of an instrument larger than the piccolo. The G combines a timbre more like the D trumpet with some of the playing advantages of the piccolo.

The Piccolo Trumpet

Of all the high trumpets, the piccolo B♭/A is the most widely used today. This is due to the extensive development of these instruments over the past two decades. Trumpeters first used the piccolo B♭ more or less exclusively for the Second "Brandenburg" Concerto and for other Baroque parts that did not require the written low C of the D trumpet. Because this note is beyond the compass of the three-valve piccolo and figures in a number of scores, the piccolo's use was fairly limited. (D or G trumpets were normally used for these parts.) It was soon found that if the piccolo B♭ was lengthened to A (through interchangeable leadpipes), parts written for the D trumpet could be played in the key signature of F, a more fluent and responsive key than the B♭ piccolo's E major:

Bach, *B Minor Mass*
Trumpet in D

Piccolo B♭ trumpet

Piccolo A trumpet

With the addition of a fourth valve, which extended the range of the piccolo downward a perfect fourth, standard Baroque works such as Bach's *Christmas Oratorio* or Handel's *Messiah* (which require the written low C of the D trumpet) began to be performed on the piccolo in A.

The fourth valve adds five notes to the player's range below the limit of the three-valve piccolo. This makes available alternate fingerings to improve intonation. The sharp 1–2–3 and 1–3 combinations can be improved by using 2–4 and 4, respectively, a procedure normally used on four-valve euphoniums and tubas. There are two configurations of four-valve piccolo. The most common consists of four in-line valves. This adds some mass to the instrument in comparison to a three-valve design, and some players feel that this improves the tone. Others feel that the in-line fourth valve creates added resistance and prefer a three-valve pattern in which a fourth (rotary) valve is placed within the third valve loop.[6]

Orchestral players soon began to use the piccolo for high passages in later works such as Ravel's *Bolero,* Stravinsky's *Petrouchka,* and *Rite of Spring.* At the same time, the piccolo was brought into prominence by solo artists such as Adolph Scherbaum and Maurice André. Most recently, the piccolo is enjoying widespread popularity in the film and recording fields.

As stated earlier, the piccolo trumpet does not automatically bestow high range. What it does do is bring these notes down into the trumpet's most secure register by raising the fundamental. Although comparable skill is required in performing in the upper register from one instrument to another, the piccolo trumpet offers the player the acoustical advantage of producing these notes in the instrument's middle range, providing greater control and security.

The choice of a mouthpiece for the piccolo trumpet is highly individual.[7] A component mouthpiece is sometimes used, which allows the player to retain the same rim while altering cup, throat, or backbore. Some players use their standard rim for all the high trumpets, and others change to a smaller rim as well as cup depth for these instruments.

Choosing a piccolo trumpet (or any high trumpet) for the first time poses difficulties because it requires experience to evaluate the qualities of different instruments. The best way of selecting a piccolo is by trying a number of instruments. Certain instruments work better for individual players than others, and this should be the focus of the selection process (it is unwise to choose a particular model because another player uses it). *The essential criteria are that the instrument plays easily and that it is in tune.* Only if these criteria are met should tone quality be evaluated. Obviously, the player will want an instrument with a good tone quality. However, the best-sounding instrument is useless if it does not produce the notes reliably and is not well in tune. Players sometimes make the mistake of choosing a high trumpet primarily for its tone quality, only to find that the instrument proves unsatisfactory in intonation and playing qualities.

There is also a piccolo trumpet built in C. Normally this is built as a combination trumpet with leadpipes and valve slides for C, Bb, and A, thereby offering an additional choice of key to the player.

Rotary Valve Trumpets

German-type rotary valve trumpets are now standard equipment for a certain portion of the repertoire of most major American orchestras. (See Figure 3.2.) This has come about in response to the desire by conductors and players to produce a more authentic sound in the nineteenth-century literature by German and Austrian composers. Although the rotary valve trumpet is less flexible in technical passages, it possesses a much broader and slightly darker timbre that is ideally suited to the

---

[6] See Vincent Cichowicz, *The Piccolo Bb–A Trumpet,* available from the Selmer Co.; David Hickman, *The Piccolo Trumpet* (Denver, Colo.: Tromba, 1973); Roger Sherman, *The Trumpeter's Handbook* (Athens, Ohio: Accura Music, 1979); and Gerald Webster, *Piccolo Trumpet Method* (Nashville, Tenn.: Brass Press, 1980).

[7] Suggested piccolo mouthpieces are the Schilke 14A4a, Stork 2P, and Josef Klier 4 EP or 5 EP.

Figure 3.2. **Rotary valve trumpets (left to right):   Heckel models: B♭ (Ganter) and C (Yamaha); Monke C and D.** *Photo: Joseph Hetman.*

works of Beethoven, Brahms, Bruckner, and Strauss. Also, these instruments have a greater capacity to blend with woodwinds and strings. When called for, they produce a larger volume of tone without becoming brassy in forte passages.

The rotary valve trumpet followed a separate line of development and has been used as the primary instrument in central European orchestras for over a century and a half. Piston valve instruments, on the other hand, were centered in France and England, and from there came to the United States. Today, rotary valve trumpets can be heard in the Vienna Philharmonic and Berlin Philharmonic, as well as in leading orchestras in the United States.

Although the cylindrical bore of the rotary valve trumpet is slightly smaller than its piston valve counterpart, the leadpipe and bell are decidedly larger. The instrument is designed with a wider pattern to avoid sharp curves in the tubing. These factors, combined with the less resistant rotary valves, create the impression of a much larger instrument, requiring greater air support.

There are two traditional designs of rotary valve trumpet and, although they appear similar, they have very different proportions in their tapered sections and produce quite dissimilar tonal characteristics. One type is made by the Cologne firm of Josef Monke. Several others follow the style of instrument perfected by F. A. Heckel (and later, Windisch) of Dresden. Lechner (Austria), Ganter (Germany), and Hetman (United States) fall into this category. Instruments are built in all of the standard keys.

Leading American players who often use rotary valve trumpets are Adolph Herseth (Chicago Symphony), Charles Schlueter (Boston Symphony), and Philip Smith (New York Philharmonic). In Europe, Walter Singer, Josef Pomberger, Hans Gansch

Figure 3.3. **Cornets in B♭ and E♭ (Besson).** *Photo courtesy of the Boosey & Hawkes Group.*

(Vienna Philharmonic), Konradin Groth, and Martin Kretzer (Berlin Philharmonic) play the instrument exclusively.

The Cornet

There has been a remarkable resurgence of interest in America recently in the cornet. (See Figure 3.3.) Most of the major manufacturers have developed new models of traditional short "shepherd's crook" cornets. These form a vital part of the developing brass band movement, which constitutes a growing market for high-quality instruments. In wind bands cornets are being revived to lend authenticity to repertoire originally written for them. Wind band conductors are now interested in achieving an authentic timbre in such works as Gustav Holst's suites for military band and Ralph Vaughan Williams's *Toccata Marziale,* for example. Orchestral players are using cornets more often when specified by the composer. In the past, these parts were usually played on trumpets, thus negating the effect of the contrasting tone colors between cornets and trumpets that was intended by composers such as Berlioz, Franck, and Debussy.

There should be a great difference in tone and style between trumpet and cornet. Genuine cornet tone is darker and much softer in timbre than the clear, ringing trumpet sound, and should be colored with an expressive, vocal-style vibrato. Such a timbre can be achieved only through the use of a mouthpiece with a distinctly deeper and more conical cup. Trumpet players often use the same mouthpiece with the smaller cornet shank when performing on the cornet, thereby losing much of the contrast inherent in the two instruments. In fact, most cornet mouthpieces available today are actually trumpet mouthpieces with a cornet shank. The only true cornet mouthpieces available are the Denis Wick models, particularly the numbers 4 and 5, which were designed about 25 years ago in collaboration with Thomas Wilson, former principal cornet of H.M. Scots Guards Band.

Most manufacturers also produce "long-model" cornets; these are constructed in more of a trumpet pattern and omit the traditional shepherd's crook of the bell section. Unfortunately, these changes affect the timbre, which is closer to that of the trumpet than the cornet.

The cornet is at its best in melodic passages where its beautiful, voicelike tone can be very expressive. Another asset is its extraordinary agility, which surpasses that of the trumpet. The best way to form a concept of genuine cornet tone and style is to seek out recordings of the many superb British brass bands. These bands have an unbroken performance tradition reaching back to the nineteenth century and have maintained their style independent of the influence of the trumpet and modern orchestral brass playing in general. (Appendix B lists representative recordings.) Other excellent sources are Salvation Army brass bands, where a premium is placed on melodic expression in performance. Of particular interest are two recordings produced by the International Trumpet Guild. One features performances of the legendary Herbert L. Clarke dating from 1904 to 1921 (Crystal cassette 450). The other is a collection of recordings by great cornetists from the turn of the century such as Walter Rogers, Allesandro Liberati, and Bohumir Kryl (International Trumpet Guild-ITG 004). Both recordings should be carefully studied by all cornet and trumpet players.

Cornets are also made in E♭; these are used exclusively in brass bands. The E♭ soprano cornet is the highest voice of the brass band and plays an important solo part. Cornets are occasionally made in C, but these are rare today, mostly used by orchestral trumpeters accustomed to playing the C trumpet.

Which Trumpets Does the Player Need?

With the wide range of trumpets available, it might be helpful to know which instruments are needed by players in various situations. Students should have little need for any instrument other than the B♭ trumpet or cornet unless they aspire to major in trumpet on the college or conservatory level. In such cases, four trumpets are needed: B♭, C, E♭/D, and piccolo B♭/A. Professional symphonic players usually have more than one instrument in these keys, each offering different playing and sound qualities. In addition, the professional might own several rotary valve trumpets, a G trumpet, B♭ cornet, and a fluegelhorn. Jazz and studio players generally prefer a B♭ trumpet with lighter playing qualities and sound than do orchestral performers, and also have available a fluegelhorn and possibly a piccolo trumpet.

It is worthwhile for conductors of high school and college bands to make available a set of cornets for loan, when desired. Similarly, conductors of school and youth orchestras should have a few C trumpets available.

Intonation

Before going into the specific problems of trumpet intonation, it is useful to consider more generally the problem of playing brass instruments in tune. By far, the most common difficulty is that students tend to allow the instrument to determine intonation rather than controlling it themselves. The majority of notes require very subtle adjustments of embouchure and air pressure to bring them into tune. Certain notes must be corrected by some mechanical means, such as extending a valve slide or using an alternate fingering. (The acoustical problem of sharpness when valves are used in combination is discussed in Chapter 6.)

The aural–mental process that enables the brass player to start the sound on specific pitches and to play in tune involves an ability to pre-hear the note that is to be played. A pitch signal is sent from the "mental ear" to bring the embouchure and other elements of tone production into a specific adjustment for a note. Tone and style are guided in the same way. Missed notes or poor intonation are caused by the elements not being in the right adjustment for a given pitch; this is usually the result of an unclear or inaccurate pitch signal.

The procedure used by brass players is the same as is used in singing. The time-honored method of training is the study of solfège, or sightsinging. This study serves to fix pitches definitely in the mind so that a clear signal is sent to the voice. Any lack of clarity is revealed by the intonation of the melody being sung. By learning to reproduce exact vocal pitches, the brass player develops the ability to predetermine pitch rapidly and this carries over to the instrument. It is a good practice for brass players to sing as well as play the etudes and exercises being studied.

It is unfortunate that the study of sightsinging is rather neglected in the United States, and this accounts for a great deal of the intonation difficulties in school and college ensembles. More emphasis could be given to working on chorales and chord studies in school groups, because the practical experience of matching pitches with other players is the primary means of developing the skills necessary for good ensemble playing.

In examining intonation charts for the trumpet, one can become dismayed by the number of notes apparently needing correction. In practice, most of these are controlled by the adjustment of the embouchure and wind speed. This is an unconscious process that is controlled by the mental ear, which focuses on the exact pitch to be played. Technical demands limit the number of notes that can be altered by lengthening the first and third valve slides. However, certain notes require this type of correction to bring them into tune:

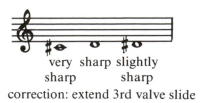

very sharp slightly
sharp   sharp
correction: extend 3rd valve slide

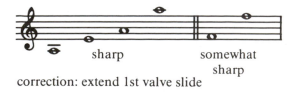

sharp   somewhat
                   sharp
correction: extend 1st valve slide

Obviously, valve slides cannot be moved in very rapid passages. In these situations the player selects notes that have sufficient duration to make correction practicable. Another approach is to preset the slide for a prominent note in a moving passage. This focuses the passage on a corrected pitch center and makes the entire passage sound more in tune. Although some players must make greater use of the slides than others, the general tendency is not to use them enough.[8]

---

[8] To facilitate moving the first valve slide, the player might consider replacing the ring with a sprung trigger. The trigger offers an advantage in that only one motion is necessary, rather than the double movement required by the ring.

Specific notes needing correction can be identified through the use of an electronic tuner. This is an essential piece of equipment that should be purchased by all serious students. In working with the tuner, the degree of correction necessary for all out-of-tune notes should be determined by observing the meter. Next, scales, intervals, and arpeggios should be slowly played while making the necessary corrections against various reference pitches sounded by the tuner. This will do a lot to improve a player's general intonation.

The low F♯, G, and G♯ tend to vary in pitch from player to player. Some must use the third valve slide, whereas others can play these notes in tune with minimal or no adjustment.

A more complex problem involves the D, E♭, and E, particularly on the C trumpet.[9]

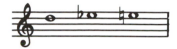

These notes are the fifth harmonics of their respective series, which tend to be low in pitch. In a well-designed trumpet, the lengths of the first and second valve loops have been calculated as a compromise intended to raise the D and E♭ slightly (shortened), but not so much as to render the other notes played with the first and second valves uncontrollably sharp (this is a primary reason why the first valve slide must be extended on the pitches shown in the preceding chart). As a result, the D and E♭ as well as the E are only minimally up to pitch and require an adjustment of embouchure and air stream to bring them into tune. On the C and higher trumpets, alternate fingerings are often used to improve the intonation of these notes, but the fingerings are awkward to use in fast passages. The problem is aggravated by too high a pitch placement on the third-space C, which has a wide band width or slot, and by not using the trigger on the F above. These factors cause some players to have fairly severe intonation problems in the C to G range, or a high pitch placement in this range in relation to the pitch centers of other areas of the instrument's compass.

The solution is to cultivate a lower pitch placement on the C and to make certain that the first valve slide is extended on the sharp notes. A lower placement on the C can be accomplished by centering the C between the G below and E above. As a temporary measure, the C might be fingered 2–3 until the feel of a lower C is established. (The 2–3 combination should be used only as an exercise because its pitch is too low for actual use.) When tuning, it is advisable to check the D, E♭, and E against the tuning note. If they seem flat, the main tuning slide should be brought inward until these notes form accurate intervals with the reference pitch. It is essential to use the first valve trigger on the top-line F and A above, to bring them into a better pitch relationship with the D, E♭, and E. This problem is present on the B♭ trumpet and most acute on the C, D, and E♭ trumpets, but for some unknown reason it causes fewer difficulties on rotary valve trumpets.

Playing in tune is, above all, a practical skill that requires careful listening and experience in matching other players in ensembles. Too much analysis often creates further problems. The best approach is to adopt a relaxed, natural approach to intonation, as one would in singing. Playing in small ensembles provides invaluable ex-

---

[9] The author is indebted to Professor Clifford Lillya for clarifying this problem.

perience, as do sectional rehearsals. A useful rehearsal procedure is to have two or three parts play alone. In this way, problems in intonation and balance can be clearly heard and corrected.

Transposition

Students often ask why transposition is necessary. Would it not be simpler to provide parts already transposed for B♭ or C trumpet?

The origin of the problem goes back to the era of the natural (valveless) trumpet, when it was customary for notes of the harmonic series to be read in C. A crook would be inserted to obtain the desired sounding pitch. For example, Mozart notated the trumpet parts to the *Prague Symphony* (No. 38 in D, K. 504) in the key of C with the instruction that the D crook be used. By always keeping the notation of the harmonic series the same, irrespective of the key of the composition, the parts were made easier for the players to read and perform using the harmonic series of the natural trumpet. The tradition of writing the fundamental and its harmonics in C continued into the valve era and persists today. Trumpeters must be prepared to transpose from parts originally written for trumpets in A, D, E♭, E, and F, to name some of the common keys.

Transposed parts for B♭ or C trumpet are not ordinarily provided for several reasons. Orchestral trumpeters often substitute trumpets in different keys on various parts and it would be difficult for publishers to keep up with changing approaches and individual preferences. Also, switching instruments is made easier for the player by having learned the part in its original notation. Above all, there is a certain tradition and pride in the trumpeter's art of being able to play from the part as the composer wrote it; therefore, professional trumpeters tend to look down on the use of transposed parts. New compositions, however, should be notated at concert pitch, leaving the choice of which trumpet to use to the player. This applies to parts for the piccolo trumpet as well. Band parts are best written for the B♭ trumpet.

There are two methods used in transposition: interval and clef. In the interval system, the notes are mentally moved upward or downward the correct distance between the key of the trumpet specified in the part and the trumpet that will be used. The key signature must be altered in the same way. For example, in Strauss's *Ein Heldenleben*, the part for E♭ trumpet must be read up a perfect fourth when played on a B♭ trumpet because the B♭ sounds a fourth below the E♭ instrument. If the part is to be played on a C trumpet, the notes must be moved upward a minor third:

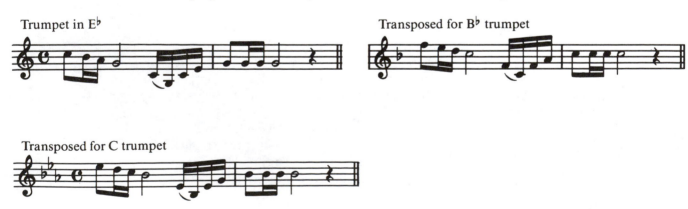

Trumpet in E♭

Transposed for B♭ trumpet

Transposed for C trumpet

When the distance is only a half step, as in transposing A parts on the B♭ trumpet, one of two procedures can be used, depending on the key signature. If the part is written without key signature or in a sharp key, the passage may be read in the parallel flat key by altering the key signature:

If the passage is written with a flat key signature, the notes are visually moved downward to the next line or space and the key is lowered a half step:

In the clef method, the notes need not be moved on the staff. Only the appropriate clef and key signature are mentally inserted at the beginning of the line:

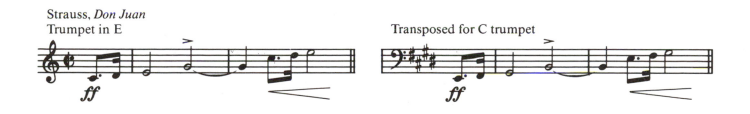

The common transpositions are shown in the following tables:

Transposition Table: Interval Method

Key of Part	Played on B♭ Trumpet	Played on C Trumpet
A	Half step lower	Minor 3rd lower
B♭	—	Major 2nd lower
C	Major 2nd higher	—
D	Major 3rd higher	Major 2nd higher
E♭	Perfect 4th higher	Minor 3rd higher
E	Augmented 4th higher	Major 3rd higher
F	Perfect 5th higher	Perfect 4th higher

Note: key signature must also be changed.

Transposition Table: Clef Method

Key of Part	Played on B♭ Trumpet	Played on C Trumpet
A	Tenor clef	—
B♭	—	Tenor clef
C	Alto clef	—
D	Bass clef	Alto clef
E♭	Mezzo-soprano clef	Bass clef
E	Mezzo-soprano clef	Bass clef
F	—	Mezzo-soprano clef

Note: key signature must also be changed.

In performing Baroque works written for trumpet in D on the piccolo trumpet in A, the part should be read a perfect fifth lower in the key of F. C parts may be read on the A piccolo by using the bass clef.

Ultimately, it is the time devoted to the study of transposition that is important, not the method used. Not all of the study time must be with the instrument. Although some daily instrumental work is necessary to orient the ear to different pitch levels, eye and finger coordination may be developed by reading silently and pretending to press the valves. In this way, nonpractice hours can be used to further transposition skills. Simple materials, such as familiar etudes and melodies, should be used at first, gradually progressing to studies specifically designed for transposition.[10]

Mutes

In scores where no specific instruction is given other than that a passage is to be muted, it is assumed that the straight mute is intended. To achieve a blend in muted sound, it is best if mutes of different materials or makers are not mixed within the same section because they tend to vary in intonation and timbre. The conventional straight mute is usually made from aluminum (although sometimes other metals and plastic are used) and produces a resonantly pungent timbre. Straight mutes are also constructed from fiber; these have a softer, less cutting sound. (See Figure 3.4.) It is customary for a composer to specify when a fiber mute is to be used in place of the customary metal type.

Because there are differences in the bell throats of various trumpets, it may be necessary to sandpaper a mute's corks to obtain good intonation. A properly adjusted mute will still play slightly sharp; the best method of correcting this is to place a pencil mark on the trumpet's main tuning slide at the beginning of rehearsal. The slide can then be extended for muted passages and returned to the mark for open playing. The amount of correction necessary can be determined by playing open and muted pitches into an electronic tuner. A special mute must be used on the piccolo trumpet due to its small bell.

There is an entire range of specialized mutes, each producing its own specific timbre. Of these, the cup mute and harmon or wa-wa mute are the most common.

---

[10] See Lucien Thévet, *Cinquante exercices à changement de ton* [*Fifty Exercises with Changes of Key*] (Alphonse Leduc); Ernst Sachse, *100 Studies* (International Music Co.); Bordogni-Porret, *24 Vocalises* (Alphonse Leduc); Mel Broiles, *Have Trumpet . . . Will Transpose* (Charles Colin); Ernest Williams, *Method of Transposition* (Charles Colin).

Figure 3.4. **Assorted mutes for brass instruments (Denis Wick).** *Photo courtesy of Boosey & Hawkes Musical Instruments.*

The latter incorporates an extendible tube that may be covered and uncovered to create the wa-wa effect. The tube can be adjusted to different lengths for distance effects, or omitted entirely for yet another color. The notation used for the wa-wa effect, and also with hats and plungers, is + (closed), and o (open).

Occasionally, a cloth bag is placed over the bell to dull and soften the sound. A very useful mute is the Charlie Spivak Whispa-Mute, which allows the performer to play comfortably, yet produce an extremely soft sound. It is sometimes used as a substitute for the straight mute in very quiet passages. Mutes designed for practicing have appeared recently and these are helpful on tours and in other difficult practice situations.

Trumpet Mutes

Straight mutes:
  Metal
  Fiber
  Plastic
  Piccolo trumpet mute
Cup mute
Felt-lined cup mute
Harmon or wa-wa mute
  (also version for piccolo trumpet)
Fiber plunger

Plunger straight mute
Bucket mute
Buzz-wow mute
Whispa-mute
Fiber derby
Felt hat
Cloth bag
Clear or solo tone mute
Rubber plunger

Recommended Literature[11]

COMPLETE METHODS

ARBAN: *Complete Conservatory Method*, ed. Goldman and Smith (C. Fischer)

*ARBAN: *Méthode complète*, ed. Maire, 3 vols. (A. Leduc)

CLODOMIR: *Méthode complète*, ed. Job (A. Leduc)

*SAINT-JACOME: *Grand Method* (C. Fischer)

ELEMENTARY METHODS

CLARKE: *Elementary Studies* (C. Fischer)

GORDON: *Physical Approach to Elementary Brass Playing* (C. Fischer)

LONGINOTTI: *L'Etude de la trompette* (Editions Henn)

McDUNN AND RUSCH: *Méthode de trompette*, 2 vols. (Leduc)

RIDGEON: *Brass for Beginners* (Boosey & Hawkes)

ROBINSON: *Rubank Elementary Method* (Rubank)

ROSENFELD: *A Method for Trumpet* (Schaffner)

VANNETELBOSCH: *Trumpet for Beginners*, vol. 1 (Leduc)

WIGGINS: *First Tunes & Studies* (Oxford)

WILLIAMS: *Modern Method* (Colin)

STUDIES

MEDIUM TO MEDIUM-DIFFICULT

BENNETT: *14 Melodic Studies* (R. King) (Leduc)

BENNETT: *18 Preliminary Studies* (R. King) (Leduc)

*BORDOGNI: *24 Vocalises*, trans. Porret (transposition) (A. Leduc)

*BOUSQUET: *36 Celebrated Studies*, ed. Goldman (C. Fischer)

*BRANDT: *34 Studies and 24 Last Studies*, ed. Vacchiano (Belwin-Mills)

BROILES: *Have Trumpet . . . Will Transpose* (transposition) (C. Colin)

*BUSSER: *12 Melodic Studies* (Leduc)

*CHAVANNE: *25 Characteristic Studies* (Leduc)

*CLARKE: *Technical Studies* (C. Fischer)

*CLARKE: *Setting Up Drills* (C. Fischer)

*CLODOMIR: *Etudes caractéristiques* (Leduc)

*CLODOMIR: *Petits exercises* (Leduc)

*CLODOMIR: *Vingt études chantantes* (Leduc)

*CLODOMIR: *Vingt études de mécanisme* (Leduc)

*CLODOMIR: *Vingt études mignonnes* (Leduc)

*COLIN: *Advanced Lip Flexibilities* (C. Colin)

*DOKCHIDZER: *Methode de trompette* (Leduc)

*ENDRESEN: *Supplementary Studies* (Rubank)

*GALLAY: *22 Exercises*, ed. Maire (A. Leduc)

*GOLDMAN: *Practical Studies* (C. Fischer)

GOWER AND VOXMAN (ED.):   *Rubank Advanced Method* (Rubank)

*GROTH: *Etudes on New Tonguing and Breathing Techniques* (Zimmermann)

HERING: *32 Etudes* (C. Fischer)

HOVALDT: *Lip Flexibility* (R. King)

JOHNSON: *Progressive Studies for the High Register* (H. Gore)

KOPPRASCH: *60 Studies*, ed. Gumbert and Herbst, 2 vols. (C. Fischer)

*LAURENT: *Etudes pratiques*, 3 vols. (A. Leduc)

*LAURENT: *Soixante études et exercices* (multiple tonguing) (Leduc)

*LAURENT: *Vingt études faciles et de moyenne force* (preparatory to *Etudes pratiques*) (Leduc)

*PARES: *Scales* (Rubank)

SALVATION ARMY: *101 Technical Exercises* (Salvation Army)

*SCHLOSSBERG: *Daily Drills and Technical Studies* (M. Baron)

SKORNICKA: *Rubank Intermediate Method* (Rubank)

SMITH: *Lip Flexibility* (C. Fischer)

STAIGERS: *Flexibility Studies*, 2 vols. (C. Fischer)

STAMP: *Warm-Ups Plus Studies* (Bim)

*THÉVET: *Cinquante exercices à changement de ton* [*Fifty Exercises with Changes of Key*] (transposition) (A. Leduc)

*VACCHIANO: *Trumpet Routines* (C. Colin)

VANNETELBOSCH: *20 Melodic and Technical Studies* (Leduc)

VANNETELBOSCH: *Trumpet for Beginners*, vol. 2 (Leduc)

*WILLIAMS: *The Best of Ernest Williams* (Colin)

*WILLIAMS: *Method of Transposition* (Colin)

ZAUDER: *Embouchure & Technique Studies* (C. Colin)

DIFFICULT

ANDRÉ: *12 Etudes caprices dans le style baroque* (piccolo trumpet) (Editions Billaudot)

BALASANYAN: *20 Studies*, ed. Foveau (International)

BALAY: *15 Etudes* (A. Leduc)

*N. BIZET: *12 Grandes études de perfectionnement* (A. Leduc)

BODET: *16 Etudes de virtuosité d'après J. S. Bach* (A. Leduc)

BODET: *25 Reading Exercises* (Leduc)

---

[11] Essential material is indicated by an asterisk. For additional literature, the reader is referred to the *Brass Player's Guide*, available from Robert King Music Sales, 140 Main St., North Easton, MA 02356. Repertoire lists appear in the texts by Dale and Sherman.

BROILES: *Trumpet Baroque*, 2 vols. (piccolo trumpet) (Queen City)

*CHARLIER: *Etudes transcendantes* (A. Leduc)

*CLARKE: *Characteristic Studies* (C. Fischer)

DUHEM: *24 Etudes* (C. Fischer)

*GALLAY: *12 Grand caprices*, ed. Maire (A. Leduc)

*GALLAY: *39 Preludes*, ed. Maire (A. Leduc)

GLANTZ: *48 Studies* (Colin)

HARRIS: *Advanced Studies* (C. Colin)

HICKMAN: *The Piccolo Trumpet* (Tromba Publications)

LONGINOTTI: *Studies in Classical and Modern Style* (International)

MAXIME-ALPHONSE: *Etudes nouvelles*, 3 vols. (Leduc)

*PETIT: *15 Etudes techniques et mélodiques* (A. Leduc)

*PETIT: *Grandes études* (A. Leduc)

*SACHSE: *100 Studies* (transposition) (International)

*SMITH: *Top Tones* (C. Fischer)

WEBSTER: *Method for Piccolo Trumpet* (Brass Press)

UNACCOMPANIED TRUMPET (CORNET)

DIFFICULT

ADLER: *Canto I* (Oxford)

*ARNOLD: *Fantasy* (Faber)

BACH: *Six Short Solo Suites for Trumpet* (R. King)

BOZZA: *Graphismes* (A. Leduc)

BURRELL: *5 Concert Studies* (Oxford)

CHEETHAM: *Concoctions* (Presser)

DELLA PERUTI: *Elegy Set* (Wimbledon)

DOKSHITSER: *Images romantiques* (M. Reift)

HENZE: *Sonatina* (Dunster Music)

*PERSICHETTI: *Parable* (Presser)

POWELL: *Alone* (Brass Press)

PRESSER: *Second Suite* (Presser)

REICHE: *Abblasen* (Philharmusica)

RENWICK: *Encore Piece* (Tromba Publications)

SAMPSON: *Litany of Breath* (Brass Press)

SCHUMAN: *25 Opera Snatches* (Presser)

TRUMPET AND CORNET WITH PIANO

EASY

ADAMS: *The Holy City* (Boosey & Hawkes)

BACH: *Aria: Bist du bei mir*, arr. Fitzgerald (Belwin-Mills)

BAKALEINIKOFF: *Serenade* (Belwin-Mills)

BARSHAM (ED.):   *Shore's Trumpet* (Boosey & Hawkes)

BARSHAM AND JONES: *Trumpet Solos*, 2 vols. (Chester)

BEECHEY (ED.):   *Trumpet Tunes of the English Baroque* (Schott)

BORST AND BOGAR (EDS.):   *Trumpet Music for Beginners* (Editio Musica)

DEARNLEY (ED.):   *8 Easy Pieces* (Chester)

DEXTER AND DE SMET: *First Year Trumpeter*, 2 vols. (E. Ashdown)

HANDEL: *A Handel Solo Album*, arr. Lethbridge (Oxford)

HAYDN: *Andante*, arr. Voxman (Rubank)

HAYDN: *A Haydn Solo Album*, arr. Lawrence (Oxford)

HERING (ED.):   *Easy Pieces for the Young Trumpeter* (C. Fischer)

LAWTON (ED.):   *Old English Trumpet Tunes*, 2 vols. (Oxford)

LAWTON (ED.):   *The Young Trumpet Player*, 3 vols. (Oxford)

LOWDEN: *Easy Play-Along Solos* (recording included) (Kendor)

MILLS AND ROMM: *Beginning Trumpet Solos*, 2 vols. (with cassette accompaniment) (H. Leonard)

MOZART: *Concert Aria*, arr. Voxman (Rubank)

MOZART: *A Mozart Solo Album*, arr. Lethbridge (Oxford)

PHILIPS (ED.):   *Classical & Romantic Album*, vol. 1 (Oxford)

TENAGLIA: *Aria*, arr. Fitzgerald (Presser)

VANDERCOOK: *Marigold* (C. Fischer)

VANDERCOOK: *Morning Glory* (C. Fischer)

WALLACE AND MILLER: *First Book of Solos* (Faber)

WALLACE AND MILLER: *Second Book of Solos* (Faber)

WILLNER (ED.):   *Classical Album* (Boosey & Hawkes)

MEDIUM TO MEDIUM-DIFFICULT[12]

ANCELIN: *Six chants populaires de basse-bretagne* (Leduc)

ANDERSON: *Trumpeter's Lullaby* (Belwin-Mills)

*ANDRÉ-BLOCH: *Meou-Tan Yin* (Leduc)

BAKALEINIKOV: *Polonaise* (Belwin-Mills)

BALAKIREFF: *Georgian Song*, trans. Smedvig (International)

BALAY: *Petite pièce concertante* (Belwin-Mills)

BARAT: *Andante et scherzo* (A. Leduc)

BARAT: *Orientale* (Leduc)

*BOZZA: *Badinage* (A. Leduc)

BURGON: *Brideshead Revisited* (Chester)

BURGON: *Lullaby & Aubade* (Galaxy)

---

[12] Works requiring the use of high trumpets are noted with a plus sign (+).

BURGON: *Toccata* (Galaxy)

BUSSER: *Variations* (Leduc)

CHANCE: *Credo* (Boosey & Hawkes)

*+J. CLARKE: *Trumpet Voluntary*, arr. Voisin (International)

COOLS: *Solo de Concours* (Leduc)

CORELLI: *Prelude & Minuet*, arr. Powell (Southern)

*DELMAS: *Choral et variations* (Billaudot)

DELMAS: *Variation tendre* (Billaudot)

FIOCCO: *Arioso* (Presser)

FITZGERALD: *English Suite* (Presser)

FITZGERALD: *Gaelic Suite* (Presser)

FLOORE: *9 Simple Pieces* (Tierolff)

FORBES (ED.):   *Classical & Romantic Album*, vols. 2 and 3 (Oxford)

GAUBERT: *Cantabile et scherzetto* (C. Fischer)

GEORGES: *Légende d'armor* (Enoch)

GETCHELL (ED.):   *Master Solos* (H. Leonard)

*GIBBONS: *Suite* (Galaxy)

*HANDEL: *Aria con variazioni*, arr. Fitzgerald (Belwin-Mills)

HANDEL: *Sonata #3*, arr. Powell (Southern)

*HOVHANESS: *Prayer of Saint Gregory* (Southern)

JACOB: *4 Little Pieces* (Emerson)

JAMES: *Windmills* (B. Ramsey)

LANCEN: *Quatre soli* (Leduc)

LAWTON: *Old English Trumpet Tunes* (Oxford)

LEDGER (ED.):   *Warlike Music 1760* (Oxford)

MILLS AND ROMM: *Intermediate Trumpet Solos* (with cassette accompaniment) (H. Leonard)

MORTIMER (ED.):   *Souvenir Album* (Boosey & Hawkes)

PERSICHETTI: *The Hollow Men* (Presser)

*PURCELL: *Sonata*, ed. Voisin (transposed) (International)

RICHARDSON (ED.):   *6 Trumpet Tunes* (Boosey & Hawkes)

RICHARDSON (ED.):   *6 More Trumpet Tunes* (Boosey & Hawkes)

ROPARTZ: *Andante et allegro* (Southern)

SIMON: *Willow Echoes* (C. Fischer)

TELEMANN: *Heroic Music*, arr. Lawton (Oxford)

VOXMAN (ED.):   *Concert & Contest Collection* (Rubank)

WASTALL (ED.):   *First Repertoire Pieces for Trumpet* (Boosey & Hawkes)

WIGGINS: *Trumpeter's Tune* (Chester)

DIFFICULT

+*ALBINONI: *Concerto in D Major*, arr. Thilde (Billaudot)

+ALBRECHTSBERGER: *Concertino* (Brass Press)

ANTHEIL: *Sonata* (Weintraub)

*ARBAN: *Carnival of Venice* (C. Fischer)

*ARBAN: *Piano Accompaniments to 12 Celebrated Fantasies* (C. Fischer)

ARNOLD: *Concerto* (Faber)

ARUTUNIAN: *Aria et scherzo* (Leduc)

ARUTUNIAN: *Concert scherzo* (Bim)

*ARUTUNIAN: *Concerto* (International)

BACH: *Concerto en ut majeur* (with organ), trans. Tambyeff (Leduc)

V. BACH: *Hungarian Melodies* (PP Music)

BALAY: *Pièce de Concours* (Leduc)

BELLSTEDT: *La Mandolinata* (Southern)

BELLSTEDT: *Napoli* (Southern)

*BITSCH: *Quatre variations sur un thème de Domenico Scarlatti* (A. Leduc)

BLAZHEVICH: *Concerto No. 5* (International)

BLAZHEVICH: *Scherzo* (Reift)

*BLOCH: *Proclamation* (Broude Bros.)

BOEHME: *Konzert in F Moll* (Benjamin)

BOZZA: *Rustiques* (A. Leduc)

CELLIER: *Chevauchée fantastique* (Billaudot)

CHARLIER: *Solo de concours* (Schott Frères)

+CHARPENTIER: *Marche et triomphe et second air de trompette* (Leduc)

*H. CLARKE: *Music of Herbert L. Clarke*, 2 vols. (Warner Bros.)

+J. CLARKE: *Suite in D Major* (Musica Rara)

+*J. CLARKE: *Trumpet Voluntary in D* (International)

CORDS: *Concert Fantasie* (C. Fischer)

+*CORELLI: *Sonata in D* (Musica Rara)

COSMA: *Concerto* (Billaudot)

DAVIES: *Sonata* (Schott)

DELERUE: *Concertino* (Leduc)

DONATO: *Prélude et Allegro* (Leduc)

EMMANUEL: *Sonate* (Leduc)

*ENESCO: *Legend* (International)

+FASCH: *Concerto* (Sikorski)

+D. GABRIELI: *Sonata No. 2 in D*, ed. Tarr (Musica Rara)

+D. GABRIELI: *Sonata No. 4 in D*, ed. Tarr (Musica Rara)

GLIÈRE: *Concerto*, ed. Dokshitser (Reift)

*GOEDICKE: *Concert Etude* (Belwin-Mills)

GREGSON: *Concerto* (Novello)

*HAYDN: *Concerto in E♭*, ed. Robbins-Landon and Tarr (Universal Edition); also version with cassette accompaniment (H. Leonard)

+M. HAYDN: *Concerto in D* (A. Benjamin)

+M. HAYDN: *Concerto No. 2*, ed. Tarr (Musica Rara)

+HERTEL: *Concerto No. 1*, ed. Tarr (Brass Press)

+HERTEL: *Concerto No. 2*, ed. Tarr (Musica Rara)

*HINDEMITH: *Sonate* (Schott)

*HONEGGER: *Intrada* (Salabert)

HOROVITZ: *Concerto* (Novello)

HOWARTH: *Concerto* (Chester)

*HUBEAU: *Sonate* (Durand)

*HUMMEL: *Concerto*, ed. Tarr (Universal); also version with cassette accompaniment (H. Leonard)

HUSA: *Concerto* (Associated)

*IBERT: *Impromptu* (A. Leduc)

+JACCHINI: *Deux concertos-sonates* (Leduc)

+JACCHINI: *Sonata in D* (Musica Rara)

JOLIVET: *Concerto No. 2* (A. Leduc)

*KENNAN: *Sonata* (Warner Bros.)

KOETSIER: *Concertino* (Bim)

KOETSIER: *Sonatina* (Donemus)

LARSSON: *Concertino* (Gehrmans)

LONGINOTTI: *Scherzo Iberico* (Editions Henn)

LUENING: *Introduction and Allegro* (Peters)

*MAGER (ED.):   *9 Grand Solos de Concert* (Southern)

MENDEZ: *Jota* (C. Fischer)

MENDEZ: *Mexican Hat Dance* (C. Fischer)

MENDEZ: *La virgen de la Macarena* (Koff Music)

+MOLTER: *Concerto No. 1 in D* (Musica Rara)

MOUQUET: *Légende héroïque* (Leduc)

*+L. MOZART: *Concerto in D*, ed. Thilde (Billaudot)

+MUDGE: *Concerto in D* (Musica Rara)

+*NERUDA: *Concerto in E♭*, ed. Tarr (Bim)

PACHMUTOVA: *Konzert* (Reift)

PEASLEE: *Nightsongs* (Margun)

PILSS: *Concerto* (King)

PILSS: *Sonate* (Universal)

PORRINO: *Concertino* (Ricordi)

*+PURCELL: *Sonata* (original key) (Schott)

RIISAGER: *Concertino* (W. Hansen)

SAINT-SAËNS-BUSSER: *Fantaisie en Mi Bémol* (Leduc)

SCHLAEPFER: *Ascensus* (Bim)

SCHULLER: *Concerto* (Associated)

STAIGERS: *Carnival of Venice* (C. Fischer)

+STANLEY: *Suite No. 1 of Trumpet Voluntaries* (Brass Press)

*+STANLEY: *Trumpet Tune*, arr. Coleman (Oxford)

*STEVENS: *Sonata* (Peters)

+STOELZEL: *Concerto in D* (Billaudot)

+STRADELLA: *Sinfonia*, 2 vols. (Musica Rara)

+TARTINI: *Concerto in D* (Selmer)

*+TELEMANN: *Concerto in D* (Musica Rara)

TELEMANN: *Heroic Music*, arr. Lawton (Oxford)

TISNÉ: *Héraldiques* (Billaudot)

*TOMASI: *Concerto* (A. Leduc)

*TORELLI: *Concertino in C* (International)

*+TORELLI: *Concerto in D*, ed. Tarr (Musica Rara)

*+TORELLI: *Sinfonia (G1)* (Sikorski)

*+TORELLI: *Sinfonia (G2)*, ed. Tarr (Musica Rara)

*+TORELLI: *Sinfonia (G3)*, ed. Tarr (Musica Rara)

*+TORELLI: *Sinfonia (G4)*, ed. Tarr (Musica Rara)

*+TORELLI: *Sonata*, ed. Neilson (International)

*+TORELLI: *Sonata (G5)*, ed. Tarr (Musica Rara)

*+TORELLI: *Sonata (G6)*, ed. Tarr (Musica Rara)

*+TORELLI: *Sonata (G7)*, ed. Tarr (Musica Rara)

*+TORELLI: *2 Concertos (G8. G9)* (Sikorski)

TOSI: *Mundial-Concerto* (Bim)

TUTHILL: *Sonata* (Warner Bros.)

+VEJVANOVSKY: *Sonata* (Edition Ka We)

WILDER: *Sonata* (Margun)

WILDER: *Suite* (Margun)

WILLIAMS: *Adirondacks Polka* (Colin)

WILLIAMS: *Concerto No. 2* (Colin)

WILLIAMS: *Prelude & Scherzo* (Colin)

WILLIAMS: *Sonata* (Colin)

ZBINDEN: *Concertino* (Schott)

RECOMMENDED BOOKS ON THE TRUMPET AND CORNET[13]

*ALTENBURG, JOHANN ERNST.   *Trumpeters' and Kettledrummers' Art.* Trans. by Edward H. Tarr. Nashville: Brass Press, 1974.

*BACH, VINCENT.   *The Art of Trumpet Playing.* Elkhart, Ind.: Vincent Bach Corporation, 1969.

*BATE, PHILIP.   *The Trumpet and Trombone: An Outline of Their History, Development, and Construction.* 2nd ed. New York: Norton, 1978.

[13] Many interesting articles appear in the *International Trumpet Guild Journal* and other periodicals listed in Appendix C.

*BELLAMAH, JOSEPH L.   *A Trumpeter's Treasury of Information*. San Antonio, Tex.: Southern Music Co., 1969.

BENDINELLI, CESARE.   *Tutta l'arte dell trombetta (1614)*. Facsimile, ed. E. H. Tarr. Kassel: Bärenreiter, 1975.

BUSH, IRVING.   *Artistic Trumpet Technique and Study*. Hollywood: Highland Music, 1962.

CARDOSO, WILFREDO.   *Ascending Trumpets: The Use of Trumpets with Ascending Valves in Symphonic Music, Opera, and Ballet*. Buenos Aires: Cardoso, 1978.

CARDOSO, WILFREDO.   *High Trumpets: Practical Applications of High Trumpets in Trumpet Solos in the Works of J. S. Bach, Baroque Music, Symphony Orchestra and Opera Repertoire*. Buenos Aires: Cardoso, 1977.

CARNOVALE, NORBERT, AND PAUL F. DOERKSEN.   *Twentieth Century Music for Trumpet and Orchestra*. 2nd ed. Nashville, Tenn.: Brass Press, 1994.

*CLARKE, HERBERT L.   *How I Became a Cornetist*. Kenosha, Wis.: Leblanc Educational Publications, n.d.

DALE, DELBERT A.   *Trumpet Technique*. London: Oxford University Press, 1967.

*D'ATH, NORMAN W.   *Cornet Playing*. London: Boosey & Hawkes, 1960.

*DAVIDSON, LOUIS.   *Trumpet Profiles*. Bloomington, Ind.: Davidson, 1975.

DAVIDSON, LOUIS.   *Trumpet Techniques*. Rochester: Wind Music, 1970.

FANTINI, GIROLAMO.   *Modo per imparare a sonare di tromba* [*Method for Learning to Play the Trumpet in a Warlike Way as Well as Musically*]. Nashville, Tenn.: Brass Press, 1975.

FOSTER, ROBERT E.   *Practical Hints on Playing the Trumpet/Cornet*. Melville, N.Y.: Belwin Mills, 1983.

HANSON, FAY.   *Brass Playing*. New York: Carl Fischer, 1975.

HYATT, JACK H.   "The Soprano and Piccolo Trumpets: Their History, Literature, and a Tutor." D.M.A. thesis, Boston University, 1974. UM 74–20, 473.

*JOHNSON, KEITH.   *The Art of Trumpet Playing*. Ames: Iowa State University Press, 1981.

LOWREY, ALVIN.   *Trumpet Discography*. Denver: National Trumpet Symposium, n.d.

MATHEZ, JEAN-PIERRE.   *Joseph Jean-Baptiste Laurent Arban, 1825–1889: Portrait d'un musicien français du XIXe siècle*. Moudon, Switzerland: Editions BIM, 1977.

MATHIE, GORDON.   *The Trumpet Teacher's Guide*. Cincinnati, Ohio: Queen City Brass Publications, 1984.

Musique pour trompette: Catalogue thématique. Paris: Alphonse Leduc, 1994.

*SHERMAN, ROGER.   *The Trumpeter's Handbook*. Athens, Ohio: Accura Music, 1979.

*SMITHERS, DON.   *The Music and History of the Baroque Trumpet Before 1721*. London: J.M. Dent, 1973.

WEBSTER, GERALD.   *Method for Piccolo Trumpet*. Nashville, Tenn.: Brass Press, 1980.

OTHER BOOKS OF INTEREST TO BRASS PLAYERS[14]

*ANDERSON, PAUL G.   *Brass Solo and Study Material Music Guide*. Evanston, Ill.: The Instrumentalist Co., 1976.

*BAINES, ANTHONY.   *Brass Instruments: Their History and Development*. London: Faber & Faber, 1976.

BARBOUR, J. MURRAY.   *Trumpets, Horns, and Music*. East Lansing: Michigan State University Press, 1964.

BELLAMAH, JOSEPH L.   *Brass Facts*. San Antonio, Tex.: Southern Music, 1961.

BRASS ANTHOLOGY.   Evanston, Ill.: The Instrumentalist Co., 1984.

BROWN, MERRILL E.   *Teaching the Successful High School Brass Section*. West Nyack, N.Y.: Parker, 1981.

*CARSE, ADAM.   *Musical Wind Instruments*. New York: Da Capo Press, 1965 (originally published by Macmillan, 1940).

DEVOL, JOHN.   *Brass Music for the Church*. Plainview, N.Y.: Harold Branch, 1974.

ELIASON, ROBERT E.   *Early American Brass Makers*. Nashville, Tenn.: Brass Press, 1981.

*FARKAS, PHILIP.   *The Art of Brass Playing*. Rochester, N.Y.: Wind Music, 1962.

*FARKAS, PHILIP.   *The Art of Musicianship*. Bloomington, Ind.: Musical Publications, 1976.

LAWRENCE, IAN.   *Brass in Your School*. London: Oxford University Press, 1975.

MACDONALD, DONNA.   *The Odyssey of the Philip Jones Brass Ensemble*. Moudon, Switzerland: Éditions BIM, 1986.

MECKNA, MICHAEL.   *Twentieth-Century Brass Soloists*. Westport, Conn.: Greenwood Press, 1994.

MENDE, EMILIE.   *Pictorial Family Tree of Brass Instruments in Europe*. Moudon, Switzerland: Éditions BIM, 1978.

RASMUSSEN, MARY.   *A Teacher's Guide to the Literature for Brass Instruments*. Durham, N.H.: Brass Quarterly, 1968.

*SEVERSON, PAUL, AND MARK McDUNN.   *Brass Wind Artistry*. Athens, Ohio: Accura Music, 1983.

*STEWART, DEE.   *Arnold Jacobs: The Legacy of a Master*. Northfield, Ill.: The Instrumentalist Publishing Co., 1987.

TARR, EDWARD.   *The Trumpet*. Portland, Ore.: Amadeus Press, 1988.

---

[14] A very useful guide to articles, books, and dissertations on brass instruments is Allen B. Skei's *Woodwind, Brass, and Percussion Instruments of the Orchestra: A Bibliographic Guide* (New York: Garland, 1985).

TAYLOR, ARTHUR R.   *Brass Bands*. London: Granada Publishing, Ltd., 1979.

*TRUSHEIM, WILLIAM H.   "Mental Imagery and Musical Performance: An Inquiry into Imagery Use by Eminent Orchestral Brass Players." Ed.D. dissertation, Rutgers University, 1987.

WATSON, J. PERRY.   *The Care and Feeding of a Community British Brass Band*. Farmingdale, N.Y.: Boosey & Hawkes, n.d.

WATSON, J. PERRY.   *Starting a British Brass Band*. Grand Rapids, Mich.: Yamaha International Corp., 1984.

WEAST, ROBERT.   *Keys to Natural Performance for Brass Players*. Des Moines, Iowa: Brass World, 1979.

CHAPTER 4

The Horn

Of the 43 or so varieties of horn available today,[1] some may be categorized as student instruments, others as general-purpose horns (see Figure 4.1), and still others as specialized high-register models, known as descant horns. There are differences in the keys in which the instruments are built: single horns in F or B♭; full or compensating double horns in F/B♭; double descant horns in B♭/F-alto, B♭/E♭-alto, and B♭/B♭-soprano; and full or compensating triple horns in F/B♭/F-alto (or B♭ soprano). Horns are made with rotary, piston, and Vienna valves, and the third valve can be descending or ascending. There are also variations in bore and bell-throat taper, as well as the material from which the instrument is made (yellow brass, gold brass, and nickel silver). Today's horn players have a wide array of excellent equipment at their disposal. To clarify the choices available and to gain an understanding of how each horn is used, the various types are considered individually.

The Single F Horn

With the exception of the Vienna horn (discussed below), single F horns today are intended specifically for beginners. Horn players tend to be more diverse in their playing and tonal concepts than other brass players. It is surprising, therefore, that there is such a unanimity of opinion as to the importance of beginning on the F horn. It is felt that in this way the student will develop a good concept of horn tone. Professional horn players strive basically for an F horn tone regardless of the key of the instrument used. One integrated tone is sought on the double horn, and players of single B♭ and descant horns try to maintain the characteristic timbre of the F horn as far as possible.

Although beginners sometimes start on a B♭ horn with good results, the F horn offers advantages for mastering the fundamental elements of horn playing, particularly accuracy and flexibility. If a single F horn is unavailable, the F section of a double horn will serve equally well.

The Double Horn

The horn most widely used today is the F/B♭ full double. Earlier, single B♭ horns were often used on first and third (high) parts in orchestras, and full doubles on second

---

[1] Paxman's catalog lists no fewer than 39 models; Alexander lists 29. The options of added stopping valves, F extensions for single B♭ horns, ascending third valve systems, differing bells, and wrapping patterns account for the availability of so many models. The output of most other firms is considerably smaller.

Figure 4.1. **Single and double horns (left to right): single F, single B♭ with stopping valve, compensating F/B♭ double, and full F/B♭ double (Alexander).** *Photo: Joseph Hetman.*

and fourth (low), but now entire sections of full doubles are found almost everywhere.

The first double horn was developed by a German hornist, Edmund Gumpert, in collaboration with the instrument maker Kruspe, who introduced it at Erfurt, Germany, in 1897. At that time, German horn players were increasingly using the B♭ crook, or horns built in B♭, in order to cope with the difficult parts being written by Strauss, Mahler, and other late-nineteenth-century composers. Although this made performing such parts easier, horn players missed the intonation and tone of the F horn in the middle and lower register.

Gumpert had the idea of building a B♭ horn with longer rotors and valve casings, so that two ranks of valve tubing could be accommodated. A change-valve directed the air column to one or both ranks of valve tubes. When the change-valve was in the F position, the air column went through both sides of the instrument—the normal B♭ tubing plus additional lengths to convert the horn's pitch to F. With the change-valve in the B♭ position, the F section was bypassed and the instrument functioned as an ordinary B♭ horn. This original type of double horn is known as a compensating double, to distinguish it from the full double horn that appeared a short time later. The full double horn is a simpler and more direct system that provides a better F section, but it is heavier due to the extra tubing required. In the full double configuration, the change-valve routes the air column directly through either the F or B♭ ranks of tubing before it re-enters the bell section. (See Figures 4.2 and 4.3.)

Although the double horn consists of two complete horns in one, it is not approached in that way by the player. A crossover point is established (usually written G♯ above middle C, or more rarely, C♯, a fourth higher) and the instrument is considered one horn (in the player's mind). The appropriate B♭ and F fingerings are used above and below the crossover point. Every effort is made to minimize differences in timbre between the F and B♭ sides, and it is difficult to detect when a skilled player passes from one side to the other. The double horn combines the tone and in-

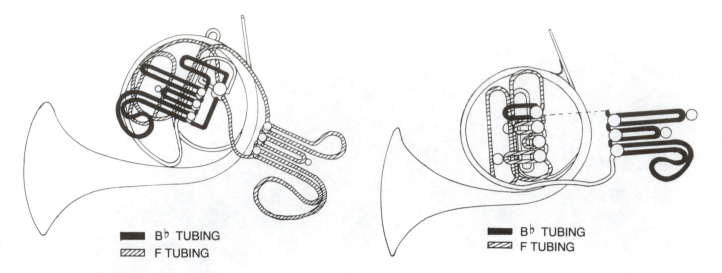

Figure 4.2. **Windways of a full double horn.**

Figure 4.3. **Windways of a compensating double horn.**

tonation of the F horn in the low and middle ranges with the B♭ horn's tone and se-curity in the high register.

Both types of double horn are in use today, but compensating doubles are be-coming increasingly rare. Compensating doubles are occasionally preferred by hor-nists who play primarily on the B♭ horn, but want the availability of an F section. In such cases, the F side is used only for the low range and one or two other notes (particularly the middle G). Played in this manner, the compensating double is a good solo instrument, being lighter in weight than a full double yet incorporating an F section. Compensating doubles are preferred by some orchestral players, par-ticularly in Scandinavia.

The Single B♭ Horn

In the period following the introduction of the double horn, the changeover to the new instrument was not universal. Many players preferred the lighter B♭ horn and felt that it offered better endurance and clarity of tone. Use of the single B♭ became widespread, especially in Germany (players of first and third parts who adopted double horns continued to play primarily on the B♭ side). It was found that a good blend of sound could be achieved with a mixture of single B♭s and full doubles. The Berlin Philharmonic used this format well into the 1950s, and the same arrangement was popular in England after German horns began to be used there. The B♭ horn was less common in the United States due to a preference for double horns, but one of the greatest players during the first half of the twentieth century, Willem Valke-nier, solo horn of the Boston Symphony in the Koussevitzsky era, played a single B♭ throughout his long career with that orchestra. Another important early player who used the single B♭ was Franz Xavier Reiter (a student of Franz Strauss), who played with the New York Philharmonic.

The single B♭ has always been a favorite solo instrument for its lightness, techni-cal agility, and accuracy. The great soloist Dennis Brain used an Alexander single B♭ exclusively for both orchestral and solo work after switching from a French-type sin-gle F piston horn around 1950. A similar single B♭ was used by Alan Civil. Another player who has made extensive use of one at various points in his career is German soloist Hermann Baumann . B♭ horns are still found in orchestras: Jeffrey Bryant, principal horn of the Royal Philharmonic Orchestra, uses an Alexander five-valve model. The single B♭ also offers definite advantages in chamber music, where its light response proves to be an asset in achieving delicate balances.

Single B♭ horns must be fitted with a stopping valve (handstopping is discussed below). This valve routes the vibrating air column through an additional length of tubing to lower the pitch three-quarters of a tone to produce an in-tune stopped note (this can be accomplished on the F horn by transposing down a half-step). With the slide of the stopping valve pushed in, the horn can be played in A, which is useful for high register parts such as Beethoven's Seventh Symphony. An F extension is often added to enable the player to reach notes below the ordinary B♭ range and to provide an improved low C. The extension can be either attached to the stopping valve or built into the instrument through an added fifth valve. A recent innovation is the addition of a C valve, which provides some further advantages in the high register.

The Ascending Third Valve Horn

The final two instruments that fall into the category of general-purpose horns are not in general use, but have flourished in specific geographical areas. The first of these, known in France as the *cor ascendant,* is constructed with an ascending third valve. This type of instrument dates from 1848, when Jules Halary invented a horn in which the air column was normally directed through the tubing of the third valve (without the valve being depressed). With a G crook, the extra length (one tone) of the third valve loop allowed the instrument to be played in F as long as only the first two valves were used. When the third valve was depressed, the extra tubing was bypassed and the instrument's pitch rose one tone to G. This offered a significant improvement in the upper register of the F horn. Around 1930, Louis Vuillermoz developed a compensating double horn based on this principle, and this instrument was widely used in France and Belgium until the mid-1970s.[2]

Aside from the ascending third-valve feature,[3] French-type horns have traditionally been made with piston valves and a slightly narrower bore and bell. The famous French makers, Selmer, Courtois, and Couesnon, all produced models of this type. The ascending third valve system has also been made available on regular medium- and large-bore rotary valve models by Alexander (Germany) and Paxman (England). For the past two decades, the usual descending rotary valve full double horns that are used elsewhere have most often been seen in French orchestras, rather than traditional piston valve instruments.

The Vienna Horn

The most distinctive horn in use today is actually a survivor from an earlier epoch. The principal instrument of the Vienna Philharmonic, the Vienna horn is unchanged from the instrument introduced by Leopold Uhlmann about 1830. Of sim-

[2] The controversy over the changes in the horn playing and instruments used in France is best represented in two articles: André Cazalet, "The Horn, the Brasses and France," *Brass Bulletin,* 81 (1993), pp. 48–55; and Lucien Thévet, "On the French School of Horn Playing," *Brass Bulletin,* 84 (1993), pp. 54–61. Thévet's thoughtful article raises issues that are relevant to all brass players.

[3] The use of the ascending third valve is presented in Lucien Thévet's *Méthode complète de cor* (Paris: Alphonse Leduc, 1960).

ilar bore and bell to the natural horns of that era and incorporating a removable F crook, the Vienna horn retains an authentic nineteenth-century tone quality and requires the playing skill of the great hornists of that period. It would have been easier for the Viennese players to adopt the B♭ or double horn, but to their credit, they have remained steadfast in their commitment to maintain the special timbre of the Vienna horn. In fact, the Vienna horn has become the trademark of the Vienna Philharmonic.

At low and medium volume levels, the Vienna horn has a pure, classic F horn tone; as the volume increases, the tone condenses into a bright, heroic quality at a lower dynamic level than on the B♭ or double horn. The lower threshold of the brighter timbre is used to good effect by the Vienna players in works of Bruckner, Wagner, and other nineteenth-century composers.

An important stylistic feature of Viennese horn playing is the glissandolike slur, which adds expressive character to romantic compositions. The double-piston Vienna valve[4] is thought to improve slurring by providing a better continuity of the air column through valve changes than the rotary valve. Perhaps due to a combination of bore, bell, and its more direct airways, the high register of the Vienna horn is usually far better than other types of single F horn. This is a reason for its survival as a viable professional instrument. For demanding high passages, a small F alto descant horn or the Paxman double F/F-alto is usually substituted for the Vienna horn.

Considering today's exacting standards for accuracy and the difficulty of playing the single F horn, it should be noted that Viennese hornists achieve a technical standard comparable to sections composed of modern horns, while retaining their special sound. Viennese horn playing is held in great esteem by all hornists, especially the performances of its finest players, such as the late Gottfried von Freiberg and Roland Berger (see Figure 4.4).

Descant Horns

In the years following 1900, horns pitched an octave above the F horn appeared in Germany to aid the performance of Baroque horn parts, which are notorious for their high-register demands. The small bore and bell of these instruments were not ideal, but in the absence of an alternative, these horns served well enough until the late 1950s. At that time, horn player–designer Richard Merewether collaborated with Robert Paxman, a London horn maker, in an effort to develop an improved descant horn using a standard-sized bell.

The idea of a double descant horn had been tried earlier in Germany, but the instrument was generally unsatisfactory in intonation and tone due to the considerable differences in length between its two sides. From their work on the single descant, Merewether and Paxman developed a successful dual-bore double descant in F/F-alto. A B♭/F-alto soon followed, which allowed most of the range to be played on the B♭ side, with the F-alto side reserved for the highest register. In this form the instrument is widely used for the Baroque repertoire, some Mozart and Haydn symphonies, and other works requiring a high tessitura. Double descant horns are now made by several manufacturers (see Figure 4.5).

The descant horn is comparable to the higher trumpets in that it does not provide automatic high range, but places these notes lower in the harmonic series, where there is greater distance between notes of the series. This allows the player to produce high notes in the most reliable and responsive part of the horn's harmonic

---

[4] The Vienna valve is discussed in Chapter 1.

Figure 4.4. **Vienna horn with F crook, played by Professor Roland Berger of the Vienna Philharmonic.** *Photo courtesy of R. Berger.*

series. Attention has recently been focused on the Bb/Eb alto descant. This instrument offers improvements in construction in that a full-length bell branch and leadpipe can be used. The fingerings are the same as on the Bb horn above the high G, where the Eb side is primarily used. For unusually high parts, as are found in a few of Bach's cantatas, or as an alternative to the Bb/F-alto, a Bb/Bb-soprano and an F-alto/Bb-soprano have recently been introduced.

The Triple Horn

Not really a descant horn in the usual sense, but a general-purpose instrument, the triple horn was developed by the late Richard Merewether from his work with descant horns. The full triple is constructed by lengthening the rotary valves still further to accommodate three ranks of valve tubing. This results in a horn having three independent sections in F, Bb, and F alto (Eb alto or Bb soprano) (see Figure 4.6). There is also a compensating model consisting of an independent F-alto or Eb alto section combined with the Bb and F parts of the normal compensating double. The difficulty in designing a triple horn was the problem of the weight of the extra tubing.

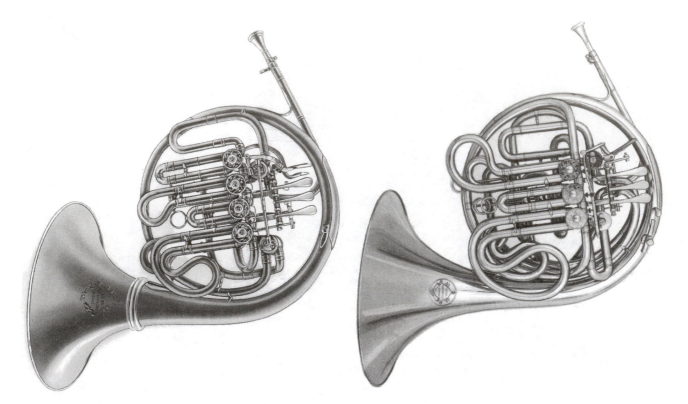

Figure 4.5. **B♭/F-alto descant horn (Alexander).** *Photo courtesy of Gebr. Alexander, Mainz.*

Figure 4.6. **F/B♭/F-alto triple horn (Alexander).** *Photo courtesy of Gebr. Alexander, Mainz.*

Merewether was able to bring the instrument's weight down to an acceptable level through the use of hollow valve rotors. In addition to Paxman, Alexander, Engelbert Schmidt, and several other firms also make good triple horns.

Other Design Factors

Aside from the various types of instruments available, there are other important constructional factors that must be considered by the horn player. Chief among these are the size of the instrument's tapered sections, such as the leadpipe and bell throat, and the metal alloy from which it is made.

Small bells, such as those found on old French piston valve horns and natural horns, are no longer made, except for modern reproductions of natural (hand) horns. The bell throats of the horns in use today may be classified as medium, large, and extra-large. The variation is in the bell's inner dimensions, not its overall diameter at the end, which averages between 12⅛ inches (309.2 mm) and 12⅜ inches (314.6 mm). Horn makers are not entirely consistent in how their models are identified. The middle-size bell is designated as large by some and medium-large by others. At least one maker refers to its extra-large bell model as a large. (The classification of bell throats is at the center of the confusion concerning bore sizes, discussed below).

The shape and dimensions of the bell throat have a profound influence on the horn's tone quality. Extra-large profiles often give the impression of a fuller sound at close range, but fail to project well into the hall in comparison with medium and large bell throats, which produce a more focused tone with greater carrying power. Because the sound radiates away from the audience and undergoes a complex reflective interaction with the acoustics of the hall, horn timbre must be evaluated from a distance. The bell throat also influences the color and character of the horn's timbre. Medium bells have a warm, well-defined sound that projects clearly within an orchestral, band, or brass ensemble texture. The large bell compromises some of the definition for a greater degree of fullness, combined with a somewhat darker color. In the author's judgment, the extra-large bell goes too far in this respect and the horn sound loses clarity.

Of equal importance to the bell size is the alloy used in the construction of the horn. The three materials—yellow brass, gold (red) brass, and nickel silver—impart different qualities to the tone. Yellow brass consists of 70% copper and 30% zinc; gold brass is 85% copper and 15% zinc; nickel silver is 63% copper, 27% zinc, and 10 to 12% nickel.[5] Yellow brass is the most widely used material and is, along with gold brass, preferred by a majority of professional players worldwide. It contributes a warm, characteristic horn tone that can be modified for various musical contexts. Gold brass endows the timbre with a richer, more veiled quality of darker color. Nickel silver was once believed to darken the tone, but this has now been attributed to the extra-large bell throats of the horns usually made with this material. In the author's opinion, nickel silver imbues the timbre with a drab, metallic quality in comparison to the tone color of yellow or gold brass.

Confusion often surrounds the subject of horn bore sizes. This is caused primarily by manufacturers and players referring to the horn's tapered portions (leadpipe and bell section) as the bore. This is not incorrect, but the tapered portions must be considered in relation to the horn's main bore. The main bore is determined by the diameter of the cylindrical tubing containing the valves between the leadpipe and the beginning of the tapered bell section. Most manufacturers offer two or three bell sizes (with appropriate leadpipes), but only one main bore. European horns usually have a main bore of 12 or 12.1 mm. Other horns are often smaller in main bore. Thus it is not uncommon for horns identified as large bore to combine a comparatively small main bore with a large or extra-large bell throat. The timbres that result from the medium, large, and extra-large bells differ considerably, depending on the diameter of the main bore to which they are attached. Outward appearances can be deceiving, as well. Some horns are wrapped more compactly than others, but this gives no indication of their internal bore dimensions.

The configuration of the tubing of the double horn is another factor in the design of high-quality horns. Modern full double horns have evolved from the four widely copied patterns of double horns dating from the early years of the twentieth century: Kruspe (model 9),[6] Alexander (model 103), C.F. Schmidt (which used a piston change-valve), and Knopf (usually known as a Geyer model in the United States). Players and designers often have a preference for one configuration over another. For example, the Knopf–Geyer type has smooth, wide bends in the tubing arrangement due to the placement of the change-valve at the far end of the valve cluster. This results in lessened resistance, a quality that is preferred by some players, but not others. Each of the layouts has its merits, and the choice of one over another is

---

[5] Richard Merewether, *The Horn, the Horn* . . . (London: Paxman Musical Instruments, Ltd., 1979), p. 14. Walter A. Lawson gives the percentages for nickel silver as 65% copper, 17% zinc, and 18% nickel. Walter A. Lawson, *Development of New Mouthpipes for the French Horn* (Boonsboro, Md.: Lawson, n.d.), p. 14.

[6] There is some confusion about the models made by Kruspe. Listed in Kruspe's 1933 catalog are four models of double horn: No. 9 full double (232038), Model Horner, Philadelphia, with extra-wide bell and leadpipe; No. 10 full double (1027 194), Model Walter Kruspe (this appears to be a medium or medium-large bell model); No. 11 compensating double (295 125), Model Gumpert–Kruspe (this is the original double horn); and No. 12 compensating double (888 990), Model Professor Wendler, Boston. (Georg Wendler was Kruspe's son-in-law, and was first horn of the Boston Symphony for some years. The Wendler model is often incorrectly identified as the first double horn).

purely a matter of preference. Many firms make instruments in more than one configuration. Over the years, various alterations have been made to the basic designs.

Most horns are available with either a fixed or detachable bell. With the latter, the horn may be carried in a flat case rather than the usual form-fitting type. The threaded rings of the detachable bell add some weight to the horn. Some players find no important difference in the playing qualities of detachable-bell models, but others find a difference in sound and playing quality and either prefer or dislike this option.

Linkages

The way in which motion from the valve levers is delivered to turn the valves is another matter of individual preference. Before the development of the Unibal and Minibal mechanical linkages, string action afforded a more positive, quicker action. The new linkages are equally quick and offer the durability of a mechanical linkage. Players usually have a preference for one type over another, and some manufacturers offer both types.

Right Hand Position

The use of the right hand in horn playing is now being recognized for its acoustical function, actually forming part of the instrument by narrowing the bell throat. As described in Chapter 1, in sounding the instrument, a longitudinal standing wave is set up between the mouthpiece and a reflective threshold created by the expanding bell. As the pitch rises, the threshold moves increasingly toward the bell opening; on the horn, at written G above the staff, it has reached the player's hand. From this point upward, the hand essentially lengthens the bell throat by reducing its diameter so that the standing wave can continue to operate without encountering a drop in impedance (caused by the widening of the bell flare) within the horn's compass.[7] This can be confirmed by trying to play the range above G without the hand in the bell. The note centers seem to disappear, making production of the notes difficult.

The need to form an acoustically effective passageway dictates how the hand should be formed in the bell. The positions described in Chapter 11 will ensure good results and should be carefully imitated. If the hand position is incorrect, the instrument's intonation and note centers are affected. The right hand also refines the timbre by absorbing some of the higher partials and deflecting the sound toward the body. The player can control these effects still further by covering the bell to a greater or lesser degree to create a more mellow or brighter timbre. Intonation is controlled in the same way—opening to raise the pitch and closing to lower it.

Handstopping and Muting

The pungent, metallic timbre that is produced when the hand completely seals the bell is an effect unique to the horn. During the second half of the eighteenth and early nineteenth centuries, playing with the hand open and closed to various de-

---

[7] See Richard Merewether, *The Horn*, pp. 28–32; Arthur Benade, "The Physics of Brasses," *Scientific American* (July 1973), pp. 24–35; and B. Lee Roberts, "Some Comments on the Physics of the Horn and Right Hand Technique," *The Horn Call*, 6, no. 2 (May 1976), pp. 41–45.

grees, including the full stopped position, was the primary means of playing diatonic and chromatic notes on the horn. It is important to distinguish between handstopping and the use of a mute. Separate and distinct sounds are produced by stopping and muting, and these effects are used differently by composers. The horn mute functions the same as other mutes and causes no acoustical change within the instrument, as is caused by handstopping. The acoustical aspects of handstopping and the controversy surrounding this subject are discussed below. For readers who wish to know only how to produce the stopped effect, the next section will suffice.

PRODUCING THE HANDSTOPPED EFFECT

The stopped sound is made by bringing the palm of the hand around into the bell opening to completely seal the bell. Because the bell throat is fully closed, it is essential to blow harder than normal and to concentrate intensely on the desired pitch. As described below, a shift of harmonic series takes place, so it is necessary to transpose down one half-step. When playing on either side of the double horn (F or B♭), the stopped note is usually played (one half-step lower) on the F side. The intonation of the stopped note should be carefully matched to the same pitch played open. The playing of stopped notes exclusively on the double horn's F side is the orthodox procedure, and the one that makes theoretical sense, but one should nonetheless take a flexible approach to fingering, trying all of the fingerings available on both sides of the horn. Whichever fingering yields the best intonation and stopped timbre should be used.

Stopping with the hand is most effective in the written range from E above middle C to the top of the staff. There is a brass stopping mute available that efficiently produces an in-tune stopped sound (notes must still be transposed downward one half-step) (see Figure 4.7). The stopping mute is generally preferred in the lower register, and many favor the mute in all ranges whenever there is sufficient time in the music to insert and remove it. Some horns are equipped with a special stopping valve. This permits stopped notes to be played without transposition. The pitch of stopped notes can be carefully adjusted by means of a tuning slide. It is particularly intended for stopping on the B♭ horn where three-quarters of a tone are theoretically required for in-tune stopped notes. Stopping valves are normally fitted to single B♭ and B♭/F-alto (B♭ soprano) descants. For double and triple horns, there is a trade-off between the obvious benefits of a stopping valve and the weight it adds to the horn.

Figure 4.7. **Stopping mute (Denis Wick).** *Photo courtesy of Boosey & Hawkes Musical Instruments.*

HANDSTOPPING: ACOUSTICAL CONSIDERATIONS

There has been a long-term dispute over whether the pitch rises or descends when the bell is stopped. The rising-pitch hypothesis appears logical because the instrument is shortened by this process. It would seem to be verified by the observation that if the player transposes downward a half-step and stops the bell, the same pitch results as the open tone.

Actually, the pitch has not risen. It can be demonstrated that as the hand is gradually closed, the pitch descends until at full seal, it settles exactly one-half step above the next *lower* harmonic. This phenomenon can be seen in the chart below.[8]

Harmonic series—F horn

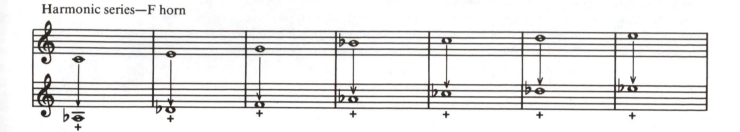

To take a practical example: To play a stopped G, the player transposes downward a half-step, using the second valve of the F horn. Although this appears to be an F♯, in reality it is the seventh overtone of the harmonic series of the second valve. If the bell were open, this note would sound as an A, but through the process of sealing the bell, it has descended to G.

2nd valve harmonic series: open

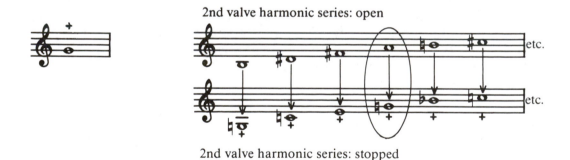

2nd valve harmonic series: stopped

This can be confirmed by playing the stopped harmonic series of the second valve; it will be found to conform to the series shown above.

MUTING

The standard horn mute (nontransposing) is basically a straight mute, but its timbre is less incisive than that of a trumpet or trombone mute. Usually, they are made of

[8] Adapted from Richard Merewether, *The Horn*, p. 40.

fiber, although plastic and metal alloys have been tried recently. Mutes must be selected with care because good intonation is possible only if the mute fits the bell throat exactly. The best mutes are made to fit specific bell sizes. Also, there is some variation of timbre between different brands of mute.[9]

Using the F and B♭ Sections of the Double Horn

The main concern in combining the sides of the double horn is to match the timbres of the F and B♭ sections so that one "F horn" tone is produced throughout the range. The usual crossover is at written G♯, although a minority of players prefer C♯, a fourth higher. The B♭ side is sometimes used for several low notes, particularly the low C♯, to improve intonation and response.

When good tonal matching has been achieved, the changeover is almost imperceptible. An effective way of developing this ability is to play individual notes and passages first on the F side, and then on the B♭ side, while concentrating on retaining the timbre of the F horn. It is helpful to occasionally practice solely on the F horn. Similarly, it is advisable to be fluent with the B♭ fingerings in all ranges, for there are tricky passages that can be facilitated through the use of the B♭ horn. The following chart indicates the usual procedure for combining the F and B♭ sections:

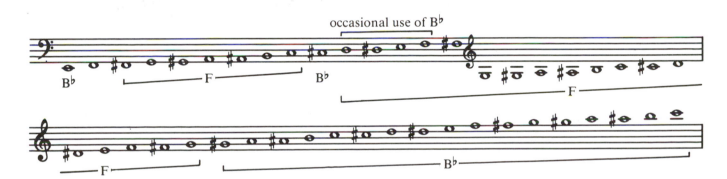

Another way of using the double horn is to play mostly on the B♭ side, reserving the F side for certain individual notes for better intonation, and low notes beyond the B♭'s range. This approach is widely used by British and European players as well as some Americans. The greater mass of the double horn played in B♭ contributes a broader tone than a single B♭, and has the advantage of an F section available as desired. The change-valves of European and British horns are customarily made to be reversible, so that the horn can stand in either F or B♭ without the thumb valve (change-valve) depressed. The wide use of the B♭ horn was the main reason European makers enlarged the main bore to 12 mm or more. The enlarged bore produces a fuller tone, particularly in the B♭'s lower middle range, where horns of smaller bore tend to sound rather hollow (the intonation of the lower middle range of the B♭, however, still requires practice).

From the beginning of double horn's existence, there has been an inherent difference in response between the F and B♭ sides. This is caused by the significant dif-

---

[9] For detailed information on horn mutes, see Nicholas E. Smith, "The Horn Mute: An Acoustical and Historical Study" (D.M.A. thesis, University of Rochester, 1980) UM 80–19, 070.

ference in length between the F and B♭ tubing in relation to the tubing's diameter. The response of the B♭ side is immediate and direct, whereas the F side is less positive. The problem is that the longer F horn tubing of the same diameter as the B♭ side creates greater resistance. Paxman of England recently introduced a dual-bore system for their double and triple horns in which the main bore of the F section is increased to match its response to that of the B♭.

Transposition and Notation

As was discussed in Chapter 3, the practice surviving from the prevalve era of notating parts in the key of C and using crooks to obtain the desired sounding pitch has left trumpet and horn players with a legacy of parts in a variety of keys. Therefore, transposition skills must be developed as a normal part of the horn player's training. The table below presents the common transpositions.

Transposition Table

Key of Part	Interval Method	Clef Method
B♭	Perfect 5th lower	Mezzo-soprano
C	Perfect 4th lower	—
D	Minor 3rd lower	—
E♭	Major 2nd lower	Tenor clef
E	Half-step lower	Tenor clef
G	Major 2nd higher	Alto clef
A	Major 3rd higher	Bass clef

Note: the key signature must also be changed.

The current practice of notation for the horn consists of writing for the F horn (sounding a fifth below concert pitch, therefore written a fifth above) regardless of whether a double horn, single B♭, or one of the descant horns will be used. It is helpful to the player if the bass clef is used below G:

As in treble clef notation, notes in the bass clef are written a fifth above where they are to sound. This manner of using the bass clef is known as new notation. This is to distinguish the present system from a nineteenth-century tradition of writing bass clef notes an octave lower (old notation).

concert
pitch

old
notation

new
notation

Horn Chords

A curious phenomenon associated with the horn is that a haunting three- or four-note chord can be made to sound by simultaneously singing a fifth or sixth above or below a played note in the lower register. Soloists in the natural horn era apparently sometimes inserted this effect into cadenzas. Eugène Vivier caused a great stir in Paris with this phenomenon in 1843. In fact, most horn players can develop the technique, but it requires a great deal of patient practice and concentration. Its chief interest today is that Carl Maria von Weber included horn chords in the cadenza of his *Concertino in E Minor*. It has also been revived here and there by contemporary composers and a few soloists.

Intonation and Tuning

As with the trumpet, subtle adjustments of embouchure and air pressure are required to achieve good intonation. Because the pitch of any note may be raised or lowered by opening or closing the hand position in the bell, the horn player has a further means available of controlling intonation; this is used as necessary as a normal aspect of playing procedure. The horn exhibits the same deficiencies as other valve brass instruments; however, the outer tubing of the valve slides is shortened to allow the slide to be brought inward as well as pulled outward to find the best position for good intonation when the valve is used alone and in combination. Students sometimes mistakenly assume that the valve slides of the horn are similar to those of the trumpet or euphonium and try to play the horn with the slides fully in; this results in disastrous intonation.

The best settings for the valve slides must be determined through a tuning procedure. To do this, unisons and various intervals should be played against a reference pitch and each slide moved as necessary. An electronic tuner is useful in this process.

To set the valve slides of the F horn or F side of a double horn, adjust the main tuning slide to a reference pitch of written G (concert C). The main tuning slide is usually at the end of the leadpipe. Play the slurred or tongued interval G–C to see whether a good fourth results and readjust the slide, if necessary. In general, by playing intervals rather than matching single notes, a more consistent and accurate tone placement results and the pitch of the second note is more clearly revealed. The reference pitch should be set to sound the note circled. This note is played first, followed by either slurring to or tonguing the second note. The slide should be moved to whatever position produces the most exact interval.

Main tuning slide

set reference pitch   adjust slide

1st valve slide

2nd valve

3rd valve slide
2-3 combination

1-2 combination

If discrepancies are found between the slide positions needed for single valve notes and valve combinations, a compromise setting should be used.

To set the B♭ slides, it is necessary to first bring the B♭ section into agreement with the F section through the use of a common open tone. Play the third space C on one side of the horn and then change to the other side. The separate F and B♭[10] tuning slides should be adjusted so that the two pitches match.

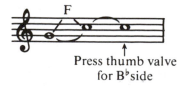

F

Press thumb valve for B♭ side

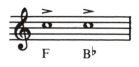

F   B♭

Once the correct settings for the F and B♭ tuning slides have been determined, the player should move only the main tuning slide when tuning with the orchestra or band. The B♭ valve slides can be set using the following procedure:

---

[10] A separate tuning slide for the B♭ section of the double horn is not absolutely necessary, and some models of double horn do not have them. Horns of this type are tuned by adjusting the F tuning slide so that the written C played on the F side matches the pitch of that note played on the B♭ side.

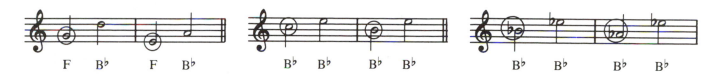

The D and A should be checked for possible sharpness, and the E and E♭ for flatness.

A few books attempt to give measurements for the slide settings, but these usually prove of little use due to the variability of instruments and players. In a good horn section, there will be some differences in slide settings, but the players will match each other's pitches very well.

The 1–2 valve combination can often be played better in tune in the low register by using the third valve. The sharp 1–2–3 combination on the low C♯ can be avoided by playing this note 2–3 on the B♭ side.

To develop good intonation in school and college horn sections, it is essential that the slide settings be checked and brought into agreement with each other. This can be done by tuning to a reliable open tone, such as middle G, and then playing single notes, intervals, and chords together while making the necessary adjustments. It is useful to play a diatonic or chromatic scale slowly in unison from middle C to fourth space E, stopping when necessary to change the slide settings.[11] After the slide settings have been established, some careful work on trios, quartets, and quintets should be undertaken. A progressive program of quartet playing can do a great deal to improve a horn section in a relatively short time. In the final analysis, good intonation is achieved by careful listening and adjusting to other players.

The Wagner Tuba

The Wagner tuba should be considered with the horn because this instrument, although a member of the tuba family, was intended to be played by hornists. (See Fig-

---

[11] A useful book for establishing some of these fundamentals is Robert W. Getchall and Nilo Hovey, *Section Studies for French Horns* (Melville, N.Y.: Belwin-Mills, 1967).

Figure 4.8. **Wagner tuba (tenor in B♭) (Alexander).**

Figure 4.9. **Wagner tuba (bass in F) (Alexander).**

ures 4.8, 4.9, and 4.10.) In 1853, during the composition of *Das Rheingold*, Wagner wanted to expand the brass section in certain places. The composer had become acquainted with the saxhorns during a visit with Adolphe Sax in Paris. The Berlin firm of Moritz is believed to have supplied the original set of Wagner tubas for the first complete performance of *Der Ring des Nibelungen* in 1875. These were made in the traditional oval shape of the German military *Tenorhorn* and *Bariton*, but with the valves

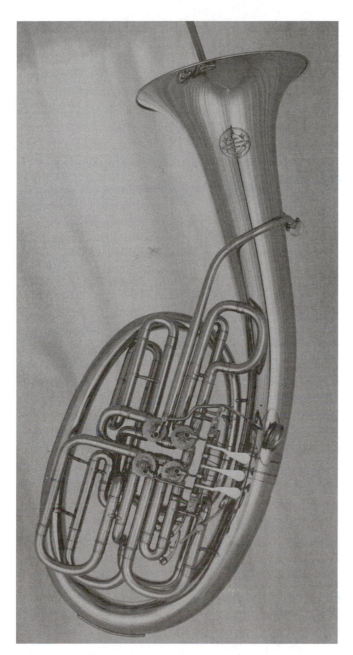

Figure 4.10. **Wagner tuba (double) (Alexander).** *Photos courtesy of Gebr. Alexander, Mainz.*

on the left so that they could be played by horn players. The mouthpipe was altered to accommodate a regular horn mouthpiece. Eight horns were called for in the score, four of which doubled on the new instruments. The quartet included two tenors in B♭ (similar to the B♭ horn), and two basses in F (which correspond to the F horn).

Wagner was followed by Bruckner and Strauss in using the instrument. The solo in *Don Quixote,* which today is usually played on the euphonium, was originally intended for this instrument. In an effort to improve intonation, the bell tapers of most modern Wagner tubas have been enlarged, thereby losing some of the haunting intensity of timbre envisioned by the composer. An authentic set can be heard in the

Vienna Philharmonic. The latest development is an F–B♭ double tuba based on the compensating principle.[12]

[12] For additional information on the historical background of the Wagner tuba, see James Harvey Keays, "An Investigation into the Origins of the Wagner Tuba" (D.M.A. thesis, University of Illinois, 1977) UM 78–4044.

Recommended Literature[13]

COMPLETE METHODS

FRANZ: *Complete Method* (C. Fischer)

*FREUND: *French Horn Method for the Young Beginner* (Waldhornschule), 3 vols. (Doblinger)

GRAHAM-CRUMP: *Complete Horn Method*, 2 vols. (Oxford)

*HOELTZEL, MICHAEL: *Horn-Schule*, 2 vols. (text in German) (Schott)

HUTH, FRITZ: *School for Horn* (Benjamin-Rahter)

NEULING, HERMANN: *Grosse F und B Hornschule*, 2 vols., (text in German) (Pro Musica)

POTTAG AND HOVEY: *Pottag-Hovey Method*, 2 vols. (Belwin-Mills)

STERN AND SCHNEIDER: *Schule für Waldhorn* (Schott)

ELEMENTARY METHODS

CLEVENGER, MCDUNN, AND RUSCH: *Dale Clevenger Method*, 2 vols. (Kjos)

GOLDSTEIN: *Book of Exercises* (Cor)

*HAUSER: *Foundation to Horn Playing* (C. Fischer)

*HORNER: *Primary Studies* (Elkan-Vogel)

*HOWE: *Method* (Marvin C. Howe)

SKORNICKA: *Rubank Elementary Method* (Rubank)

*TUCKWELL: *50 First Exercises* (Oxford)

WILLIAMS: *Enjoy Playing the Horn* (Oxford)

STUDIES

MEDIUM TO MEDIUM-DIFFICULT

BROPHY: *Technical Studies for Solving Special Problems on the Horn* (C. Fischer)

*BURDEN: *Horn Playing—A New Approach* (Paterson's Publ.)

DEGRAVE: *Etudes for Modern Valve Horn* (medium to difficult) (Wind Music)

*GALLAY: *22 Studies* (International)

*GALLAY: *24 Studies* (International)

GOLDSTEIN: *Etudes*, 2 vols. (Cor)

GOUNOD: *Dix études* (Billaudot)

GOWER AND VOXMAN: *Rubank Advanced Method*, 2 vols. (Rubank)

*HUTH: *Tonleiter-Studien* (Hofmeister)

*KOPPRASCH: *60 Selected Studies*, 2 vols. (medium to difficult) (C. Fischer)

*LEVET: *La technique journalière du corniste* (Lemoine)

*MAXIME-ALPHONSE: *Deux cents études nouvelles*, vols. 1–3 (A. Leduc)

*MIERSCH: *Melodious Studies for French Horn* (C. Fischer)

MOORE AND ETTORE: *Master Warm-Up & Flexibility Studies* (Mel Bay)

*MUELLER: *34 Studies*, 2 vols. (medium to difficult) (International)

*PARÈS: *Parès Scales* (Rubank)

POTTAG: *Daily Exercises* (Belwin-Mills)

*POTTAG (ED.):   *Preparatory Melodies to Solo Work* (Belwin Mills)

POTTAG AND ANDRAUD (ED.):   *Selected Melodious, Progressive, & Technical Studies*, vol. 1 (Southern)

*SCHANTL: *Grand Theoretical & Practical Method* (medium to difficult) (Wind Music)

*SCHANTL: *92 Übungen für Ventilanfänger* (Pizka)

*SINGER: *Embouchure Building* (medium to difficult) (Belwin-Mills)

*THEVET: *Fifty Exercises with Changes of Key* (Transposition) (Leduc)

DIFFICULT

*ARTÔT: *19 Progressive Etudes* (Belwin-Mills)

*BELLOLI: *8 Studies* (International)

BERGONZI: *Capricci*, 2 vols. (Doblinger)

*BRAHMS: *10 Horn Studies* (Belwin-Mills)

*CUGNOT: *30 Etudes* (Wind Music)

*GALLAY: *12 Etudes brillantes* (International)

*GALLAY: *12 Grand Caprices* (International)

*GALLAY: *12 Studies for Second Horn* (International)

*GALLAY: *40 Preludes* (International)

GUGEL: *12 Studies* (International)

HACKLEMAN: *21 Characteristic Etudes for High Horn Playing* (Bim)

[13] Essential literature is noted with an asterisk. For additional material, see the *Brass Players' Guide* (Robert King). Repertoire lists appear in the texts by Brüchle, Gregory, and Schuller.

HACKLEMAN: *34 Characteristic Etudes for Low Horn Playing* (Bim)

JEURISSEN: *4 Characteristic Studies* (McCoy)

*KLING: *40 Studies* (International)

*MAXIME-ALPHONSE: *Deux cents etudes nouvelles*, vols. 4–6 (A. Leduc)

*NEULING: *30 Special Studies for Low Horn*, 2 vols. (Pro Musica)

POTTAG AND ANDRAUD: *Selected Melodious, Progressive, & Technical Studies*, vol. 2 (Southern)

*RANIERI: *Etuden* (Pizka)

*F. STRAUSS: *17 Concert Studies* (Eulenburg)

UNACCOMPANIED SOLOS
DIFFICULT

ADLER: *Canto XI* (Ludwig)

APOSTEL: *Sonatine* (Universal)

*ARNOLD: *Fantasy* (Faber)

BACH: *Cello Suites*, transcribed by Hoss (Southern)

BARBOTEU: *5 pièces poetiques* (Choudens)

BOZZA: *Graphismes* (A. Leduc)

*BUYANOVSKY: *Pieces* (McCoy)

*DAVIES: *Sea Eagle* (Chester)

*DODGSON: *Cor Leonis* (Bim)

FAUST: *Prelude* (Faust)

HALSTEAD: *Suite* (Dunster)

KAUDER: *3 Melodies for Solo Horn* (Seesaw)

ORVAL: *Libre–Free–Frei* (McCoy)

*PERSICHETTI: *Parable* (Presser)

PLOG: *Postcards* (Bim)

HORN AND PIANO
EASY

ANDERSON: *Prelude & March in Canon* (Boosey & Hawkes)

BAKALEINIKOFF: *Canzona* (Belwin)

BAKALEINIKOFF: *Cavatina* (Belwin)

BRIGHTMORE: *3 Easy Solos* (Taurus)

CARSE: *2 Easy Pieces* (Galaxy)

FRANCK: *Panis Angelicus* (Warner Bros.)

GUNNING AND PEARSON: *The Really Easy Horn Book* (Faber)

HANDEL AND HAYDN: *8 Solos from "Messiah" and "The Creation,"* arr. Lethbridge (Oxford)

JONES (ED.):   *First Solos for the Hornplayer* (Schirmer)

LANGRISH (ED.):   *8 Easy Pieces* (Oxford)

LAWTON (ED.):   *The Young Horn-Player*, 3 vols. (Oxford)

MARSHALL (ED.):   *An Album for the Horn* (Oxford)

OHANIAN: *Beginning Horn Solos* (with cassette accompaniment) (H. Leonard)

OHANIAN: *Easy Horn Solos* (with cassette accompaniment) (H. Leonard)

ONOZO AND KOVACS (EDS.):   *Horn Music for Beginners* (Editio Musica)

PHILLIPS (ED.):   *Classical & Romantic Pieces* (Oxford)

MEDIUM TO MEDIUM-DIFFICULT

BAKER: *Cantilena* (Chester)

BEETHOVEN: *Little Rondo* (Schirmer)

*BUTTERWORTH: *Romanza* (Hinrichsen)

CAMPBELL: *Horn Solos*, 2 vols. (Faber)

*CHABRIER: *Larghetto* (Salabert)

DISHINGER: *Masterworks Solos* (Medici)

DUNHILL: *Cornucopia* (Boosey & Hawkes)

FORBES (ED.):   *Classical & Romantic Album*, vols. 2 and 3 (Oxford)

*FRANÇAIX: *Canon in Octave* (International)

*GLAZOUNOV: *Reverie* (Belwin-Mills)

JAMES: *Windmills* (B. Ramsey)

JAMES AND DEHAAN (ED.):   *Horn Solos* (Chester)

JOHNSON (ED.):   *Intermediate Horn Book* (Oxford)

JONES (ED.):   *Solos for the Hornplayer* (Schirmer)

MARSHALL (ED.):   *An Album for the Horn* (Oxford)

MOORE: *Second Book of Horn Solos* (Faber)

*MOZART: *Concerto No. 1 in D* (Breitkopf & Härtel)

*MOZART: *Concerto No. 3 in E♭* (Breitkopf & Härtel); also version with cassette accompaniment (Ohanian) (H. Leonard)

*MOZART: *Concert Rondo in E♭* (Breitkopf & Härtel)

OHANIAN: *Intermediate Horn Solos* (with cassette accompaniment) (H. Leonard)

PLOYHAR (ED.):   *Horn Solos*, 2 vols. (Belwin-Mills)

READ: *Poem* (C. Fischer)

RICHARDSON (ED.):   *6 Horn Tunes* (Boosey & Hawkes)

*SAINT-SAËNS: *Romance* (Belwin-Mills)

STOUT (ED.):   *Master Solos* (with cassette accompaniment) (H. Leonard)

VOXMAN (ED.):   *Concert & Contest Collection* (Rubank)

DIFFICULT

ADLER: *Sonata* (R. King)

*ALBRECHTSBERGER: *Concerto* (International)

*ARNOLD: *Concerto* (Lengnick)

ARTUNIAN: *Concerto* (International)

BALAY: *Chanson du Forestier* (A. Leduc)

*BEETHOVEN: *Sonata*, ed. Tuckwell (Schirmer)

BELLINI: *Concerto* (Billaudot)

BITSCH: *Variations* (A. Leduc)

BLANC: *Sonata* (Pizka)

*BOZZA: *Chant lointain* (A. Leduc)

*BOZZA: *En forêt* (A. Leduc)

BUSH: *Autumn Poem* (Schott)

CARR: *Soliloquy* (Broadbent & Dunn)

*CHERUBINI: *2 Sonatas*, ed. Tuckwell (Schirmer)

*CZERNY: *Andante e Polacca* (Doblinger)

DANZI: *Concerto* (Heinrichshofen)

DANZI: *Sonata* (International)

DELMAS: *Ballade Féerique* (Billaudot)

*DUKAS: *Villanelle* (International)

DUVERNOY: *Concerto No. 3* (Ka We)

ECCLES: *Sonata in G Minor*, transcribed by Eger (International)

FOERSTER: *Concerto* (Schirmer)

GALLAY: *Concerto* (Ka We)

*GLIÈRE: *Concerto* (International)

GOEDICKE: *Concerto* (International)

*HAYDN: *Concerto No. 1* (Boosey & Hawkes)

*HAYDN: *Concerto No. 2* (Boosey & Hawkes)

*M. HAYDN: *Concertino*, ed. Tuckwell (Schirmer)

HIDAS: *Concerto* (Editio Musica)

*HINDEMITH: *Concerto* (Schott)

HINDEMITH: *Sonata for Alto Horn* (Schott)

*HINDEMITH: *Sonate* (Schott)

HODDINOTT: *Sonata* (Oxford)

*JACOB: *Concerto* (Galaxy)

KLING: *Concerto* (H. Pizka)

KOETSIER: *Romanza* (Reift)

KOETSIER: *Sonatina* (Reift)

LEWY: *Concerto* (H. Pizka)

*MADSEN: *Sonata* (Musikk-Huset)

MARAIS: *Le Basque* (Paxman)

McCABE: *Floraison* (Novello)

McCABE: *Shapeshifter* (Novello)

*L. MOZART: *Concerto in D*, ed. Tuckwell (Schirmer)

*MOZART: *Concerto No. 2 in E♭* (Breitkopf & Härtel)

*MOZART: *Concerto No. 4 in E♭* (Breitkopf & Härtel)

MUSGRAVE: *Music for Horn and Piano* (Chester)

NERUDA: *Concerto* (Bim)

*NIELSEN: *Canto serioso* (Skandinavisk Musikforlag)

PILSS: *Concerto* (R. King)

PILSS: *Tre pezzi* (Doblinger)

PLOG: *Nocturne* (Bim)

PORTER: *Sonata* (R. King)

PUNTO: *Concerto No. 11* (Medici Music)

*ROSETTI: *Concerto No. 1* (Ka We)

*ROSETTI: *Concerto No. 2* (International)

*ROSSINI: *Prelude, Thème et Variations* (Schirmer)

*SAINT-SAËNS: *Concertpiece* (International)

SCHUMAN: *3 Colloquies* (Presser)

*F. STRAUSS: *Concerto*, ed. Tuckwell (Schirmer)

*R. STRAUSS: *Concerto No. 1* (Schirmer); also version with cassette accompaniment (Ohanian) (H. Leonard)

*R. STRAUSS: *Concerto No. 2* (Boosey & Hawkes)

*TELEMANN: *Concerto in D*, ed. Tuckwell (Schirmer)

TISNÉ: *Lied* (A. Leduc)

*VINTER: *Hunter's Moon* (Boosey & Hawkes)

*WEBER: *Concertino*, ed. Tuckwell (Schirmer)

WILDER: *First Sonata* (CFG)

WILDER: *Suite* (Margun)

RECOMMENDED BOOKS ON THE HORN[14]

*BRÜCHLE, BERNHARD.   *Horn Bibliographie* (3 vols.). Wilhelmshaven, Germany: Heinrichshofen's Verlag, 1970.

*BUSHOUSE, DAVID.   *Practical Hints on Playing the Horn.* Melville, N.Y.: Belwin-Mills, 1983.

*COAR, BIRCHARD.   *A Critical Study of the Nineteenth-Century Horn Virtuosi in France.* DeKalb, Ill.: Coar, 1952.

*COAR, BIRCHARD.   *The French Horn.* DeKalb, Ill.: Coar, 1947.

*COUSINS, FARQUHARSON.   *On Playing the Horn.* London: Samski Press (distributed by Paxman Musical Instruments), 1983.

*FARKAS, PHILIP.   *The Art of Horn Playing.* Evanston, Ill.: Summy-Birchard, 1956.

FARKAS, PHILIP.   *A Photographic Study of 40 Virtuoso Horn Players' Embouchures.* Rochester, N.Y.: Wind Music, 1970.

---

[14] Many interesting articles appear in *The Horn Call* (published by the International Horn Society), *The Horn Magazine* (published by the British Horn Society), and other periodicals listed in Appendix C.

*Fitzpatrick, Horace.   *The Horn and Horn-Playing and the Austro-Bohemian Tradition 1680–1830*. London: Oxford University Press, 1970.

*Gregory, Robin.   *The Horn*. London: Faber & Faber, 1969.

Hill, Douglas.   *Extended Techniques for the Horn*. Hialeah, Fla.: Columbia Pictures Publications, 1983.

Janetzky, Kurt and Bernard Brüchle.   *The Horn*. Portland, Ore.: Amadeus Press, 1988.

*Merewether, Richard.   *The Horn, the Horn. . . .* London: Paxman Musical Instruments, 1979.

*Morley-Pegge, Reginald.   *The French Horn*. London: Ernest Benn, 1973.

Pettitt, Stephen.   *Dennis Brain*. London: Robert Hale, 1976.

*Pizka, Hans.   *Hornisten-Lexikon/Dictionary for Hornists 1986*. Kirchheim b. München: Hans Pizka Edition, 1986.

Prichard, Paul, ed.   *The Business: The Essential Guide to Starting and Surviving as a Professional Hornplayer*. Surrey, England: Open Press Books, 1992.

Schuller, Gunther.   *Horn Technique*. London: Oxford University Press, 1971.

Stewart, Dee.   *Philip Farkas: The Legacy of a Master*. Northfield, Ill.: The Instrumentalist Co., 1990.

*Tuckwell, Barry.   *Horn*. New York: Schirmer Books, 1983.

*Tuckwell, Barry.   *Playing the Horn*. London: Oxford University Press, 1978.

*Wekre, Frøydis Ree.   *Thoughts on Playing the Horn Well*. Oslo: Frøydis Ree Wekre, 1994.

Whaley, David R.   "The Microtonal Capability of the Horn." D.M.A. thesis, University of Illinois, 1975. UM 76–7010.

Yancich, Milan.   *A Practical Guide to French Horn Playing*. Rochester, N.Y.: Wind Music, 1971.

CHAPTER 5

Trombone

The trend in trombone playing since the 1950s has been toward larger and, in the case of the bass trombone, more complex and specialized instruments. In earlier years, small-bore trombones, following the pattern established by the French instrument maker Antoine Courtois and other French firms in the mid-nineteenth century enjoyed great popularity. When used with a conical mouthpiece, the instrument offered the pure tone and agile technique demanded by famous soloists of the era, such as Arthur Pryor (1870–1942).

Although trombones of this type were the mainstay of American bands and theater orchestras around the turn of the century, players in symphony orchestras of that era used instruments of considerably larger bore and bell dimensions. This was probably a result of the strong German influence in American orchestras at that time. Large-bore German trombones served as the prototypes from which the modern American symphonic trombone was developed.

Today, there are four general categories of trombone, based on their bore and bell dimensions (Figure 5.1):

Type	Bore	Bell
Small-bore tenor	up to .500" (12.7 mm)	7–8" (177.8–203.2 mm)
Medium-bore tenor	.510–.525" (12.9–13.3 mm)	8" (203.2 mm)
Large-bore tenor	.547" (13.8 mm)	8.5" (216 mm)
Bass	.562" (14.2 mm)	9.5–10.5" (241–267 mm)

In the trombone sections of symphony orchestras, a typical layout would include two large-bore tenors and a bass, all having a basic pitch of B♭. An F attachment might or might not be found on the principal player's instrument,[1] but it is likely that one would be included on that used by the second player. The bass trombonist would use one of the new in-line double-valve instruments or an earlier double- or single-trigger model. (The instruments with F attachment or double valves might be equipped with Thayer Axial-Flow valves, discussed in Chapter 1.) The same arrangement would be used in concert bands and wind ensembles. In jazz and

[1] First trombonists often prefer the response and sound of a large-bore trombone without F attachment for the range in which they play. For certain repertoire, an F attachment would be used. The F attachment does not determine whether a trombone is designated as large-bore, medium-bore, or bass. This is determined by the diameter of the cylindrical tubing, the size of the taper of the bell-throat, and the overall width of the bell. Often, the same model of tenor trombone is made with and without the F attachment. Some instruments are made with removable F attachments.

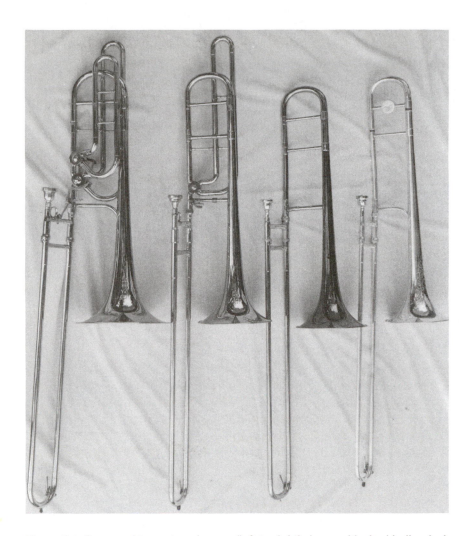

Figure 5.1 **Bass and tenor trombones (left to right): bass with dual in-line independent valves (F, G♭, and D) (King), large-bore tenor with F attachment (Conn), medium-bore tenor (Conn), and small-bore tenor (King).** *Photo: Joseph Hetman.*

studio work, small and medium-bore trombones are usually preferred for their more responsive upper register and brighter tone. Beginners generally start on the small- or medium-bore, and later move to an instrument more specifically suited to their performance interests.

The situation is similar in Europe, where American-type symphonic trombones displaced small-bore instruments in England during the 1950s and in France slightly later. In Germany and Austria, however, traditional German trombones have developed along somewhat independent lines (Figure 5.2). Constructed with wider, more gently curved bows and large bells, these instruments incorporate a more conical bore that includes a dual-bore slide (the lower slide is of larger diameter than the upper slide and is connected by a tapered bow).[2]

American-style trombones are also used in these countries. However, the leading orchestras, such as the Berlin Philharmonic and Vienna Philharmonic, generally favor traditional German instruments. The use of German trombones plays an important role in achieving a blend of sound and matching the wider projection patterns of the rotary valve trumpets that are characteristic of these orchestras.

[2] Leading examples are made by the firm of Herbert Lätzsch of Bremen, Germany.

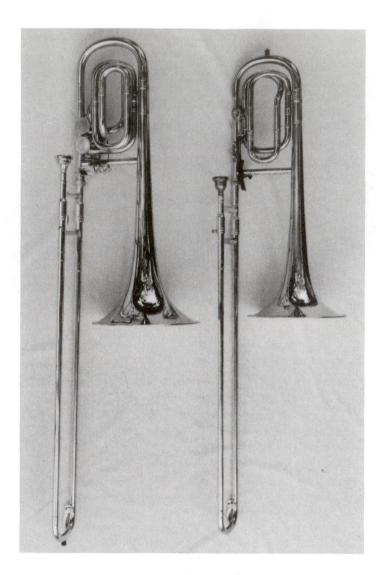

Figure 5.2. **German trombones (left to right): bass with dual in-line independent valves, large-bore tenor with removable F attachment (Lätzsch).** *Photo: Joseph Hetman.*

German trombones produce a dark, almost somber tone quality at softer dynamic levels and assume a resonant brightness at *fortissimo*. This contrasts with American-style trombones, which tend to hold a more consistent timbre throughout the dynamic range. (A similar change of timbre occurs in rotary valve trumpets and the horns used in the above orchestras, particularly the Vienna horn.[3]) The distinctive qualities of the German trombone contribute a great deal to the overall effect the Vienna and Berlin brass sections achieve in Wagner, Bruckner, and Mahler.

Along with the trend in modern trombone playing to larger bore and bell diameters, more highly developed and efficient bass trombones have come into regular use. The inadequacy of the F attachment in completely filling the gap between low E and the fundamental (pedal) range has led to the development of the double-valve bass trombone.

[3] The Vienna horn is discussed in Chapter 4.

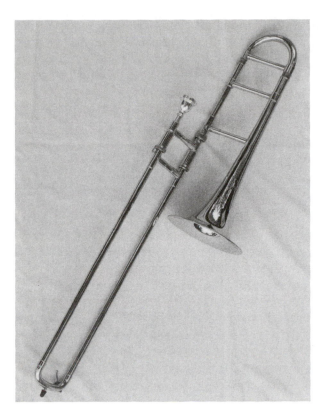

Figure 5.3. **Alto trombone (Bach).** *Photo courtesy of the Selmer company, Elkhart, Indiana.*

The Alto Trombone

At the other end of the scale is the E♭ alto trombone, which, during the late eighteenth and early nineteenth centuries, led the orchestral trio of alto, tenor, and bass (Figure 5.3). It is used today for parts requiring a high tessitura and lightness of tone. The alto trombone allows the player to achieve delicate balances without strain, and it makes high entrances more secure. Its timbre blends well with woodwinds and strings and is particularly effective with voices.

In Germany, the alto trombone is regularly used on parts that were originally written for it, but the instrument was less common in the past in the United States and Britain. Because the alto is pitched in E♭ or F, the player must learn a different set of positions. Players have preferred to play such parts on their regular instrument or a small-bore tenor. In recent years, however, there has been much renewed interest in the alto trombone in America. This has come about in response to the desire to perform orchestral music in a way that is more faithful to the original intentions of the composer, and for the solo literature written for the instrument.[4] When the alto trombone is used in early-nineteenth-century works, it is preferable if the second and bass parts are played on somewhat smaller-bore instruments to facilitate a blend of tone. As high-quality alto trombones become more widely available, it is likely that there will be greater use of this instrument in the future.

A soprano trombone pitched in B♭ appeared in Germany in the late seventeenth century. Its principal use was to play chorale melodies in trombone choirs and it can

[4] A list of literature and a discography for the alto trombone are provided in Stephen C. Anderson, "The Alto Trombone, Then and Now," *The Instrumentalist* (Nov. 1985), pp. 54–62.

still be found there fulfilling this function. In America, the instrument is sometimes used in trombone choirs associated with the Moravian Church.

The F Attachment

The origin of the F attachment can be traced to the bass trombone in F, which was used throughout the nineteenth and early twentieth centuries. The idea of fitting additional F tubing to a B♭ trombone dates from 1839, when the first instruments of this type were produced by C. F. Sattler of Leipzig. The purpose of the F attachment is to extend the compass of the B♭ trombone downward to the pedal range and to provide some alternate positions to improve technical fluency in the low register. It consists of a rotary (or axial-flow) valve that diverts the air column through a secondary section of tubing to lower the instrument's pitch a perfect fourth. Unfortunately, the F attachment cannot completely bridge the gap between the normal and pedal ranges. The low C is theoretically beyond the standard length slide, and a much longer slide would be needed to reach the low B immediately above the first pedal tone (B♭).

The reason for this is that the distance between positions increases as the slide is extended. Because extra tubing is added to lower the trombone's pitch a perfect fourth, a slide of greater length would be necessary to obtain the full seven positions (the F bass trombone had such a slide). As it is, the trombonist must play the more widely spaced F positions on the shorter B♭ slide, where it is scarcely possible to fit six positions. In practice, finding the F positions is not as difficult as it may appear because the player thinks of them as altered B♭ positions: 1, ♭2, ♭3, ♯5, 6, ♭7.

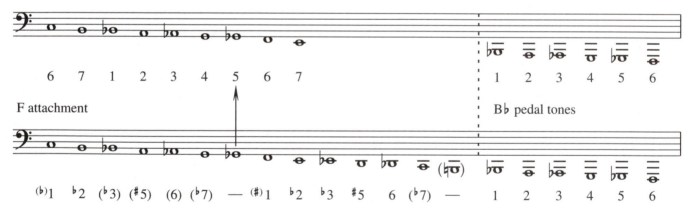

The problem of the absent low B and overextended C is not serious for the tenor player, but it presents a formidable obstacle to the bass trombonist because the literature calls for chromatic tones down and into the pedal range. This has led to the development of the double-valve bass trombone, discussed below. Both the low C and B can (almost) be played on the single valve F attachment if sufficient time is allowed to pull out the attachment's tuning slide (in effect making it an E attachment). The low B, however, is still theoretically beyond the end of the slide.

Another problem with the F attachment is that there is usually a difference in tone quality between normal B♭ notes and those played with the attachment. For this reason, trombonists generally restrict its use to the lower register and spend a good deal of practice time attempting to equalize the sound. This problem has been improved in recent years by the Thayer Axial-Flow valve and other new designs that feature better windways.

One of the chief advantages of the F attachment is that alternate positions are provided so that awkward movements can be avoided:

The most effective way to learn to use the F attachment is to work through one of the books of studies designed for this purpose.[5]

A common method of tuning the F attachment is to play the middle F alternately in B♭ and F, and adjust the attachment's tuning slide as necessary. In using this tuning procedure, however, the low F on the F attachment tends to be flat and the main slide must be brought inward to bring it into tune (this is possible only on instruments with spring barrels). Also, the second-space C is usually sharp and the first position must be lowered accordingly. An alternative method of tuning the F attachment that is favored by many players is to tune the low F against the B♭ a perfect fourth above. This ensures that the low F is in tune when needed. With this tuning, the low C is sharp and even more difficult to reach in the flat seventh position. Therefore, a decision must be made as to which is more important: an in-tune F or a more attainable low C. Tenor trombonists usually favor the F, and bass trombonists the C. (Bass trombonists often tune the low C in first position and pull in for the F.) On some trombones, the low D♭ is a bit sharp when played in sixth position on the F attachment. In such cases, the D♭ should be considered a flat sixth.

Bass Trombones

Bass trombonists must be able to play chromatically into the pedal range. Before the development of the double-valve bass trombone, the player had to extend the tuning slide of the F attachment to produce a usable low C, and, even with this measure plus embouchure adjustment, the low B was generally unsatisfactory in pitch and tone quality.[6]

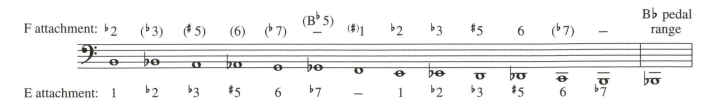

[5] A. Ostrander, *The F Attachment and Bass Trombone* (C. Colin); O. Blume (ed.) and R. Fink, *36 Studies for Trombone with F Attachment* (C. Fischer); and R. Fote, *Selected Kopprasch Studies for Trombone with F Attachment* (Kendor Music).

[6] The low C and B were easily accessible on the nineteenth-century bass trombone in F, which had a longer slide fitted with a handle. As a result, these notes are found in the literature.

By incorporating a second valve and added tubing within the F attachment, the pitch could be instantaneously lowered a half-step to E.[7] The two problem notes could be played on the E attachment without pulling out the tuning slide, but still required considerable embouchure adjustment.

It was soon found that by lengthening the tubing of the second valve to E♭ or D, the low notes could be played with less extension of the main slide, yielding better tone and response as well as improved slide motion.

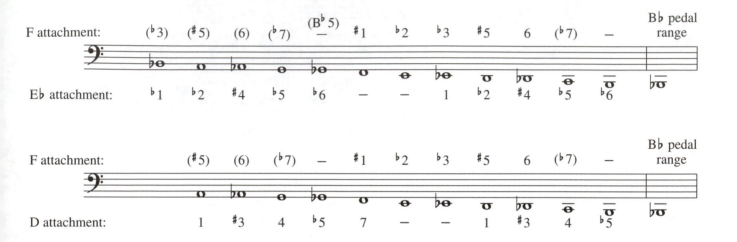

The latest development is the in-line double-valve bass trombone, in which both valves are located in the main tubing of the bell section. This allows the valves to be used independently. The instrument is currently available in two forms, depending on whether G or G♭ is chosen as the pitch of the second valve. (Some models come with both a G and a longer G♭ tuning slide for the second valve tubing so that either format is available to the player.)

When the first valve (operated by the thumb) is activated, the normal F attachment positions may be played. If the lever of the second valve is depressed by the middle finger, an alternative set of G or G♭ positions are made available. Using both valves together lowers the trombone's pitch to either E♭ (G format) or D (G♭ format). It is essentially four trombones in one: B♭, F, G♭ (G), and D (E♭).

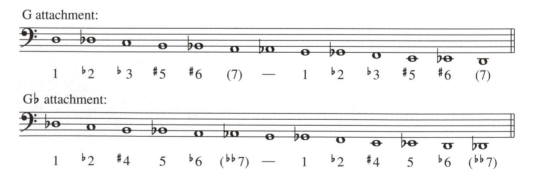

---

[7] The second valve cannot be used independently because the added tubing is an extension built into the F attachment. Both triggers must be depressed to use the E (E♭ or D) valve.

Additional improvements in the design of bass trombones are the use of Thayer Axial-Flow valves[8] and shaping the tubing from the valves in a more open pattern to provide better response with less resistance.[9] Recent experiments have lengthened the second valve's tubing so that C is in first position when the valves are used together.

Other Attachments

Sattler's choice of the key of F for the attachment fitted to the B♭ tenor trombone in 1839 was probably made because F was the standard key of the bass trombone at that time (earlier instruments were often pitched lower, in E♭ or D). Although Sattler's purpose for the tenor–bass was the same as it is today (to enable the trombonist to play notes in the lowest register in F with less slide extension and to fill in the missing notes between low E and pedal B♭), he probably did not anticipate that the F attachment would provide the added benefit of a few alternate positions for the tenor range, assisting technical facility. Thus, the F attachment has been accepted by succeeding generations of trombonists without giving much thought as to whether F is the optimum key for the attachment. Recently engineering professor Dr. B. P. Leonard has shown that F is not the best choice of key for either of the attachment's purposes. For technical facility, a G attachment offers more alternate positions as well as the added possibility of being constructed with a shorter slide (six positions in B♭ and five in G). The lower inertia of the shorter slide combined with the G alternate positions constitutes a clear improvement in facility over the conventional F attachment. To bridge the gap between low E and pedal B♭, a single-valve E♭ attachment is superior to either the F attachment or the double-trigger dependent (contained within the F attachment) E or E♭ attachments.[10] In addition to B♭/G and B♭/E♭ models, Dr. Leonard designed an in-line B♭/G–E–D instrument (actually the first U.S. in-line design) that features a shorter slide. This offers the technical advantages of the B♭/G configuration along with the capability to effectively bridge the gap to the pedal range.[11]

Slide Movement

How effectively the trombonist is able to move the slide from position to position determines the quality of both technique and intonation. The slide must obviously be in excellent condition and free of any tendency to bind. The instrument's weight should be supported by the left arm so that the right hand is free to control the slide.

To achieve clarity in moving passages, the player must make the slide reach a precise position before each note begins without shortening the duration of the previous note. Due to the distances involved, it takes a great deal of practice to develop

[8] Available from Thayer Valve International L.P., P.O. Box 475, Waldport, OR 97394.

[9] See Douglas Yeo, "The Bass Trombone: Innovations on a Misunderstood Instrument," *The Instrumentalist* (Nov. 1985), pp. 22–28.

[10] B. P. Leonard, "Rational Design of Trigger Attachments," Center for Computational Mechanics, The University of Akron, Ohio. Dr. Leonard has patented the B♭–E♭ (perfect fifth) and (in-line) B♭/G–E–D tunings.

[11] The first in-line independent double-trigger trombone was invented by Hans Kunitz (British Patent, 1965). This is a large F bass intended to function as a contrabass, incorporating the keys of F/C–D–B♭. In the early 1970s, B. P. Leonard independently invented the in-line configuration with the tuning B♭/G–E–D. The prototype was built by J. Onqué of the Giardinelli Band Instrument Company in New York. Giardinelli subsequently made several alterations in the tuning of Leonard's design: B♭/F–G–E♭ and B♭/F–G♭–D. In the latter forms, the double-trigger design has been adopted by instrument manufacturers for bass trombones.

the necessary coordination to place the slide in position accurately. Through practice, the player can develop an automatic feel for the location of each position but must continually strive for the quickest possible movement between positions. A helpful technique for improving the slide movement is to occasionally practice in the dark. Students often depend on the eye in making slide movements. When the visual crutch is removed, the player must rely on the ear and the feel of the hand to locate the positions. This technique will accelerate a student's mastery of slide motion.

In legato, quickness of slide motion is essential. Students sometimes interrupt the air flow to compensate for slow slide motion. Although this eliminates obvious glissandos, the legato is unsatisfactory. Developing good intonation is a continual process of careful listening. In practicing, trombone students should make it a policy not to accept notes that reflect any fault in slide movement or intonation.

Alternate Positions

Alternate positions play a more important role in trombone technique than do alternate fingerings in the playing of valve instruments. Through their use, a number of changes of slide direction and long shifts between positions can be avoided. For example, in a moving passage, if sixth-position C is followed by the F above, it is preferable to play the F also in sixth rather than return the slide to first position. Unlike most alternate fingerings, differences in intonation between the regular and altered position can be corrected by the trombone slide.

By selecting alternate positions, the trombonist tries to maintain the direction of slide motion where possible. These patterns become established through the practice of scales and arpeggios. Students often resist using alternate positions and cling to familiar positions no matter how awkward the slide motion. It is important, therefore, that the use of alternate positions be included in their normal technical development to avoid problems when more difficult literature is encountered. Most method books incorporate this skill progressively within their studies.

Because they are played on different harmonic series, there is some difference in timbre between the regular and alternate position. In rapid passages, small variations in timbre may not be noticed, but in notes of longer duration, tone quality must be the primary consideration, even if a somewhat awkward shift of the slide is necessary. Positions that involve long extensions of the slide tend to be less resonant and more difficult to control physically, due to the imbalance of the instrument. With a few exceptions, a more consistent tone is achieved by minimizing the intermixing of notes taken in B♭ or F on trombones with F attachments. Ordinarily, the F attachment is rarely used above second-space C. Practice must be directed toward matching the timbre and intonation of regular and alternate positions. By playing a note in each position, the trombonist can equalize tone, stability, and intonation to an acceptable level on most notes.

The following are the most commonly used alternate positions:

Intonation

The trombone is unique among wind instruments in being capable of completely variable pitch. This is both an advantage and a challenge to the player. Having a greater capacity to adjust intonation than other brass players, the trombonist must rely more on the ear in locating exact pitch centers. In this sense, trombone playing is similar to string playing, where it takes considerable time and effort to learn to play in tune. Apart from the general suggestions presented in the discussion of the trumpet in Chapter 3, the following notes most often need correction:

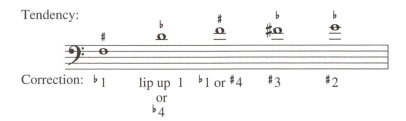

The highest octave varies with individual players and instruments, and requires fine adjustment. It is common for students to tend to play sharp in the upper register; this is usually the result of too much embouchure adjustment in proportion to air pressure.

In a brass section, the first trombone must concentrate carefully on the pitches played by the first trumpet. It is helpful if these players can sit next to each other in order to hear each other as clearly as possible. Likewise, the bass trombone should be seated next to the tuba since the parts often double. Specific guidelines for seating the brass section for optimum balance and intonation are presented in Chapter 14.

In large ensembles, the trombone section must work outside of full rehearsals if good intonation is to be achieved. Only through sectional rehearsals is adequate time available for careful tuning and balancing of chords. It is helpful if the tubist occasionally joins these sessions. In bands, euphoniums should also be included. The low brass should be considered an ensemble within the orchestra or band.

Trills on the Trombone

Trills are not often called for in the literature for the trombone, but when they are, the player must be able to produce a smooth and reliable lip trill. Fortunately, the upper register of the trombone lends itself to whole-tone lip slurs and these, with work, can be refined into usable trills.

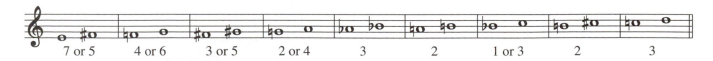

Lip trills are difficult for everyone at first. Above all, a great deal of patience is needed for this work. By working slowly and gradually increasing the speed, the player can develop the trill over time. The great hornist Barry Tuckwell has suggested that if the usual way of practicing lip trills is reversed, the trill can be developed more easily.[12]

The Glissando

The special capability of the trombone's moving slide to produce a glissando has not been lost on composers who like to make use of this effect. However, there are instances in the repertoire where glissandos have been written without an adequate awareness of what the instrument can do. Continuous glissandos can take place only within the seven positions of the slide:

Occasionally, problematic glissandos are found that cross over the first (ascending) or seventh (descending) positions. Experienced trombonists have found their way around such "broken glissandos,"[13] but it would be better if composers considered the length of slide available above or below the starting note before writing this effect.

Another problem is glissandos such as the one from low B to F in Bartók's *Concerto for Orchestra*, which was written for the longer slide of the obsolete F bass trombone. Although this is impossible on the B♭–F bass due to the length of the slide, it can be managed on the in-line double-valve instrument with some adroit handling of the valves in conjunction with the slide (Some bass trombonists play this on the Kunitz-type F bass–contrabass if one is available). The various configurations of double-valve bass trombone have created new possibilities for glissandos.

The F, C, and G Clefs

Although the trombonist is free of the burden of transposition that confronts horn and trumpet players, parts in tenor, alto, and occasionally treble clef are encoun-

---

[12] Barry Tuckwell, *Playing the Horn* (London: Oxford University Press, 1978), pp. 17–18.

[13] Some solutions, as well as a table of glissandos, may be found in Denis Wick, *Trombone Technique* (London: Oxford University Press, 1971), pp. 62–66. See also Edward Kleinhammer, *The Art of Trombone Playing* (Evanston, Ill.: Summy-Birchard, 1963), pp. 58–61.

tered in addition to the usual bass clef. An advanced player must be prepared to function comfortably in the tenor and alto clefs (parts written in alto, tenor, and bass clef were originally intended for alto, tenor, and bass trombone). In writing for the trombone today, the use of clefs is extremely helpful as a means of avoiding excessive ledger lines:

More use could be made of the nontransposed treble clef, particularly in the jazz and studio fields, as an alternative to the ledger lines required in bass clef by high-register parts. An anomaly is the transposed treble clef, in which the trombone sounds down a ninth from where it is written. Trombone parts in brass bands (other than the bass trombone) are written in this manner. Players who are familiar with tenor clef can perform such parts by replacing the treble clef with a tenor clef and subtracting two sharps (or adding two flats).

Students of orchestration are often confused when they are told that the trombone is a nontransposing instrument sounding an octave below the B♭ trumpet (a transposing instrument). The trombone (with its movable slide) predates the horn and trumpet as a chromatic instrument and did not go through a "natural" era during which notes were limited to the harmonic series. To make performing on the harmonic series easier, natural trumpet and horn parts were notated in C and crooks were inserted to make the notes sound in the key of the orchestra . The practice of writing the fundamentals of the horn and trumpet as C continues today. Consequently, when the trumpeter plays open (written) C on the B♭ trumpet, concert B♭ sounds. Open position on the trombone (first position) has always been notated and read as concert B♭, the fundamental pitch.

Mutes

Trombone mutes follow the same patterns as those for trumpet, but are constructed in appropriately larger dimensions. (See Figure 5.4.) With the variety of bell sizes in use, it is important to use a mute that has been designed for a specific bell. Even with a well-designed mute, it may be necessary to make further adjustments by sanding the corks. The low register, particularly F attachment notes, should be checked when selecting a mute because some will work better than others in this range. Where possible, the same brand of straight mute should be used between trumpets and trombones to ensure evenness of tone color. Cup mutes, harmon mutes, and so forth may not blend as well between the two sections.

One irritating problem that seems to occur regularly is that the composer fails to allow adequate time to insert or withdraw the mute. Composers should check their muting instructions carefully and mentally go through the motions they are asking of the performer. Generally, more time is needed for mute changes by trombonists than by trumpeters.

Figure 5.4. **Assorted mutes for brass (Jo-Ral).** *Photo Courtesy of Jo-Ral Mutes.*

Miscellaneous

Although some trombones are produced with a silver-plated finish, most professional performers prefer lacquered brass. The latter is considered to offer a warmer tone. Some players favor bells made of gold (red) brass. This material includes a greater percentage of copper and produces a darker timbre.

Another matter of preference is whether rotary valves are operated by string action, as is common with horns, or by mechanical connection. With the older ball-and-socket linkages, many felt that string action offered a quicker valve change. The new mechanical Unibal and Minibal linkages available for horns and tubas have solved this problem and can be fitted to trombone rotary valves.

Leadpipes are the subject of experimentation, and some instruments are made with removable leadpipes to allow performers to select one that is more suited to their specific requirements. Existing instruments can be modified to accept different leadpipes.

The Trombone in New Music

Within the last two decades composers have shown a great deal of interest in the trombone's unlimited capacity to vary pitch and produce novel sounds. Microtonal effects, singing or speaking through the instrument, and passing air through the tubing are a few of the devices that have been used. A number of solo compositions have appeared and have been received with interest at new music concerts. Works such as Luciano Berio's *Sequenza V,* Adler's *Canto II,* Erickson's *General Speech* have brought the trombone into a new era as a solo instrument admirably suited to to-day's compositional techniques. There has been a comparable reawakening in the traditional literature. Soloists such as Christian Lindberg and Branimir Slokar have popularized the trombone as a solo instrument through recordings and concert appearances. This has been of immense service to young trombonists who now can look forward to a widening circle of opportunities for the future.

Recommended Literature[14]

COMPLETE METHODS

*ARBAN: *Famous Method,* ed. Randall and Mantia (C. Fischer)

ARBAN: *First and Second Year,* ed. Prescott (C. Fischer)

*JOSEL: *Posaunenschule,* 3 vols. (L. Krenn)

*LAFOSSE: *Méthode complète,* 3 vols. (A. Leduc)

ELEMENTARY METHODS

BEELER: *Method,* 2 vols. (Warner Bros.)

CIMERA: *Method* (Belwin-Mills)

*E. CLARKE: *Method* (C. Fischer)

LONG: *Rubank Elementary Method* (Rubank)

McDUNN: *Méthode de trombone,* 3 vols. (Leduc)

RIDGEON: *Brass for Beginners* (Boosey & Hawkes)

SLOKAR: *Method for Trombone* (Reift)

STUDIES

MEDIUM TO MEDIUM-DIFFICULT

BLUME: *36 Studies,* vols. 1 and 2 (C. Fischer)

BORDOGNI: *43 Bel Canto Studies,* transcribed by Roberts (bass trombone) (R. King)

*BORDOGNI: *Melodious Etudes,* transcribed by Rochut, vol. 1 (C. Fischer)

COLIN: *Advanced Lip Flexibilities* (medium to difficult) (C. Colin)

ENDRESEN: *Supplementary Studies* (Rubank)

*FINK: *Introducing the Tenor Clef* (Accura Music)

*FINK: *Studies in Legato* (C. Fischer)

*GOWER AND VOXMAN: *Rubank Advanced Method,* 2 vols. (Rubank)

HANSEN: *Solobuch für Posaune,* 4 vols. (Benjamin)

JOSEL: *Special Legato Exercises* (Krenn)

JOSEL: *Technical Exercises,* 2 vols. (Krenn)

JOSEL: *Tonleiter* (Krenn)

*LAFOSSE: *School of Sightreading and Style,* 5 vols. (easy to difficult) (A. Leduc)

*LITTLE: *Embouchure Builder* (Pro Art Publ.)

MUELLER: *Technical Studies,* vols. 1 and 2 (C. Fischer)

*OSTRANDER: *F Attachment and Bass Trombone* (C. Colin)

*PARÉS: *Scales* (Rubank)

REIFT: *Warm-Ups* (Reift)

*REMINGTON: *Warm-Up Exercises* (bass trombone, easy to difficult) (Accura Music)

*REMINGTON: *Warm-Up Studies* (easy to difficult) (Accura Music)

*SCHLOSSBERG: *Daily Drills and Technical Studies* (medium to difficult) (M. Baron)

SLAMA: *66 Etudes in All Keys* (C. Fischer)

SLOKAR: *Warm-Ups & Technical Routines* (Reift)

SKORNICKA AND BOLTZ: *Rubank Intermediate Method* (Rubank)

*TYRRELL: *40 Progressive Studies* (Boosey & Hawkes)

VOXMAN (ED.): *Selected Studies for Trombone* (Rubank)

WIGGINS: *First Tunes & Studies* (easy to medium) (Oxford)

DIFFICULT

AHARONI: *New Method for the Modern Bass Trombone* (Noga Music)

ANDERSON: *Complete Method for Alto Trombone* (Modern Editions)

*BACH: *Studies,* transcribed by Lafosse (Leduc)

*BLAZEVICH: *Clef Studies* (International)

*BLAZEVICH: *Sequences* (International)

BLUME: *36 Studies,* vol. 3 (C. Fischer)

*BORDOGNI: *Melodious Etudes,* transcribed by Rochut, vols. 2 and 3 (C. Fischer)

*DUFRESNE AND VOISIN: *Sightreading Studies* (C. Colin)

FINK: *Introducing the Alto Clef* (Accura Music)

FINK: *Studies in Legato for Bass Trombone & Tuba* (C. Fischer)

KAHILA: *Advanced Studies* (alto and tenor clef) (R. King)

---

[14] Essential literature is noted with an asterisk. For additional material, see the *Brass Players' Guide* (Robert King). Repertoire lists may be found in the texts by Fink, Gregory, Griffiths, Kleinhammer, and Wick.

KOPPRASCH: *Selected Studies*, ed. Fote (bass trombone) (Kendor)

*KOPPRASCH: *60 Selected Studies*, 2 vols. (C. Fischer)

MANTIA: *Trombone Virtuoso* (C. Fischer)

*MAXTED: *20 Studies for Tenor Trombone* (Boosey & Hawkes)

MUELLER: *Technical Studies*, vol. 3 (C. Fischer)

*OSTRANDER: *Double-Valve Bass Trombone Low Tone Studies* (C. Colin)

*RAPH: *Double-Valve Bass Trombone* (C. Fischer)

*ROCHUT: *Lectures* (Fetter)

WATROUS: *Trombonisms* (C. Fischer)

UNACCOMPANIED SOLOS

DIFFICULT

*ADLER: *Canto II* (bass trombone) (Oxford)

*ARNOLD: *Fantasy* (Faber)

*BACH: *6 Cello Suites*, transcribed by Brown (tenor trombone) (International)

*BACH: *6 Cello Suites*, transcribed by Marsteller, 2 vols. (bass trombone) (Southern)

*BERIO: *Sequenza V* (Universal Ed.)

BERNSTEIN: *Elegy for Mippy II* (Schirmer)

*CAGE: *Solo for Sliding Trombone* (Peters)

CHILDS: *Sonata* (Presser)

*ERICKSON: *General Speech* (Seesaw Music)

FETTER: *Variations on Palestrina's Dona Nobis Pacem* (Fetter)

*GLOBOKAR: *Exchanges* (Peters)

HARTLEY: *Sonata Breve* (bass trombone) (Presser)

HIDAS: *Fantasia* (Editio Musica)

KENNY: *Sonata* (Tezak)

PRESSER: *Partita* (Philharmusica)

RABE: *Basta* (Reimer)

ROSS: *Prelude, Fugue, and Big Apple* (with tape) (bass trombone) (Boosey & Hawkes)

SANDSTROEM: *Disjointing* (Nordiska Musikforlaget)

*STOCKHAUSEN: *In Freudenschaft* (Stockhausen)

*TELEMANN: *12 Fantasies* (C. Fischer)

TROMBONE AND PIANO

EASY

ADAMS: *The Holy City* (Boosey & Hawkes)

BACH: *Aria, Bist du bei mir*, transcribed by Fitzgerald (Belwin-Mills)

BAKALEINIKOFF: *Andantino Cantabile* (Belwin-Mills)

BAKALEINIKOFF: *Meditation* (Belwin-Mills)

BARNES: *The Clifford Barnes Trombone Album* (Boosey & Hawkes)

DEARNLEY (ED.):   *More Easy Pieces* (Chester)

GOODWIN AND PEARSON: *First Book of Trombone Solos* (Faber)

GOODWIN AND PEARSON: *Second Book of Trombone Solos* (Faber)

LAWTON (ED.):   *The Young Trombonist*, 3 vols. (Oxford)

LAYCOCK: *The Dove* (Boosey & Hawkes)

MENDELSSOHN: *On Wings of Song* (Boosey & Hawkes)

MOZART: *A Mozart Solo Album*, arranged by Lethbridge (Oxford)

PERRY (ED.):   *Classical Album* (Boosey & Hawkes)

PHILLIPS (ED.):   *Classical & Romantic Album* (Oxford)

SMITH (ED.):   *First Solos for the Trombone Player* (Schirmer)

SNELL: *Belwin Master Solos, Easy* (Belwin)

STRAUSS: *Allerseelen* (Rubank)

VERDI: *A Verdi Solo Album*, arranged by Lethbridge (Oxford)

WATTS: *Beginning Trombone Solos* (with cassette accompaniment) (H. Leonard)

WATTS: *Easy Trombone Solos* (with cassette accompaniment) (H. Leonard)

MEDIUM TO MEDIUM-DIFFICULT

BACH: *Sinfonia*, transcribed by Fote (bass trombone) (Kendor)

BAKER (ED.):   *Master Solos* (H. Leonard)

*BARAT: *Andante & Allegro* (C. Fischer)

BARNES: *Trombone Album* (Boosey & Hawkes)

BERLIOZ: *Recitative & Prayer* (Presser)

CLACK: *First Repertoire Pieces* (Boosey & Hawkes)

*GALLIARD: *6 Sonatas*, 2 vols. transcribed by Brown (International)

*GAUBERT: *Cantabile et Scherzetto* (C. Fischer)

HANDEL: *Sonata 3*, arranged by Powell (Southern)

HOROVITZ: *Adam-Blues* (Novello)

*IVESON: *Trombone Solos* (Chester)

*LUSHER: *Sweet and Sour* (Warwick)

*LUSHER AND NORTON: *Trombone Album* (Boosey & Hawkes)

MARCELLO: *Sonata in C* (International)

MARCELLO: *Sonata in E Minor* (International)

OSTRANDER (ED.):   *Concert Album* (Editions Musicus)

*PRYOR: *Annie Laurie* (Ludwig)

RACHMANINOFF: *Vocalise* (International)

RICHARDSON (ED.):   *6 Classical Solos* (Boosey & Hawkes)

*SMITH (ED.):   *Solos for the Trombone Player* (Schirmer)

SNELL: *Belwin Master Solos, Intermediate* (Belwin)

TANNER: *Trombone Solos,* 2 vols. (Belwin)

TCHEREPNIN: *Andante* (Belaieff)

*TELEMANN: *Sonata in F Minor* (International)

VOXMAN (ED.):   *Concert & Contest Collection* (Rubank)

WATTS: *Intermediate Trombone Solos* (with cassette accompaniment) (H. Leonard)

DIFFICULT

*ALBRECHTSBERGER: *Concerto* (Rosehill)

*ARUTUNIAN: *Concerto* (Bim)

BLAZHEVICH: *Concerto No. 1* (Bim)

BLAZHEVICH: *Concerto No. 2* (International)

*BLOCH: *Symphony* (Broude Bros.)

CHAVEZ: *Concerto* (Schirmer)

CORELLI: *Sonata in F,* transcribed by Brown (International)

COSMA: *Concertino* (Bim)

*CRESTON: *Fantasy* (Schirmer)

CURNOW: *Fantasy for Trombone* (Rosehill)

*DAVID: *Concertino* (C. Fischer)

DEFAYE: *2 danses* (also for bass trombone) (A. Leduc)

ECCLES: *Sonata in G Minor* (International)

FINGER: *Sonata* (Bim)

*GAUBERT: *Morçeau symphonique* (International)

GEORGE: *Sonate* (Southern)

*GREGSON: *Concerto* (Novello)

*GRONDAHL: *Concerto* (Samfundet til Udgivelse Af Dansk Musik)

*GUILMANT: *Morçeau symphonique* (Warner Bros.)

HARTLEY: *Arioso* (bass trombone) (Fema Music)

HIDAS: *Concerto* (Editio Musica)

*HINDEMITH: *Sonate* (Schott)

HODDINOTT: *Ritornelli* (Oxford)

*HOWARTH: *Concerto* (Chester)

*JACOB: *Cameos* (bass trombone) (Emerson Ed.)

*JACOB: *Concertino* (Emerson Ed.)

*JACOB: *Concerto* (Galaxy)

*JACOB: *Sonata* (Emerson Ed.)

KOETSIER: *Concertino* (Bim)

KOETSIER: *Sonatina* (Donemus)

KROL: *Capriccio da Camera* (Benjamin)

LARSSON: *Concertino* (Gehrmans Musikforlag)

*MARTIN: *Ballade* (Universal)

*MILHAUD: *Concertino d'hiver* (Associated)

*L. MOZART: *Concerto* (Ludwig)

*NIELSEN: *2 Fantasy Pieces* (International)

PILSS: *Concerto* (bass trombone) (R. King)

*PRYOR: *Blue Bells of Scotland* (C. Fischer)

*PRYOR: *Thoughts of Love* (C. Fischer)

*RIMSKY-KORSAKOFF: *Concerto* (Boosey & Hawkes)

*ROPARTZ: *Piece in Eb Minor* (International)

*SAINT-SAËNS: *Cavatine* (Durand)

*SALZEDO: *Piece Concertante* (A. Leduc)

SANDERS: *Sonata in Eb* (Warwick)

SNELL: *Belwin Master Solos,* advanced (Belwin)

*STEVENS: *Sonata* (Southern)

*STEVENS: *Sonatina* (Southern)

*TOMASI: *Concerto* (Leduc)

TUTHILL: *Concerto* (R. King)

*WAGENSEIL: *Concerto* (Boosey & Hawkes)

*WHITE: *Sonata* (Southern)

WHITE: *Tetra Ergon* (Brass Press)

WILDER: *Sonata* (bass trombone) (Margun Music)

UBER: *Sonata* (Southern)

*ZWILICH: *Concerto* (Presser)

BOOKS ON THE TROMBONE[15]

ARLING, HARRY J.   *Trombone Chamber Music.* Nashville, Tenn.: Brass Press, 1983.

BAKER, DAVID.   *Contemporary Techniques for the Trombone.* 2 vols. New York: Charles Colin, 1974.

*BATE, PHILIP.   *The Trumpet and Trombone: An Outline of Their History, Development, and Construction.* 2nd ed. New York: Norton, 1978.

*DEMPSTER, STUART.   *The Modern Trombone.* Berkeley: University of California Press, 1979.

*EVERETT, THOMAS G.   *Annotated Guide to Bass Trombone Literature.* Nashville, Tenn.: Brass Press, 1978.

*FINK, REGINALD H.   *The Trombonist's Handbook.* Athens, Ohio.: Accura Music, 1977.

*Gregory, Robin: *The Trombone.* New York: Faber & Faber, 1973.

[15] Many interesting articles appear in the *International Trombone Association Journal* and other periodicals listed in Appendix C.

GRIFFITHS, JOHN R.   *The Low Brass Guide.* Hackensack, N.J.: Jerona Music, 1980.

*KAGARICE, VERN L., ET AL.   *Solos for the Student Trombonist: An Annotated Bibliography.* Nashville, Tenn.: Brass Press, 1979.

*Kleinhammer, Edward. *The Art of Trombone Playing.* Evanston, Ill.: Summy-Birchard Company, 1963.

KNAUB, DONALD: *Trombone Teaching Techniques.* 2nd ed. Athens, Ohio: Accura Music, 1977.

NAYLOR, TOM L.   *The Trumpet and Trombone in Graphic Arts, 1500–1800.* Nashville, Tenn.: Brass Press, 1979.

SENFF, THOMAS E.   "An Annotated Bibliography of the Unaccompanied Solo Repertoire for Trombone." D.M.A. thesis, University of Illinois, 1976. UM 76–16, 919.

*WICK, DENIS.   *Trombone Technique.* London: Oxford University Press, 1975.

*WIGNESS, C. ROBERT.   *The Soloistic Use of the Trombone in Eighteenth-Century Vienna.* Nashville, Tenn.: Brass Press, 1978

CHAPTER 6

Baritone and Euphonium

The origin of the euphonium and baritone (Figures 6.1 and 6.2) is more obscure than that of the tuba, which has a definite starting point and clear lines of development.[1] It is known that tenor-range brass instruments built in B♭ with three valves were part of German military bands during the late 1820s. The next clue is an instrument called the Euphonion, which was developed in 1843 or 1844 by Sommer of Weimar. This may be the same Sommer (his first name is unknown) who caused a stir with a similar instrument at the 1851 Crystal Palace Exhibition in London.

About the same time, Adolph Sax patented his complete family of saxhorns, which included two low B♭ instruments: the Saxhorn Baryton, which was of similar dimensions to the modern baritone, and the Saxhorn Basse, a larger instrument originally of greater bore size than the euphonium. The originality of Sax's instruments was disputed at the time, and it is clear that the German instruments both preceded them and developed independently. However, Sax's instruments were distinct in their tone and playing qualities as well as in their use of piston valves. Sax should also be credited with developing a complete group of instruments of this type, and he is largely responsible for their acceptance in countries west of the Rhine.

Today, the baritone and euphonium (both are in the key of B♭) are constructed similarly, but differ significantly in their bore and bell dimensions. Consequently, there are important differences in timbre and playing characteristics between the two instruments. Baritones from British and European manufacturers, and others based on these designs, are made with a distinctly narrower bore than euphoniums. For example, the Boosey & Hawkes and Besson baritones are built with a 13.11 mm (.516″) main bore, as opposed to 14.72 mm (.579″) for their euphoniums.

In the United States, the difference is less defined. This is due to a lack of clarity in identifying the instruments as well as a tendency for American firms to produce larger-bore baritones and smaller euphoniums than those used in England (this trend is changing, however, in response to the almost total domination of British-type euphoniums). Further confusion is generated by the habit among conductors and players of referring to both instruments as baritones or baritone horns.

Still more confusion is created by the names applied to these instruments in other countries. In Germany, the baritone is known as the *Tenorhorn* (Figure 6.3) and the euphonium as the *Baryton* (Figure 6.4). In England, the tenor horn is the E♭ alto horn. Sax's original designation of *Baryton* (baritone) and *Basse* (euphonium) is still used in France.

---

[1] The development of the baritone and euphonium is sketched as clearly as it probably can be in Clifford Bevan's *The Tuba Family* (New York: Scribner's, 1978), pp. 90–94.

Figure 6.1. **Baritone (Besson).** *Photo courtesy of the Boosey & Hawkes Group.*

Figure 6.2. **Euphonium (Besson.)** *Photo courtesy of the Boosey & Hawkes Group.*

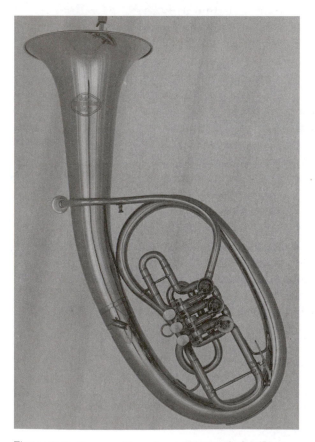

Figure 6–3. **German Tenorhorn (Alexander).** *(Photo courtesy of Gebr. Alexander, Mainz.)*

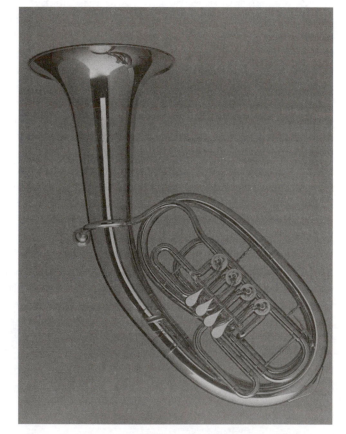

Figure 6–4. **German Baryton (Meinl Weston).** *(Photo courtesy of Wenzel Meinl, GmbH)*

Greater precision would prevail if the name *euphonium* were used only for instruments with a bore larger than 14 mm (.551"). Differences between the baritone and euphonium can be readily seen by comparing the cylindrical tubing of the valve sections of the two instruments. If tubing from the baritone is inserted into the euphonium, the differences in main bore are quite evident. Even more conspicuous are the tapers of the bell sections. On the baritone, the profile is more slender, with a significantly smaller bell throat. These factors give the baritone its light, clear tone in comparison to the darker timbre and more tubalike appearance of the euphonium (in particular, the size of the bottom bow should be noted). The brass band is the only ensemble where a clear distinction between the instruments is made. Brass band scores include separate baritone and euphonium parts (two of each), and players specialize on one instrument or the other.

Intonation

The degree to which a player can correct intonation by lipping a faulty note into tune decreases as the vibrating air columns become longer and greater quantities of air are used. Hence, intonation on the trumpet can be more readily influenced by subtle adjustments of the player's embouchure than on the lower brass. Hornists have the further ability to affect pitch by altering the hand position, and trombonists by varying the position of the slide. Intonation on the baritone, euphonium, and tuba is therefore a prime concern and how this is dealt with is an important consideration in the design of the instrument.

Aside from problems with the harmonic series itself (which should be minimal in a well-designed instrument), errors occur when the valves are used in combination. For example, the total length for a euphonium in B♭ is 115.325" (2929.25 mm). When the first valve is depressed, 14.175" (360.4 mm) of tubing is added to lower the pitch one tone to A♭. Opening the third valve lowers the instrument's pitch one and one-half tones to G, adding 21.825" (554.35 mm). The difficulty arises when the first and third valves are used together to lower the instrument to F.

Just as progressively more tubing is required between each trombone position to arrive at the correct measurement for a given pitch, so the valve tubing would need some means of extending itself for the lower pitch. The length of vibrating air column necessary for the low F is 153.960" (3910.58 mm). If 14.175" (360.4 mm) of the first valve and the third valve's 21.825" (554.35 mm) are added to the euphonium's fundamental length of 115.325" (2929.25 mm), the total tubing available for the F is 151.325" (3843.65 mm)—that is, 2.635" (66.93 mm) too short, producing a sharp pitch. When all three valves are used to play a low E, the discrepancy is even greater.[2]

The usual way around this problem is for the manufacturer to increase the length of the third valve tubing to more than the one-and-one-half-tone extension it was originally intended to provide; this introduces a compromise that is workable on the high brass instruments due to their greater responsiveness to embouchure control. However, the third valve is diverted from its original purpose and is almost never used alone. In its place, the first and second valves are used in combination for the one-and-one-half-tone extension, but their combined length is slightly short. This is why trumpeters must use the first valve trigger on notes played in this combination.

There have been various approaches to finding a practical solution to this difficulty. For the trumpet, the compromises work well enough, provided that the instrument is fitted with both a first- and third-valve trigger or ring. A similar ap-

---

[2] F. C. Draper, *Notes on the Besson System of Automatic Compensation of Valved Brass Wind Instruments* (Edgware, England: Besson , 1953).

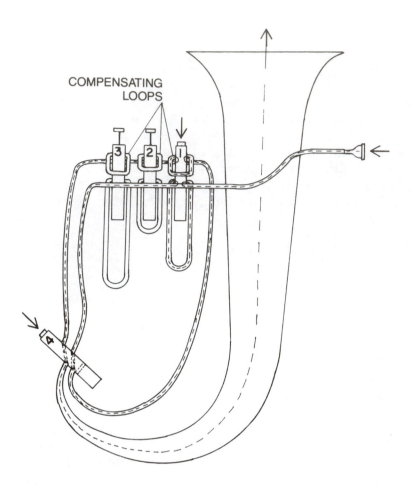

COMPENSATING
LOOPS

Figure 6.5. **Blaikley's four-valve compensating system.** *Adapted from Draper, Notes on the Besson System.*

proach is taken by some euphonium manufacturers by adding rings to the third-and/or first-valve slides, or to the main tuning slide. Although these offer some measure of correction, they are awkward to use in an instrument of this size and do not offer a very viable solution. Most commonly, a fourth valve is incorporated into the design; this affords some improvement by providing alternate fingerings for the 1–3 and 1–2–3 combinations (4 and 2–4, respectively). However, there are serious limitations of the four-valve system in the range above the pedal tone and this has led tubists to consider the further addition of a fifth valve to be essential.

The most effective solution for the euphonium is the system of automatic compensation designed by David J. Blaikley for the Boosey company in 1874. In this system, each valve contains a second loop of tubing of sufficient length to correct intonation when the valve is used in combination with the compensating (master) valve. There are both three- and four-valve compensating systems. In the preferable four-valve system, the fourth valve acts as the master valve and has its compensating loop routed through the other valves. The valves perform normally when used independently of the fourth valve. In combination with the fourth valve, however, the vibrating air column is directed a second time through the regular valves' compensating loops, thereby adding the correct length of tubing for accurate intonation.

The advantage of the compensating system may be seen in the following chart, which compares the intonation of compensated and uncompensated four-valve systems:

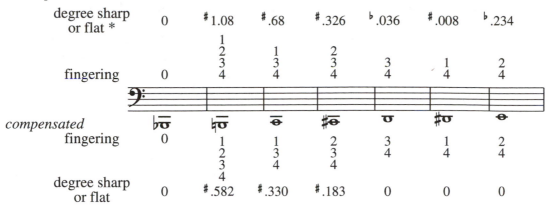

uncompensated

degree sharp or flat *	0	♯1.08	♯.68	♯.326	♭.036	♯.008	♭.234
fingering	0	1 2 3 4	1 3 4	2 3 4	3 4	1 4	2 4

compensated

fingering	0	1 2 3 4	1 3 4	2 3 4	3 4	1 4	2 4
degree sharp or flat	0	♯.582	♯.330	♯.183	0	0	0

* Of a semitone.

uncompensated †

♭.052	♭.211	♯.112	0	0	0	♭.243	♭.052	♭.211	♯.112	0	0	0
1 3	2 3	1 2	1	2	0	2 4	1 3	2 3	1 2	1	2	0

4	2 3	3	1	2	0	2 4	4	2 3	3	1	2	0
0	♯.147	0	0	0	0	0	0	♯.147	0	0	0	0

compensated

† The fourth valve would normally be used in place of the 1 - 3 combination on uncompensated instruments, providing improved intonation.

uncompensated

♭.211	♯.112	0	0	0	♯.112	0	0	0	0	0	0	♭.211
2 3	1 2	1	2	0	1 2	1	2	0	1	2	0	2 3

2 3	3	1	2	0	3	1	2	0	1	2	0	2 3
♯.147	0	0	0	0	0	0	0	0	0	0	0	♯.147

compensated

uncompensated

♯.112	0	0	0
1 2	1	2	0

3	1	2	0
0	0	0	0

compensated

Chart 6.1. **Comparison of intonation of compensated and uncompensated four-valve systems.** *Adapted from Draper, Notes on the Besson System.*

An additional advantage of the compensating system is that on instruments of this type, the third valve is constructed in the exact length for the one-and-one-half tone extension (not longer, as in uncompensated instruments) as originally intended, and may be used in place of the sharp 1–2 combination whenever the fingering pattern or the duration of the note permits. (The 1–2 combination may still be preferred in certain instances because it follows the first finger more naturally in rapid fingering sequences.) The accurate tuning of the third valve gives the player of a compensated instrument an advantage in intonation (it is a pity that many players are unaware of this feature and still cling to the 1–2 combination).

Although not perfect, the four-valve compensating system does greatly improve intonation. Alternate fingerings may still need to be used on some notes. Beyond the beginning level, a four-valve instrument is a necessity. As with all brass instruments, good intonation ultimately depends on the player getting to know the instrument and adjusting pitches as necessary.

Tone and Playing Style

Euphonium playing is related to cornet playing in that the main emphasis should be melodic and expressive. Although both instruments are especially suited to technical display—and this is exploited in the literature—their most important quality is a subtle capacity to emulate the human voice. This ability can best be heard by listening to some of the best British brass bands, where all 25 players (regardless of instrument) play with this concept. The use of a natural, singing vibrato is fundamental to this style and lends expressiveness and sensitivity to the tone.

The euphonium was originally created to blend with the other conical-bore instruments of the brass band, so it should have a deep, mellow tone quality, without any trace of edge or hardness. If the trombone tone needs a certain ring in the timbre, the euphonium and baritone timbre should have softness and richness. The difference in tone quality between euphonium and baritone is one of degree: The sound is similar, but the baritone timbre is somewhat lighter in both color and weight.

To achieve a characteristic tone quality, it is essential to use a mouthpiece of adequate depth and throat bore. It is quite common to find students using trombone mouthpieces that are too small to yield a satisfactory tone. (In orchestras, a trombonist is usually appointed to perform the euphonium parts and this often results in a hollow, rather hard timbre.) By examining the expanding tubing along the bell section, one can see the need for a large-capacity mouthpiece. In order to fill flared tubing of this size, a great quantity of air is necessary. A small mouthpiece places a restriction on the air column and results in a thin, fairly colorless tone. A large backbore (as on the Denis Wick 4AL or 5AL) is helpful in achieving the characteristic rich, dark timbre.

In orchestral circles, the euphonium is known as the tenor tuba and is generally played without vibrato. The Bydlo solo in *Pictures at an Exhibition* (Mussorgsky–Ravel), however, gains character from the addition of some vibrato and a rich euphonium tone. In other passages, such as those found in the Janácek *Sinfonietta* and Holst's *Mars* (*The Planets*), a pure, straight tone is more effective. In Strauss's *Don Quixote*, the vibrato question is less clear and some experimentation is called for. Sometimes a German rotary valve euphonium (known as a *Baryton* in Germany) is used. This instrument has an unusually sturdy tone, but lacks an effective system of compensation. For this reason, it is important that a four-valve model be used, and the fit of the mouthpiece into the receiver must be carefully checked. (This problem is discussed in Chapter 2.)

The euphonium is in its natural element in bands, where it is treated as a leading solo voice. Composers have taken advantage of the instrument's technical agility, and the player is provided with many interesting and challenging parts. This is even more true of euphonium writing in the brass band. The instrument is used in truly virtuosic fashion in the leading British bands, such as Black Dyke Mills, Besses O' th' Barn, and Grimethorpe Colliery.

The euphonium is a superb solo instrument with a long tradition, although it has mostly been associated with brass and wind bands. In the days when bands such as Sousa's and Gilmore's toured the country, euphonium players were featured as soloists and gained considerable fame. In subsequent years, the solo euphonium was rather forgotten in America, as it fulfilled its ensemble role in concert bands. In Britain, the euphonium remained fairly prominent due to the popularity of brass bands and the leading role given the instrument in this type of group. Euphonium solos are a standard feature of brass band concerts and there are always excellent soloists around. Today's generation of soloists both in Britain and America, such as the Childs brothers, Steven Mead, and Dr. Brian Bowman, are bringing about a rebirth of interest in the solo euphonium. New solo works with orchestra as well as band have been introduced, and there is a rising tide of enthusiasm for this medium. What is needed now is more exposure and perhaps a more broad-minded attitude on the part of conductors and concert managers. Concert programs of both orchestras and bands can be enriched by occasionally offering something new and unusual, and the euphonium never fails to connect with audiences.

Miscellaneous

The first use of a mute for the euphonium can be found in Strauss's *Don Quixote*. Mutes are rarely called for in the literature, and it is probably necessary for the band or orchestra to make one available when required. An example of muted writing can also be found in Karel Husa's *Music for Prague 1968* (for band).

The baritone and euphonium are obviously bass clef instruments and this should be the normal practice of notation. Beginners should be taught in bass clef. However, there is a long-standing tradition of writing for euphonium and baritone as transposing B♭ instruments in the treble clef (like the cornet), sounding a ninth lower. This is the case in brass bands, and it is common for wind-band parts to be furnished in both treble and bass clef. This practice probably came about in order to make it easier for cornet players to switch to other instruments within the brass band. Therefore, it is important for euphonium players to be equally comfortable in bass or treble clef. An important reason for learning the treble clef in addition to bass clef is that a great quantity of vital study and solo literature for cornet, trumpet, and horn will be made accessible. The tenor clef is also useful for trombone and bassoon literature. Orchestral players occasionally have to deal with transposed bass clef parts and other oddities.

Passing mention might be made of the double-bell euphonium, although this instrument is now considered a valuable collector's item. It was popular as a solo instrument during the Sousa–Pryor era because the normal tone of the instrument could be modified by being directed through a second, smaller bell to produce echo and trombonelike effects. Superior instruments in their time, double-bell euphoniums are sought after today as much for their playing qualities as for the novelty of their design.

Recommended Literature[3]

COMPLETE METHODS

*Arban: *Method,* ed. Mantia & Randall (trombone) (C. Fischer)

Saint-Jacome: *Grand Method* (cornet) (C. Fischer)

ELEMENTARY METHODS

*Beeler: *Method* (Warner Bros.)

Long: *Elementary Method* (Rubank)

Ridgeon: *Brass for Beginners* (Boosey & Hawkes)

Uber: *70 Beginning & Early Studies* (PP Music)

Wiggins: *First Tunes & Studies* (Oxford)

Williams: *Little Classics* (Colin)

STUDIES

MEDIUM TO MEDIUM-DIFFICULT

Blume: *36 Studies,* vol. 1 (trombone) (C. Fischer)

*Bordogni: *Melodious Etudes,* ed. Rochut, vols. 1 and 2 (trombone) (C. Fischer)

*Clarke: *Technical Studies,* ed. Gordon (C. Fischer)

*Fink: *From Treble to Bass Clef* (Accura)

*Kopprasch: *60 Selected Studies* (trombone) (medium to difficult) (C. Fischer)

Miller: *60 Studies* (R. King)

Mueller: *30 Leichte Etuden* (F. Hofmeister)

Mueller: *Technical Studies,* vols. 1 and 2 (trombone) (C. Fischer)

*Parés: *Scales* (Rubank)

Reift: *Warm-Ups* (Reift)

Ronka: *Modern Daily Warm-Ups & Drills* (C. Fischer)

*Tyrrell: *40 Progressive Studies* (trombone) (Boosey & Hawkes)

Voxman (ed.):   *Selected Studies* (Rubank)

Wastall: *Scales & Arpeggios* (Boosey & Hawkes)

DIFFICULT

Blume: *36 Studies,* vol. 2 (trombone) (C. Fischer)

*Bordogni: *Melodious Etudes,* ed. Rochut, vol. 3 (trombone) (C. Fischer)

Charlier: *32 Etudes de perfectionnement* (H. Lemoine)

*Gordon: *30 Velocity Studies* (trombone) (C. Fischer)

Harris: *Advanced Daily Studies* (C. Colin)

Mueller: *Technical Studies,* vol. 3 (trombone) (C. Fischer)

Uber: *Symphonic Studies* (REBU)

UNACCOMPANIED SOLOS

DIFFICULT

Bach: *Dance Movements from the Cello Suite,* transcribed by Torchinsky (Schirmer)

Baxley: *Ronald McDifficult* (Clark-Baxley)

Constantinides: *Fantasy* (Whaling)

Croley: *Sonata* (Philharmusica Corp.)

Frackenpohl: *Bonebits* (Anglo-American)

Globokar: *Echanges* (Peters)

Grainger: *Walking Tune* (Philharmusica)

Paganini: *Caprice 24* (Whaling)

Paganini: *Four Caprices* (Whaling)

Sparke: *Pantomime* (Studio)

BARITONE/EUPHONIUM AND PIANO[4]

EASY

Adams: *The Holy City* (trombone) (Boosey & Hawkes)

Dearnley (ed.) *More Easy Pieces* (trombone) (Chester)

Gluck: *2 Classic Airs* (trombone) (Editions Musicus)

Haydn: *Aria & Allegro* (Rubank)

Johnson (ed.):   *Sacred Solos* (trombone) (Rubank)

Laycock: *The Dove* (trombone) (Boosey & Hawkes)

Mendelssohn: *On Wings of Song* (trombone) (Boosey & Hawkes)

Mozart: *Arietta & Allegro* (Southern)

Perry (ed.):   *Classical Album* (trombone) (Boosey & Hawkes)

Strauss: *Allerseelen* (Rubank)

Wagner: *Song to the Evening Star* (Kendor)

MEDIUM TO MEDIUM-DIFFICULT

*Barat: *Andante & Allegro* (trombone) (C. Fischer)

Campbell: *Master Solos* (H. Leonard)

*Capuzzi: *Andante & Rondo* (Hinrichsen)

Corelli: *Prelude & Minuet* (Southern)

*Cowell: *Tom Binkley's Tune* (Presser)

---

[3] Essential material is noted with an asterisk. For additional literature, see the *Brass Music Guide* (Robert King) and texts by Bevan, Griffiths, Louder, and Winter.

[4] See Earle L. Louder, "Original Solo Literature and Study Books for Euphonium," *The Instrumentalist* (May 1981), pp. 29–30; also "Begged, Borrowed, and Stolen Solo Euphonium Literature," by Paul Droste in the same issue (pp. 30–32).

DISHINGER: *Masterworks Solos* (Medici)

*EWALD: *Romance* (Editions Musicus)

GALLIARD: *6 Sonatas,* transcribed by Brown, 2 vols. (trombone) (International)

GLIERE: *Russian Sailors' Dance* (C. Fischer)

*HANDEL: *Andante & Allegro* (Southern)

*HANDEL: *Sonata 3* (Southern)

MARCELLO: *Adagio* (Whaling)

*PRYOR: *Annie Laurie* (trombone) (Ludwig)

*PRYOR: *Blue Bells of Scotland* (trombone) (C. Fischer)

*PRYOR: *Starlight* (trombone) (C. Fischer)

ROSSINI: *Largo al Factotum* (Boosey & Hawkes)

*SENAILLE: *Allegro Spiritoso* (Southern)

*SIMON: *Willow Echoes* (C. Fischer)

VOXMAN (ED.): *Concert & Contest Collection* (Rubank)

DIFFICULT

ALARY: *Morçeau de concours* (C. Fischer)

BACH: *Sonatas 1, 2, 3,* arranged by Marsteller (Southern)

BARAT: *Introduction et serenade* (A. Leduc)

BARAT: *Morçeau de concours* (A. Leduc)

*BELLSTEDT: *Napoli* (Southern)

BENSON: *Aubade* (H. Leonard)

BLAZHEVICH: *Concerto No. 2* (C. Fischer)

BODA: *Sonatina* (tape) (Whaling)

*BRASCH: *Fantasy on Weber's Last Waltz* (H. Brasch)

*CHILDS AND DEVITA: *Softly as I Leave and Other Favorites* (Rosehill)

*R. AND N. CHILDS: *Childs' Choice* (Rosehill)

*CLARKE: *Sounds from the Hudson* (cornet) (C. Fischer)

*CLARKE: *Music of Herbert L. Clarke* (cornet) (Warner Bros.)

FRACKENPOHL: *Sonata* (Dorn)

GUILMANT: *Morçeau symphonique* (trombone) (Warner Bros.)

HARTLEY: *2 Pieces* (Presser)

*HARTLEY: *Sonata Euphonica* (Presser)

*HOROVITZ: *Concerto* (Novello)

*JACOB: *Fantasia* (Boosey & Hawkes)

*MANTIA: *All Those Endearing Young Charms* (Whaling)

PRESSER: *Sonatina* (Presser)

*PRYOR: *Thoughts of Love* (trombone) (C. Fischer)

SAINT-SAËNS: *Morçeau de concert* (Shawnee)

TAKACS: *Sonate* (Sidemton)

UBER: *Sonata* (Editions Musicus)

*VAUGHAN WILLIAMS: *6 Studies in English Folksong* (Galaxy)

VAUGHAN WILLIAMS: *A Winter's Willow* (Medici)

*WHITE: *Lyric Suite* (Schirmer)

WILDER: *Concerto* (Margun)

WILDER: *Sonata* (Margun)

BARITONE AND EUPHONIUM BOOKS

*BEVAN, CLIFFORD. *The Tuba Family.* New York: Scribner's, 1978.

*BOWMAN, BRIAN L. *Practical Hints on Playing the Baritone (Euphonium).* Melville, N.Y.: Belwin-Mills, 1983.

GRIFFITHS, JOHN R. *The Low Brass Guide.* Hackensack, N.J.: Jerona Music, 1980.

*LEHMAN, ARTHUR. *The Art of Euphonium Playing.* Poughkeepsie, N.Y.: Robert Hoe.

*LOUDER, EARLE L. *Euphonium Music Guide.* Evanston, Ill.: The Instrumentalist Co., 1978.

*PHILLIPS, HARVEY, AND W. WINKLE. *The Art of Tuba and Euphonium Playing.* Secaucus, N.J.: Summy-Birchard, 1992.

ROSE, W. H. *Studio Class Manual for Tuba and Euphonium.* Houston, Tex.: Iola Publications, 1980.

*WERDEN, D. *Euphonium Music Guide.* New London, Conn.: Whaling Music.

WERDEN, D. *Scoring for Euphonium.* New London, Conn.: Whaling Music.

*WINTER, DENIS. *Euphonium Music Guide.* New London, Conn.: Whaling Music, 1983.

Articles of interest to the euphonium players appear in *The Instrumentalist,* the *T.U.B.A. Journal,* and other periodicals listed in Appendix C.

CHAPTER 7

The Tuba

To the non-tubist, today's tuba world is a confusing jumble of instruments of differing keys, types and numbers of valves, sizes, and so forth. As with the rest of the brass family, the great variety of tubas now available reflects the need for more specialized and improved instruments to fit different performance situations.

There are two broad categories of tuba: bass tubas in F and E♭, and contrabass tubas in C and B♭. The latter are usually identified as CC and BB♭ tubas. (Large-bore E♭ tubas are sometimes designated EE♭.) Orchestral tubists generally prefer a five-valve CC as a standard instrument (see Figures 7.1 and 7.2) but also use a five-valve F or four-valve E♭ for high passages and some solo work. In the United States, the BB♭ is used primarily as a band instrument, but it is widely used in orchestras in Germany and Eastern Europe. The E♭ tuba, once familiar in American bands, is now rarely seen as a principal instrument outside England, where it is extensively used in orchestras, brass ensembles, and brass and military bands. A few orchestral players in America use the E♭ as an alternative to the F tuba.

Valve Types

Among the most obvious differences in tubas is that some are built with rotary valves and others with piston valves. Piston valves offer a cleaner articulation and are generally better in technical passages. Rotary valves, on the other hand, encourage a smooth legato. The difference between rotary and piston tubas is more than just the valve types, however. The tapered portions of the instruments including the leadpipes and bell contours, as well as the layouts of the tubing, are quite different between the two instruments. These variables, along with the effects of the valve systems, impart different timbres and distinctive playing qualities to the two types of tuba, irrespective of key.

For many years, there was a predominance of rotary valve tubas in American symphony orchestras. This came about as a result of the unavailability of large-bore piston valve CC tubas suitable for orchestral use. To fill this void, orchestral tubists turned to large-bore German tubas, which are traditionally made with rotary valves. As these became standardized in American orchestras, they were also adopted by bands and wind ensembles.

The picture today is completely different. Due to the persistent efforts of several eminent American orchestral players and as a result of new design improvements, there is a real choice as to valve type in both CC and F tubas. The choice now centers on personal preference, rather than practicality. Makers such as Hirsbrunner, B&S, Kurath, Yamaha, Meinl-Weston, and others, offer excellent new piston valve instruments in a variety of sizes, as well as improvements on existing rotary valve models.

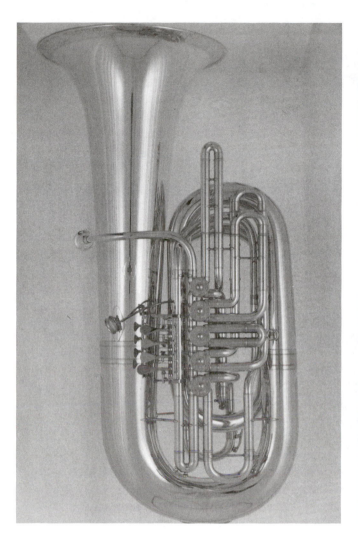

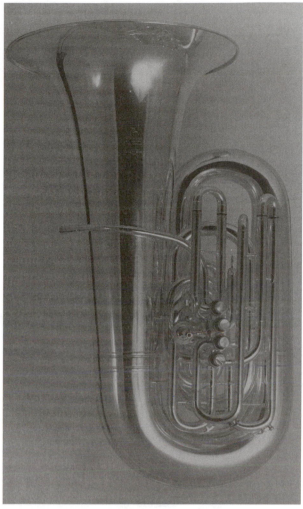

Figure 7.1. **Five-rotary-valve CC tuba (Alexander).** *Photo courtesy of Gebr. Alexander, Mainz.*

Figure 7.2. **Five-piston-valve CC tuba (Hirsbrunner).** *Photo courtesy of Custom Music Company.*

The large-bore piston valve CC tubas are based in their design to some extent on an old, well-known American York tuba that was played by the great tubist Arnold Jacobs during his long career in the Chicago Symphony Orchestra.

The placement of the valves is an important consideration for the player. On rotary valve tubas, the valve levers are arranged vertically at the center of the instrument. This allows the right arm and hand to be in a relaxed position, assisting finger dexterity. An additional benefit of this layout is that the valve slides are directed upward so that they can be moved by the left hand in making adjustments in intonation. The opposite of this is the top-action piston valve tuba, in which the valves are placed in line beneath the top bow. Many tubists feel that this places the right hand in an uncomfortable position, creating tension. Side-action (front-action) piston valve tubas have the valves located in the center of the instrument so that the valve caps face outward, permitting the most natural hand position to be used. Tubas of this type also have upward-directed valve slides similar to those of rotary valve tubas.

Dimensions and Bore

There is substantial variation in the size of tubas, not only in bore and bell diameter, but in overall dimensions and weight. For example, BB♭ tubas are made with main bore diameters of .610 to .920" (15.5 to 23.4 mm). Bell diameters may vary from $14\frac{3}{8}$ to 24" (365.55 to 609.6 mm). Weights range from 6.132 to 14.512 kg.[1]

Among rotary valve tubas, three general sizes can be distinguished: a smaller bore of approximately .740" (17.8 mm), a standard bore of .778" (19.7 mm), and an extra-large bore of .835" (21.2 mm). These are sometimes identified as 3/4, 4/4, and 5/4 models. However, there is considerable diversity between manufacturers as to the actual bore used under each label. The largest bore sizes are descendants of Václav Červený's *Kaiserbass*, introduced in the 1880s. (Červený produced the first contrabass tubas in CC and BB♭ in 1845).

CC tubas are built in the same large-bore sizes as BB♭s. This gives the CC an equal volume of tone while preserving its advantages in fingering and projection. The bores of orchestral (five-rotary-valve CC) tubas are usually in the range of .778 to .835", but even larger bores are sometimes used. The largest piston valve CC tubas are in the .748 to .787" range (19 to 20 mm). Typical F tuba bore sizes are .681 to .770" (17.3 to 19.5 mm). E♭ tuba bores usually average around .730" (18.5 mm). In comparison, three-valve student models in BB♭ generally run from .610 to .670" (15.5 to 17 mm).

Tubas may be wrapped in a compact or more open pattern, with heights varying from 33 to 48" (838.2 to 1219.2 mm). Some players feel that the more compact instruments are rather stuffy in response due to sharp bends in the tubing. The height of the largest instruments sometimes presents problems to smaller players, who must alter their playing position to reach the mouthpiece.

The variables of key, bore, and so forth allow tubists to adapt more fully to the needs of differing repertoire. For example, an orchestral tubist might use a large-bore CC in performances of Bruckner and Wagner and other large-scale works, but change to a smaller instrument for compositions having a light, transparent texture. Similarly, an F or E♭ tuba would probably be chosen for high-register solos such as are found in Stravinsky's *Petrushka*.

Valve Systems

If the valve systems fitted to modern tubas appear complex, it should be noted that the first tuba (in 1835) by Wieprecht and Moritz was a five-valve model in F. Today, tubists generally agree that three valves are inadequate and six valves are excessive. On standard four- and five-valve models, the purpose of the added valves is to extend the low range and improve intonation.

Unlike the trumpet, the fundamental of the tuba's harmonic series is a fully usable note. A fourth valve is added to extend the range downward from the lowest valve combination (1–2–3, fingered 2–4 when a fourth valve is added) to the fundamental because notes of the chromatic octave from the fundamental to the second harmonic are called for by composers. The sharpness caused when valves are used in combination is severe in this octave, although intonation can be corrected to some extent by pulling valve slides on individual notes. The best solution is a fifth valve, which affords a greater selection of fingerings and yields the most accurate intonation in this range. Six-valve tubas were developed for players who wish to use the F

---

[1] Clifford Bevan, *The Tuba Family* (New York: Scribner's, 1978), p. 126.

tuba as their principal instrument. The sixth valve enables this instrument to cover the same range as the CC. Most professional tubists (outside France) find the six-valve arrangement overly complex and prefer a five-valve system.

Using the Fourth and Fifth Valves

Greater mechanical correction is necessary on the tuba than on other brass instruments due to the length of the vibrating air columns. The most effective method of controlling intonation is by moving valve slides while playing. In order to do this, the valve slides must go upward, as on rotary valve and side-action tubas. On instruments of this type, all but the second valve slide are accessible to the left hand, with the first slide being used most often. The fourth and fifth valves come into play in the lowest octave and are used in combination with the adjustment of valve slides to center pitches in this range.

The fourth valve not only extends the range down to the fundamental, but offers an alternative to the sharp 1–3 and 1–2–3 fingerings:

To correct intonation, the valve slide should be pulled out for all fingerings circled (◯).
When an arrow is added to the circle(◯↑), The valve slide should be pushed inward.

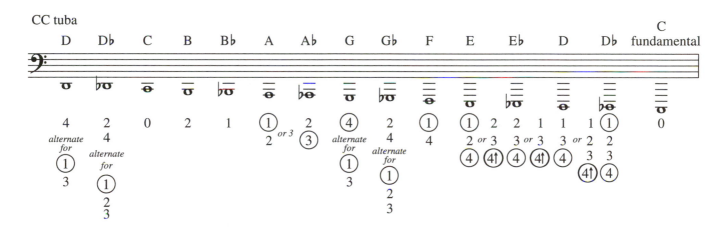

It is obvious that all tubas, except perhaps for inexpensive models intended for beginners, should be made with at least four valves. The four-valve system does have its limitations, however. The semitone above the fundamental is almost unusable, and it is only through the addition of a fifth valve that truly accurate intonation and a centered sound can be achieved.

In a five-valve system, the first four valves function as in the four-valve system. The fifth valve lowers the fundamental either five-quarters of a tone or two whole tones, depending on the length of the valve slide. The former is sometimes known as a flat whole step system and the latter as a 2/3 system (the 2/3 refers to the fifth valve's intervallic similarity to the normal 2–3 fingering, which also lowers the fundamental by two tones). Either system is effective and the choice of one over the other is a matter of individual preference.

In the flat whole step mode, the fifth valve is used as follows (use whichever fingering yields the best intonation):

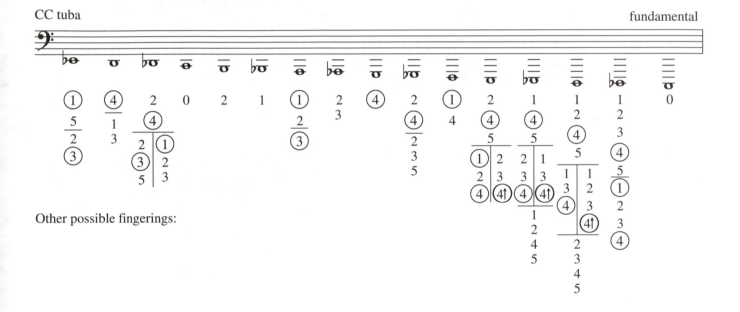

CC tuba

Other possible fingerings:

The fingering pattern for the 2/3 system is as follows:

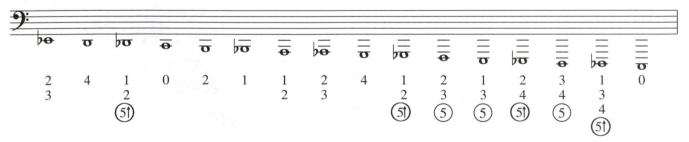

CC tuba

Well-known tubist Roger Bobo has recommended that a trigger mechanism be fitted to the fifth valve slide to facilitate its adjustment.

Another difference in five-valve systems is how the fifth valve is operated. On many tubas, an actuating lever is placed adjacent to the thumb ring with linkage connecting it to the fifth valve. Other models have a spatula attached directly to the fifth valve that is operated with the left hand. The disadvantage of the latter arrangement is that the left hand is not free to adjust valve slides when the fifth valve is in use. Roger Bobo has advocated a dual linkage that would enable the player to operate the valve with either hand, as desired.

The Automatic Compensating System

An entirely different approach to the problem of low-register intonation is the compensating system, devised in 1874 by English acoustician David Blaikley, which is incorporated in some baritones, euphoniums, and tubas.[2] In this system, corrective lengths of tubing are automatically added when the fourth valve is used in combination with the other valves. Although the Blaikley system does not solve all intonation problems, it works quite well. However, thus far it has been available only in top-action, medium-bore instruments. Tubas of this type are used as the principal instrument in British orchestras, bands, and brass ensembles (although regular large-bore rotary and piston valve BB♭ and CC tubas are used for certain orchestral works). It would be very interesting to see whether the Blaikley system would work well on large-bore tubas, but as yet this has not been tried.

Intonation

In addition to the intonation difficulties of the lower range, the tubist must also be prepared to cope with some problem notes in the middle and upper registers. No absolute rules can be set, for individual instruments vary in this respect. This is a fertile period in the development of the tuba, and one of the primary goals is improved intonation.

Faulty intonation is corrected by substituting an alternate fingering, moving a valve slide, or combining these measures. Whenever possible, it is preferable to adjust a note mechanically rather than with the lip because of the negative effect on tone and stability caused by forcing an off-center note into tune with the embouchure. Through careful practice, tubists learn to incorporate the necessary slide movements into their normal technique.

The current trend among manufacturers of high-quality tubas is to shorten the outer tubes of the valve slides (as is customary with the horn) to allow more room for slide adjustment. The chart below applies to this type of instrument. On older tubas, more use of alternate fingerings would probably be necessary.

---

[2] The Blaikley system is discussed more fully in Chapter 6.

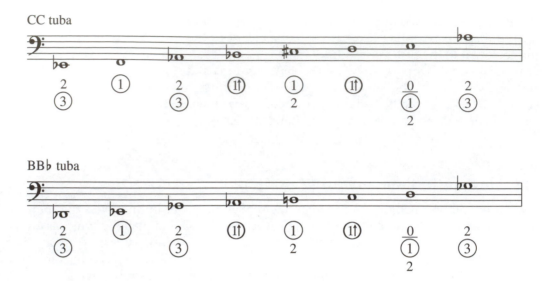

The fifth partial might be flat when played open.

CC tuba   BB♭ tuba

If it is, it may be played 1–2 while pulling out the first valve slide. The 1–2 combination tends to be sharp an octave lower and some adjustment of the slide will probably be necessary to correct it. An electronic tuner should be used to determine the best means of correction for other notes.

Regardless of how well the tubist can learn to play in tune when practicing, further adjustments will undoubtedly have to be made when performing in an ensemble. Within a brass section, the tubist must listen intently to the first trombone and first trumpet to provide a clear sense of pitch for the inner players to match. The ability of the tubist to balance and match the intonation of the first trumpet does a great deal to define the pitch center for the entire brass section.

BB♭ and CC Tubas

The preference of American orchestral tubists for the CC instrument is based on three factors. First, like the C trumpet, the CC tuba responds well in making "cold" entrances and is particularly responsive and flexible. Second, because orchestras often play in sharp keys, the awkward fingerings that would result if a BB♭ instrument were used is avoided. The third factor is that the timbre of the CC tuba projects with greater clarity. Some players find little difference in tone between the two instruments, but others, particularly German and Eastern European performers, have a definite partiality for the tone of the BB♭ because of its greater blending qualities and depth of sound.

The BB♭ tuba remains the primary band instrument, but CC tubas are sometimes used in bands and wind ensembles within schools of music because tuba majors are accustomed to playing the CC as their principal instrument. However, it is important that, when parts are doubled by more than one player, the same key instrument is used to avoid conflicts in intonation. At one time, bell-front or recording-bell tubas

Figure 7.3. **EE♭ tuba (Besson), played by the late John Fletcher, a legendary British tubist.** *Photo courtesy of Decca Records International.*

Figure 7.4. **F tuba (B & S), played by Scott Mendoker, a New York freelance artist.** *Photo courtesy of S Mendoker.*

were often seen in large bands, but these have been replaced by standard upright bell models. The directionality of the forward-radiating bell tended to lose the characteristic roundness of the tuba's timbre.

E♭ and F Tubas

E♭ and F tubas are predominantly used as auxiliary instruments to the normal CC when unusually high passages are encountered, or when a lighter sound is desired (see Figures 7.3 and 7.4). The standardized use of large-bore E♭ (EE♭) tubas in Britain has come about because the first British tubists were former euphonium players who sought an instrument that retained some of the euphonium's technical flexibility and response. A small-bore piston valve tuba in F was developed and this provided an agreeable "bottom" to orchestral brass sections until the end of World War II.[3] Up to that time, smaller-bore trumpets, trombones, and French-type piston valve horns were mainly in use. As brass sections adopted larger instruments in the postwar years, British tubists changed to the brass band EE♭, which combines a fuller tone with much of the F's flexibility.

Rotary valve F tubas are often used on the European continent (particularly in German orchestras), along with contrabass models. The Vienna concert tuba,[4] like the Vienna horn, is a unique model related to instruments of an earlier epoch, in this

[3] Ralph Vaughan Williams wrote his technically demanding *Bass Tuba Concerto* for the F tuba.

[4] The history and evolution of the Vienna concert tuba are discussed in Gerhard Zechmeister, "Die Entwicklung der Wiener Konzerttuba," *Brass Bulletin,* 75 (1991), pp. 44–47. (Translations in English and French are included.)

case the first Wieprecht–Moritz instrument of the 1830s. Pitched in F, the Vienna tuba is viewed by Viennese players as a bass–contrabass because its six rotary valves allow it to cover both ranges. The comparatively narrow bore and less flared bell give this instrument a strong, clear sound in which higher partials are more present than in the timbres of other tubas. This is felt to integrate better within the traditional Viennese brass sound, whereas the darker and more massive tone of other tubas tends to fall out of the unified tone of the brass section.

An important application of the E♭ and F tuba is in the brass quintet, where their lighter timbres often contribute a more effective balance than a contrabass. Unfortunately, in many quintets, the misbalance created by the consuming tone of large BB♭ or CC tubas is accepted without question.[5] If a contrabass is used, it should be one of the smaller sizes.

The French Six-Valve C Tuba

Although practically obsolete today, the French C tuba is of interest because of the large body of solo literature and orchestral parts by French composers written for it. In reality, it is an extended-range tenor tuba pitched one tone higher than the euphonium. Through the addition of two sets of valves (one for each hand), this tuba produces a full four octaves, from the lowest notes of the contrabass CC into the normal euphonium range. Parts for this unusual instrument have caused confusion because both the range and technical demands are not well suited to bass and contrabass tubas. French solo literature is often neglected for this reason.

The concept of a tenor-sized bass for the brass section is not as peculiar as it may seem. French composers have always shown a predilection for mixtures of clearly defined timbres rather than a blend of sound. The French C tuba was well suited to this aesthetic, while offering additional possibilities as a solo instrument. Such parts as are found in Stravinsky's *Petrushka, Rite of Spring*, and the *Bydlo* solo in Ravel's transcription of Mussorgsky's *Pictures at an Exhibition* exemplify the capabilities of this unique instrument.

In French orchestras today, six-valve F or CC contrabass tubas are used for the majority of the repertoire and the French C is reserved for the solos originally written for it.

The Tuba Mute

Richard Strauss was the first to write for the muted tuba in *Don Quixote* (1897). Because composers often call for the muted timbre, a mute is now considered a necessary part of the tubist's regular equipment. The problem is to find a mute that fits the bell taper accurately and plays in tune. Tuba mutes are normally in straight-mute form, but a few of the other types (such as cup mutes and practice mutes) have now become available.

Notation

Lacking any historical convention that the fundamental must be written as C (as in the horn and trumpet), the BB♭, E♭, and F tubas function as nontransposing instru-

---

[5] A good idea of the excellent balance that can be achieved with an EE♭ may be gained by listening to some of the recordings of the Philip Jones Brass Ensemble (currently available recordings are listed in Appendix B). The superb player on these recordings was the late John Fletcher, principal tubist of the London Symphony Orchestra.

ments, with the player using the appropriate fingering to yield concert pitch. When more than one tuba is used, such as the CC or F, the player must learn a different set of fingerings for each instrument. There are exceptions to this practice. In British brass bands, all instruments except the bass trombone are considered transposing instruments and read treble clef. The bass tuba in E♭ is treated as a transposing instrument in much of the French solo literature, although parts for the six-valve C tuba are also usually included. (In French C tuba parts, there is some use of the non-transposed treble clef.) This is often the practice in French band scores and in some of Verdi's operas.

In order to have access to a greater variety of study material, it is important for tubists to develop the ability to read down an octave. This brings trombone and euphonium literature into a practicable range. It is also helpful to be able to read treble clef in order to perform etudes and solos written for trumpet and horn.

The Golden Age of the Tuba

The last two-and-a-half decades have seen more activity in the tuba world than in any period of its history. Today's generation of tubists is no longer content to remain in the background and has broken through barriers that were considered impassable even 40 years ago. There are now several internationally recognized soloists, but the most striking aspect of the movement is the incredibly high standard of playing that is now taken for granted. Interesting new solo works are appearing regularly that exploit the possibilities of the tuba and the virtuosity of the player in previously unimagined ways. Undoubtedly, this evolution will continue into the future, with more recognition and opportunities for the solo tuba as each new generation of tubists carries the movement forward.

Recommended Literature[6]

COMPLETE METHODS

*ARBAN: *Arban-Bell Method* (C. Colin)

*ARBAN: *Famous Method for Slide and Valve Trombone and Baritone*, ed. Randall and Mantia (read octave down) (C. Fischer)

BEELER: *Method*, 2 vols. (Warner Bros.)

*BOBO: *Mastering the Tuba*, 3 vols. (Bim)

GEIB: *Method* (C. Fischer)

ELEMENTARY METHODS

*ARBAN: *Method*, 1st and 2nd year, ed. Prescott (C. Fischer)

*BELL: *Foundation to Tuba Playing* (C. Fischer)

ENDRESEN: *Method for E♭ Tuba* (M. M. Cole)

HOVEY: *Rubank Elementary Method* (Rubank)

KUHN-CIMERA: *Method* (Belwin)

STUDIES

MEDIUM TO MEDIUM–DIFFICULT

BELL: *Blazhevich Interpretations* (C. Colin)

*BELL: *William Bell Daily Routine for Tuba* (Encore)

*BOBO: *Mastering the Tuba*, 3 vols., (Bim)

*BORDOGNI: *43 Bel Canto Studies*, transcribed by Roberts (R. King)

*BORDOGNI AND ROCHUT: *Melodious Etudes*, books 1 and 2 (for trombone) (C. Fischer)

BORDOGNI–W. JACOBS: *Legato Etudes* (Encore)

*BORDOGNI–W. JACOBS: *Low Legato Etudes* (Encore)

*CONCONE: *Legato Etudes*, ed. Shoemaker (C. Fischer)

ENDRESEN: *Supplementary Studies* (Rubank)

FINK: *Studies in Legato* (C. Fischer)

GETCHELL: *Practical Studies*, 2 vols. (Belwin-Mills)

GOWER AND VOXMAN: *Rubank Advanced Method*, 2 vols. (Rubank)

*HILGERS: *Daily Exercises* (Reift)

*W. JACOBS: *Warm-Up Studies* (Encore)

[6] Essential material is noted with an asterisk. For additional literature, see the *Brass Music Guide* (Robert King). Repertoire lists appear in the texts by Bell, Bevan, Griffiths, and Morris and Goldstein.

KNAUB: *Progressive Techniques* (Belwin)

*LITTLE: *Embouchure Builder* (Pro Art)

*PARÉS: *Scales* (Rubank)

RONKA: *Modern Daily Warm-Ups & Drills* (C. Fischer)

*SCHLOSSBERG: *Daily Drills and Technical Studies* (trombone) (medium to difficult) (M. Baron)

SEAR: *Etudes* (Cor)

SKORNICKA AND BOLTZ: *Rubank Intermediate Method* (Rubank)

*STREET: *Scales & Arpeggios* (Boosey & Hawkes)

UBER: *25 Early Studies* (Southern)

WILLIAMS: *Little Classics* (Colin)

DIFFICULT

BACH: *Bach for Tuba,* transcribed by Bixby and Bobo (Western International)

*BLAZHEVICH: *70 Studies* (R. King)

*BORDOGNI–ROCHUT: *Melodious Etudes,* book 3 (trombone) (C. Fischer)

CIMERA: *73 Advanced Studies* (Belwin-Mills)

GALLAY: *30 Studies* (R. King)

GALLAY: *40 Preludes* (R. King)

*W. JACOBS: *Low Register Development for Tuba* (Encore)

*KOPPRASCH: *60 Studies* (medium to difficult) (R. King)

KUEHN: *28 Advanced Studies* (Southern)

KUEHN: *60 Musical Studies,* 2 vols. (Southern)

PAUDERT: *18 Etudes* (Encore)

ROBINSON: *Advanced Conditioning Studies* (Whaling)

*SNEDECOR: *Low Etudes* (Pas Music)

TYRRELL: *40 Advanced Studies* (Boosey & Hawkes)

UBER: *Concert Etudes* (Southern)

VASILIEV: *24 Melodious Etudes* (R. King)

UNACCOMPANIED TUBA

DIFFICULT

ADLER: *Canto VII* (Boosey & Hawkes)

ANONYMOUS: *Hijazker Longa* (Whaling)

*ARNOLD: *Fantasy* (Faber)

BACH: *Six Short Solo Suites* (R. King)

CROLEY: *Variazioni* (Philharmusica)

DRAGONETTI: *Concert Etude* (Philharmusica)

FRACKENPOHL: *Studies on Christmas Carols* (Kendor)

GLOBOKAR: *Echanges* (Peters)

HADDAD: *Short Suite* (Seesaw)

HARTLEY: *Music for Tuba* (Philharmusica)

HARTLEY: *Suite* (Presser)

KAGEL: *Mirum* (Universal)

KRAFT: *Encounters II* (Bim)

*PENDERECKI: *Capriccio* (Schott)

PENN: *3 Essays* (Seesaw)

*PERSICHETTI: *Parable* (Presser)

*PERSICHETTI: *Serenade No. 12* (Presser)

POORE: *Vox Superius* (Arts Lab)

POWELL: *Midnight Realities* (Brass Press)

RECK: *5 Studies* (Peters)

TISNÉ: *Monodie III* (Billaudot)

TUTHILL: *Tiny Tunes for Tuba* (Presser)

WILDER: *Convalescence Suite* (Margun Music)

TUBA AND PIANO

EASY

ADAMS: *The Holy City* (Kjos)

*BACH: *Air and Bourée,* arranged by Bell and Swanson (C. Fischer)

*BACH: *Gavotte,* arranged by Smith (Belwin-Mills)

BELL: *Gavotte* (C. Fischer)

BELL: *Jig Elephantine* (C. Fischer)

BELL: *Low Down Bass* (C. Fischer)

BELL: *Melodious Etude* (Belwin-Mills)

BELL: *Nautical John* (C. Fischer)

BIZET: *Toreador's Song,* arranged by Holmes (Rubank)

DAELLENBACH: *Beginning Tuba Solos* (with cassette accompaniment) (H. Leonard)

DAELLENBACH: *Easy Tuba Solos* (with cassette accompaniment) (H. Leonard)

GRIEG: *In the Hall of the Mountain King,* arranged by Holmes (Rubank)

HANDEL: *Honor & Arms from Samson* (Schirmer)

KREISLER: *Rondo* (Southern)

SCHUMANN: *The Jolly Farmer* (C. Fischer)

WEKSELBLATT (ED.):   *First Solos for the Tuba Player* (Schirmer)

MEDIUM TO MEDIUM–DIFFICULT

BEETHOVEN: *Variations on a Theme by Handel,* arranged by Bell (C. Fischer)

*BENSON: *Arioso* (Belwin)

*BENSON: *Helix* (C. Fischer)

CAPUZZI: *Andante & Rondo* (Hinrichsen)

DAELLENBACH: *Intermediate Tuba Solos* (with cassette accompaniment) (H. Leonard)

DAVIS: *Variations on a Theme of Robert Schumann* (Southern)

*FLETCHER: *BBb Bass Solos* (Chester)

*FLETCHER: *E♭ Bass Solos* (Chester)

*FLETCHER: *Tuba Solos* (tuba in C) (Chester)

*HADDAD: *Suite* (Shawnee)

*JACOB: *6 Little Tuba Pieces* (Emerson Ed.)

*JACOB: *Tuba Suite* (Boosey & Hawkes)

OSTLING (ED.):   *Tuba Solos*, 2 vols. (Belwin)

OSTRANDER (ED.):   *Concert Album* (Editions Musicus)

PERANTONI: *Master Solos* (H. Leonard)

PHILLIPS: *8 Bel Canto Songs* (Shawnee)

REED: *Fantasia a due* (Belwin)

*SENAILLE: *Introduction and Allegro Spiritoso* (Hinrichsen)

VOXMAN (ED.):   *Concert & Contest Collection* (Rubank)

WEKSELBLATT (ED.):   *Solos for the Tuba Player* (Schirmer)

DIFFICULT

*ARTUNIAN: *Concerto* (Bim)

BARAT: *Introduction & Dance,* arranged by Smith (Southern)

BELLSTEDT: *Introduction & Tarantella* (Southern)

BEVERSDORF: *Sonata* (Southern)

BODA: *Sonatina* (R. King)

BOZZA: *Concertino* (Leduc)

*BROUGHTON: *Sonata* (Masters)

CHILDS: *Seaview* (M. M. Cole)

CROLEY: *3 Espressioni* (Philharmusica)

FRACKENPOHL: *Sonata* (Kendor)

*GREGSON: *Concerto* (Novello)

HARTLEY: *Sonatina* (Fema Music)

*HINDEMITH: *Sonate* (Schott)

*JACOB: *Bagatelles* (Emerson Ed.)

KOETSIER: *Concertino, op. 77* (Bim)

KOETSIER: *Sonatina* (Donemus)

KROL: *Falstaff Concerto* (Bim)

*MADSEN: *Konzert* (Musikk-Huset)

*MADSEN: *Sonata, op. 34* (Musikk-Huset)

*MADSEN: *Sonate, op. 25* (Musikk-Huset)

MORTIMER: *Tuba Concerto* (Reift)

NELYBEL: *Concert Piece* (E. C. Kerby)

PLOG: *Three Miniatures* (Bim)

REYNOLDS: *Sonata* (C. Fischer)

*SALZEDO: *Sonata* (Chester)

SOWERBY: *Chaconne* (C. Fischer)

*H. STEVENS: *Sonatina* (Southern)

T. STEVENS: *Variations in Olden Style* (Bim)

*STRUKOW: *Concerto* (Bim)

*THOMSON: *Jay Rozen: Portrait & Fugue for Bass Tuba & Piano* (Heilman)

UBER: *Sonata* (Editions Musicus)

UBER: *Sonatina* (Southern)

*VAUGHAN WILLIAMS: *Concerto* (Oxford)

*VAUGHAN WILLIAMS: *6 Studies in English Folksong* (Galaxy)

*WHITE: *Sonata* (Ludwig)

*WILDER: *Sonata* (Mentor)

*WILDER: *Suite No. 1* (Margun)

BOOKS ON THE TUBA[7]

BELL, WILLIAM.   *Encyclopedia of Literature for the Tuba.* New York: Charles Colin, 1967.

*BEVAN, CLIFFORD.   *The Tuba Family.* New York: Scribner's, 1978.

BIRD, GARY.   *Program Notes for the Solo Tuba.* Bloomington: Indiana University Press, 1994.

*CUMMINGS, BARTON.   *The Contemporary Tuba.* New London, Conn.: Whaling Music, 1984.

GRIFFITHS, JOHN R.   *The Low Brass Guide.* Hackensack, N.J.: Jerona Music, 1980.

*LITTLE, DONALD C.   *Practical Hints on Playing the Tuba.* Melville, N.Y.: Belwin-Mills, 1984.

MASON, J. KENT.   *The Tuba Handbook.* Toronto: Sonante, 1977.

*MORRIS, R. WINSTON.   *Tuba Music Guide.* Evanston, Ill.: The Instrumentalist Co., 1973.

*MORRIS, R. WINSTON, AND EDWARD R. GOLDSTEIN.   *The Tuba Source Book.* Bloomington: Indiana University Press, 1996.

*PHILLIPS, HARVEY, AND WILLIAM WINKLE.   *The Art of Tuba and Euphonium Playing.* Secaucus, N.J.: Summy-Birchard, 1992.

RANDOLPH, DAVID MARK.   "New Techniques in the Avant-Garde Repertoire for Solo Tuba." D.M.A. thesis, University of Rochester, 1978. UM 78–11, 493.

ROSE, W.H.   *Studio Class Manual for Tuba and Euphonium.* Houston, Tex.: Iola, 1980.

SORENSON, RICHARD A.   "Tuba Pedagogy: A Study of Selected Method Books, 1840–1911." Ph.D. dissertation, University of Colorado, 1972. UM 73–1832.

*STEWART, DEE.   *Arnold Jacobs: The Legacy of a Master.* Northfield, Ill.: The Instrumentalist Publishing Co., 1987.

---

[7] Many interesting articles appear in the *T.U.B.A. Journal* (published by the Tubists' Universal Brotherhood Association) and other periodicals listed in Appendix C.

CHAPTER 8

Other Brass Instruments

Flugelhorn

The flugelhorn derives its name from the curved horn that was used for signaling by the flügelmeister during hunts in eighteenth-century Germany. Subsequently adopted as the *halbmond* (half-moon, denoting its shape) for military purposes, it was later modified to the bugle shape we know today (see Figure 8.1). In 1810, English bandmaster Joseph Halliday fitted the instrument with keys and in this form it was known as the Royal Kent bugle. In Germany, the instrument was known as *Klappenflügelhorn*. When valves replaced the key system, the flugelhorn found its modern form; models are now made with both piston and rotary valves.

Piston valve flugelhorns are constructed basically in a trumpet form, but with a very widely wrapped bell section and with the mouthpipe going directly into the first valve. Models with rotary valves are played on the side in the manner of the rotary valve trumpet. Although the B♭ flugelhorn covers the same range as the trumpet, its tone is almost totally opposite due to its broad, conically shaped bell. The bell profile is very close to that of nineteenth-century European bugles. The sweet, softly mellow timbre has many musical uses. It plays an important role in British brass bands, where it contributes to the sonority of the tutti sound and is featured in many solo passages. British brass ensembles such as the Philip Jones Brass Ensemble and London Brass have also used the instrument in effective ways in the scoring, and this has enriched the tone colors available in this type of ensemble. Occasionally, the flugelhorn is called for in orchestral music. The instrument creates a particularly haunting effect in the opening of Ralph Vaughan Williams's Ninth Symphony. Other composers who have made impressive use of the flugelhorn are Stravinsky in *Threni* and Respighi in *The Pines of Rome,* where flugelhorns are used to evoke the sound of the ancient Roman *buccina* (the parts are often played on trumpets, however, negating this effect).

Flugelhorns are used only when required by the score in American and British wind bands, but form a regular part of traditional European bands. It is in the brass band that the flugelhorn has come into its own. The timbre of the flugelhorn, though capable of blending with any other brass band instrument, is unique and distinctive. The instrument provides an important resource for important solo passages and this is exploited in very creative ways by composers of brass band works. The mere presence of this rich timbre contributes to the overall quality of the brass band sound. It is therefore not surprising that most of the important developments in mouthpieces and instruments have come from this source.

An E♭ flugelhorn is also made in Europe, known as the *petit bugle* in France and *Pikkolo* in Germany. In the jazz field, the flugelhorn has come into prominence as a

Figure 8.1. **Flugelhorn (Besson).** *Photo courtesy of the Boosey & Hawkes Group.*

solo voice and is considered a normal part of the trumpeter's equipment. There are several internationally known jazz soloists who play flugelhorn exclusively.[1]

A word should be said about flugelhorn mouthpieces. The instrument requires a much deeper mouthpiece than that used for the trumpet. The Denis Wick flugelhorn mouthpieces (2F or 4F for European instruments, 2Fl or 4Fl with large fittings for American and Japanese instruments) offer the richest tone quality currently available, and are recommended.

Alto (Tenor) Horn

The principal use today of the E♭ alto horn (tenor horn in Britain) is in the brass band, where the standard instrumentation calls for a section of three. (See Figure 8.2.) Alto horns were once popular in American concert bands as a substitute for the French horn, but as horn players became more plentiful the alto horn fell into disuse. However, bell-front versions were widely used in American marching bands—again substituting for the French horn—but these have largely been replaced by derivative instruments such as the marching mellophone (now usually in F)[2] or the B♭ marching French horn.

[1] For additional information on the flugelhorn, see Frederick Allan Beck, "The Flugelhorn: Its History and Literature" (D.M.A. thesis, University of Rochester, 1979), UM 79–21, 124.

[2] Substitutes for the French horn in marching bands are discussed later in this chapter.

Figure 8–2. E♭ alto (tenor) horn, played by British soloist Gordon Higginbottom. *Photo courtesy of G. Higginbottom.*

The somewhat confusing designations for instruments of this family should be kept in mind:

Key	U.S.A.	Britain	Germany	France	Italy
E♭	Alto horn	Tenor horn	Althorn	Alto	Genis
B♭	Baritone	Baritone	Tenorhorn	Baryton	Flicorno tenore
B♭	Euphonium	Euphonium	Baryton	Basse	Eufonio

Based on Clifford Bevan, *The Tuba Family* (New York: Scribner's, 1978).

During the era when alto horns were used in concert bands, it was found that constructing the instrument in a round, hornlike shape would result in a better imitation of horn sound. The new instrument was called the mellophone (in England, the tenor

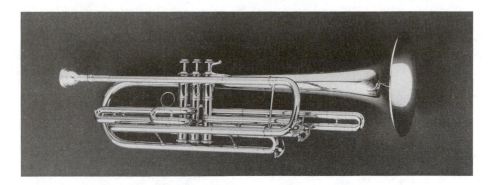

Figure 8.3. **Bass trumpet (Bach).** *Photo courtesy of the Selmer Company, Elkhart, Indiana.*

cor) and was equipped with right-hand piston valves, and a mouthpiece that was somewhat larger and more cup-shaped than the horn. Though easy to play, it lacked the true tone color of the horn, and gradually declined in American bands.

German alto horns are usually constructed in the traditional oval shape with rotary valves; these instruments have a somewhat fuller tone. It was for this instrument that Hindemith composed his 1943 *Sonata für Althorn,* although it is now usually performed on the French horn.

Bass Trumpet

Natural bass trumpets, usually in E♭ or B♭, were found in German cavalry bands in the early nineteenth century. After the invention of valves, chromatic instruments of this type continued to be a feature of mounted bands throughout the century. The chief interest in the bass trumpet today is that Richard Wagner, seeking a broader spectrum of timbres, wrote for it in *The Ring.* Modern bass trumpets are built in C or B♭, with rotary or piston valves (see Figure 8.3). Due to the size of its mouthpiece, the bass trumpet is always played by a trombonist rather than a trumpeter. The instrument produces a clearly defined tone, quite distinct from the trombone. It was this quality that Wagner exploited in his scoring.

Valve Trombone

Though greeted with interest when it made its appearance in the 1820s, the valve trombone ultimately failed to hold its own against the conventional slide instrument. (See Figure 8.4.) The inherent intonation difficulties in the valve system and the lack of an effective means of correction (other than the lip) made the instrument unequal to the almost total pitch control afforded by the movable slide. The valve trombone also compared unfavorably in timbre. Valve trombones did find acceptance in situations where use of a moving slide was inconvenient, such as mounted cavalry bands. Deficiencies aside, some bands adopted the valve trombone for the technical facility it offered. Italian bands, in particular, were noted for dazzling technical displays by their all-rotary-valve brass sections. In the twentieth century, the valve trombone has found an important niche in jazz, where its agility has made it a favorite solo instrument.

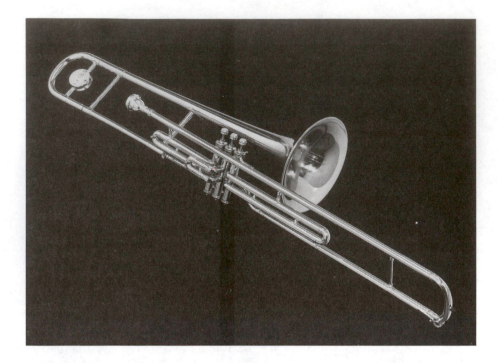

Figure 8.4. **Valve trombone (Conn).** *Photo courtesy of Conn, a member company of United Musical Instruments, U.S.A., Inc.*

Valve trombones have been made with both piston and rotary valves. Rotary valve models sometimes have the bell angled upward to increase the directionality of the sound toward the audience.

Contrabass Trombone

Apparently an *octav-posaune* existed during the Renaissance, but how and to what extent the instrument was actually used remains obscure. Wagner called for a contrabass trombone in the score to *The Ring,* and an instrument pitched an octave below the B♭ tenor trombone was specially constructed to play this work. The instrument used double tubing in its slide so that the extensions of the slide would be similar to those of the tenor instrument. Contrabass parts also occur in operas by Verdi and Puccini. These were intended for a four-valve piston or rotary valve instrument known as the *cimbasso* (see Figures 8.5 and 8.6).

Although a few *cimbassos* are still made, these and the Wagner parts are mostly played on the in-line double-valve slide trombone invented by Hans Kunitz around 1959 (British patent, 1965). This instrument is a very large bass in F, with independent valves for C and D (see Figure 8.7). When the valves are used together, the trombone is pitched in low B♭, suitable for contrabass parts. Recently, new versions of this basic instrument have been developed using different tunings on the in-line valves and incorporating the open-wrap design. One such instrument made by the German firm of Thein uses D and low B♭ as the tuning of the independent valves; using both valves produces a tuning of low A♭. Because the design of these instruments is directed toward a solution to the technical difficulties of the Italian works (intended for the *cimbasso*) and the Wagner contrabass parts, trombones of this type have been variously identified as bass, bass/contrabass, contrabass, or confusingly, as a *cimbasso* model (the true *cimbasso* is a valve instrument). Bass trombonists have

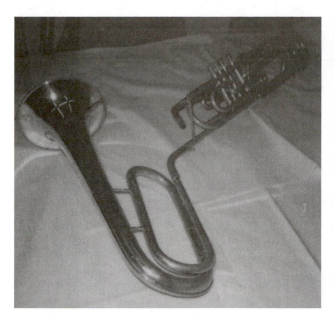

Figure 8.5. **Piston valve *cimbasso* (Kalison).** *Photo courtesy of Kalison s.n.c.*

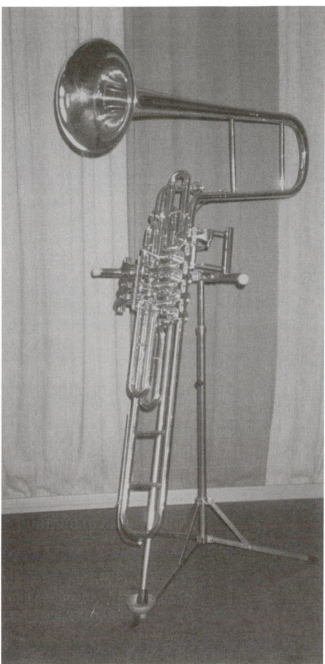

Figure 8.6. **Rotary valve *cimbasso* (Meinl Weston).** *Photo courtesy of Wenzel Meinl GmbH.*

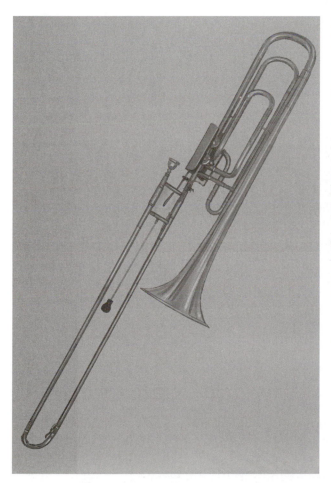

Figure 8.7. **Bass trombone in F (Kunitz system).** *Photo courtesy of Gebr. Alexander, Mainz.*

Figure 8.8. **Natural trumpet (William Bull, 1680), played by Crispian Steele-Perkins.** *Photo: John Edwards, courtesy of C. Steele-Perkins.*

Figure 8.9. **Natural trumpets, played by (left to right) David Staff and Michael Laird before a performance of Beethoven's Third Symphony at Queen Elizabeth Hall, London.** *Photo courtesy of Michael Laird.*

made more use of this instrument recently for parts such as Bartók's *Concerto for Orchestra* and other works.

Historical Brass

The past three decades have witnessed a phenomenal revival of instruments that had been unused for two centuries or more. From the first uncertain attempts, performances of early music have progressed to the point that today's leading groups routinely attain first-rate standards of precision, technique, and intonation (see Figures 8.8, 8.9, and 8.10). The underlying principle in such performances is the desire to hear music as it would have been heard by the composer and audiences of the composer's time. The cornerstone of the early music revival is the use of authentic instruments whose timbres differ markedly from their modern counterparts. Of equal importance is the use of stylistic procedures that musicians of the time would probably have followed. In this way, historical performances attempt to convey a more faithful realization of the composer's intentions.

The success of this approach is demonstrated by the fact that new recordings of Baroque music made with modern instruments are becoming increasingly rare, and authentic performances are now part of the recording and concertizing mainstream, with a number of groups having attained international status. The movement has now reached well into the nineteenth century, and one wonders just how far the quest for authenticity will ultimately extend.

Reconstructions of natural trumpets and horns are a feature of orchestras specializing in Baroque and Classical performance. There are a number of outstanding soloists active on the natural trumpet, including Michael Laird, Crispian Steele-Perkins, Friedemann Immer, David Staff, Edward Tarr, and Don Smithers.[3] Trum-

---

[3] A listing of recommended historical brass recordings is included in Appendix B.

Figure 8.10. **Sackbuts and cornets, played by His Majesties Sagbutts & Cornetts.** *Photo: Julion Nieman, courtesy of His Majesties Sagbutts & Cornetts, Jeremy West, director.*

peters no longer need to speculate as to how Bach's trumpet parts may have sounded in his time, but may choose from among several representative recordings. The same can be said of the solo literature. The Haydn concerto has been recorded using reconstructions of Weidinger's keyed trumpet. Excellent performances are also to be heard via recordings on hand horns.[4] Early valve trumpets are beginning to be revived for performances of early romantic works.

In Renaissance music, the cornett[5] and sackbut are widely used in various types of consort. Through the efforts of Don Smithers, Michael Laird, the late instrument maker Christopher Monk, Jeremy West, Bruce Dickey, and others, the cornett has regained its position as an agile, virtuosic solo voice in sixteenth- and seventeenth-century music. Consorts of cornetts and sackbuts bring a light, stylish character to pieces by the Gabrielis, Matthew Locke, John Adson, and others. Performers in modern brass ensembles can gain much stylistic insight by listening to such performances.

In recognizing the many achievements of today's early music movement, a few critical points might be noted as well. Problems of authenticity are more apparent in the brass than in other areas, such as the use of trombones with reformed bells in place of genuine sackbuts. Due to their larger bore, such hybrids sound more like trombones than sackbuts. Authentic sackbuts are capable of great subtlety in blending with almost any instrumental combination and possess a near-vocal timbre. These qualities are lost with the recycled modern instruments. Another problem of authenticity involves the use of finger holes (clarino holes), which are commonly incorporated in reconstructions of Baroque trumpets and horns to correct the pitch of certain harmonics. These additions were unknown during the seventeenth and eighteenth centuries, when players were taught to lip the sharp harmonics into tune.[6] Baroque horn parts, which were played with the instrument held high and

---

[4] Several first-rate recordings of the Mozart horn concertos played on hand horn are available today, with more of the solo literature expected.

[5] Although the cornett is made of leather-covered wood and has finger holes, its method of tone production is that of a brass instrument.

[6] A point raised by Don Smithers, Klaus Wogram, and John Bowsher in "Playing the Baroque Trumpet," *Scientific American* (April 1986), pp. 108–115.

no hand in the bell, are often played on copies of early-nineteenth-century horns using handstopping, a technique that did not become common until after 1750. The unevenness between stopped and open tones, though appropriate in music of the Classical and early Romantic periods, sounds particularly anachronistic in Baroque music.

Clarino holes and handstopping in Baroque music are functions of the perceived need to produce intonation that is acceptable to modern audiences. In the author's view, the natural intonation of the open harmonics contributes a certain rustic quality to the Baroque horn, which is lost when handstopping is used. If authenticity is indeed the goal, one might ask whether the natural trumpet should not be played using the same techniques as the great seventeenth- and eighteenth-century masters, such as John Shore and Gottfried Reiche. Compromises of this sort raise a deeper question: Are performers and audiences sincere in wishing to hear music performed as it actually was in its own time, or must it be made to conform to twentieth-century ears for commercial and other nonartistic reasons?

These issues aside, there are splendid historical performances available today, and they should be carefully studied by all brass players.

Brass in the Marching Band

Aside from military and community bands, marching bands in the United States are in reality football and competition bands, specialized for performance in the open air. In Britain, bands take the same instruments[7] on the march as they play in concerts, but the trend toward specialization in America has created a demand for instruments specifically designed for outdoor performance. In earlier years, this took the form of bell-front baritones, alto horns, and Sousaphones to increase the directionality of sound and provide a more equal balance of parts in the band's brass section. Today, largely because of the drum corps influence, an entire range of new instruments known as marching brass has been created.

Various alternatives to the French horn have been tried over the years because the horn is basically unsuited to the needs of high school and college marching bands. For a long time, the E♭ alto horn[8] was used as a substitute for the French horn. This instrument offered a horn-like timbre[9] and (with high-quality instruments) good intonation. Following the stylistic trend toward the drum corps, however, many directors changed over to instruments that produced a more powerful sound and greater directionality.

Trumpets built in low F or E♭ were tried, but these were found to be entirely unsatisfactory in tone and intonation. Next came the circular, forward-facing mellophonium and the frumpet, both of which also suffered from intonation problems. Today, the most widely used instruments are the marching mellophone in F and the marching French horn in B♭ (in the same key as the regular B♭ horn). The latter attempts to retain more of the French horn's round construction and bell flare in a forward-radiating pattern. Each of these instruments has its advocates, and only careful trial and error will establish their relative merits. Intonation is the critical factor and this is where most of the problems occur.

---

[7] French horns, cornets, and upright euphoniums and tubas are used in British military bands.

[8] Some alto horns are pitched in F and supplied with an E♭ tuning slide. The alto horn is also known as the altonium.

[9] Especially with instruments having upright bells.

Regular horn mouthpieces may be used on marching French horns, but a larger shank is required for the marching mellophone. In such cases, horn players can use an adapter or try to play on the mouthpiece supplied with the instrument. Although the instrument plays better in tune and sounds fuller with the mellophone mouthpiece, the broad rim and wide diameter often prove problematic for horn players in switching between this and their normal horn mouthpiece.

Also resulting from the drum corps influence are compact, bugle-shaped marching baritones and (valve) trombones. Some years ago, Sousaphones made of fiberglass made their appearance, offering lower cost and lighter weight. Unfortunately, the fiberglass instruments do not compare well with brass Sousaphones in fullness and quality of timbre. Therefore, many college bands have returned to conventional brass instruments. Euphoniums and small upright tubas with convertible leadpipes are also popular. These are played bell-forward, resting on the player's shoulder.

Even with the best-quality marching brass instruments, intonation is still a significant problem. Intonation difficulties probably stem from compromises in the instruments' basic tapers, plus the usual problems of three-valve systems.[10] Because every brand of instrument differs in its intonation (to say nothing of disparities between instruments of the same maker), each instrument must be tested individually. The use of a tuner is essential in evaluating instruments and making corrections.

It is customary for the better instruments to be fitted with a ring on the first valve slide, but usually none is provided on the third valve slide. This allows the first valve tubing to be extended to lower the sharp 1–2 combination, but does little for the very sharp 1–3 and 1–2–3 combinations (the best solution for this would be the addition of a fourth valve). Alternate fingerings can also be used; the intonation charts below show these possibilities.

Possible Alternate Fingerings for
Mellophone in F or E♭

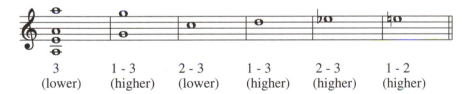

3	1 - 3	2 - 3	1 - 3	2 - 3	1 - 2
(lower)	(higher)	(lower)	(higher)	(higher)	(higher)

Possible Alternate Fingerings for
Marching Baritone and Trombone

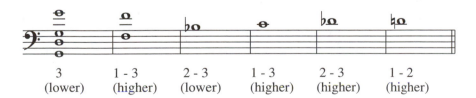

3	1 - 3	2 - 3	1 - 3	2 - 3	1 - 2
(lower)	(higher)	(lower)	(higher)	(higher)	(higher)

[10] This problem is discussed under "Intonation" in Chapters 3, 6, and 7.

Possible Alternate Fingerings for B♭
Marching French Horn

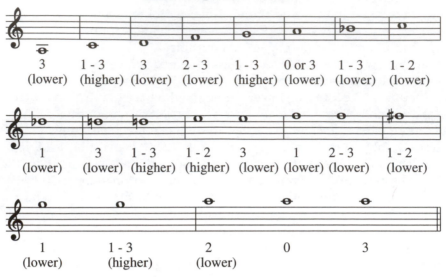

3	1 - 3	3	2 - 3	1 - 3	0 or 3	1 - 3	1 - 2
(lower)	(higher)	(lower)	(lower)	(higher)	(lower)	(lower)	(lower)

1	3	1 - 3	1 - 2	3	1	2 - 3	1 - 2
(lower)	(lower)	(higher)	(higher)	(lower)	(lower)	(lower)	(lower)

1	1 - 3	2	0	3
(lower)	(higher)	(lower)		

Note: These fingerings can be substituted for the regular fingering if a more in-tune note results and the timbre is satisfactory.

Suggestions for Marching Band Directors

Brass players in marching bands should strive for an unforced, well-articulated, and sustained sound. A crisp and uniform attack gives sharpness and excitement to the sound and focuses it as it is heard in the distance. Good balance and sustaining work together to contribute resonance and fullness to the sound. Many bands actually lose sound by encouraging a heavy emphasis from note to note rather than a consistent effort of "blowing through the notes." Smaller bands can often convey an impression of greater size by using their sound well.

In addition to stressing the sustained approach, it is important to emphasize that notes and chords be played as broadly as possible due to the absence of ambiance in the outdoor environment. A good practice is to make certain that notes do not diminish before their release, and to designate the beginning of the following beat as the release point. It is the combination of balance, sustaining, and a broad style that brings resonance and fullness to brass in the open air.

One of the most common problems in marching bands today is poor intonation and tone quality. Intonation difficulties are most obvious in the alto range with the various substitutes for French horn. In addition to careful tuning, the use of octave and chord studies as a daily warm-up does much to improve the sound. These should be played at low- to medium-volume levels while concentrating on an unforced, balanced, and in-tune sound. Careful listening and matching will lead to an improved concept of sound that will carry over into the performance.

CHAPTER 9

The Historical Development of Brass Instruments

The historical outlines that follow note the principal points in the development of the major brass instruments. The outlines are horizontally aligned to show concurrent developments in the trumpet, horn, trombone, baritone, euphonium, and tuba, thereby providing an overview of the development of the brass family.

Museum collections often give a rather incoherent picture of this development by displaying instruments (like the omnitonic horn) that are interesting visually but were little-used in actual practice. Written accounts, too, sometimes leave the reader in doubt as to which instrument is likely to have been used in an orchestra in a particular era. In the interest of space, the outlines have been kept as concise as possible while attempting to convey an accurate impression of the main instruments in use in each period. Important solo compositions are also noted along the way. For those interested in pursuing the history of brass instruments, the following books are recommended (other sources are listed in the bibliography):

General References

BAINES, ANTHONY. *Brass Instruments : Their History and Development.* London: Faber & Faber, 1976.

CARSE, ADAM. *Musical Wind Instruments.* London: Macmillan, 1940. Reprint: Da Capo Press, 1965.

MENDE, EMILIE. *Pictorial Family Tree of Brass Instruments in Europe Since the Early Middle Ages.* Moudon, Switzerland: Editions BIM, 1978.

Specific Instruments

TRUMPET

BATE, PHILIP. *The Trumpet and Trombone: An Outline of Their History, Development, and Construction.* 2nd ed. London: Ernest Benn, 1978. New York: Norton, 1978.

BENDINELLI, CESARE. *The Entire Art of Trumpet Playing, 1614.* Nashville: Brass Press, 1975.

CLARKE, HERBERT L. *How I Became a Cornetist.* Kenosha, Wis.: Leblanc Educational Publications, n.d.

DAHLQVIST, REINE. *The Keyed Trumpet and Its Greatest Virtuoso, Anton Weidinger.* Nashville, Tenn.: Brass Press, 1975.

EICHBORN, HERMANN. *The Old Art of Clarino Playing on Trumpets.* Trans. by Bryan A. Simms. Denver, Colo.: Tromba Publications, 1976.

ENRICO, EUGENE. *The Orchestra at San Petronio in the Baroque Era.* Washington, D.C.: Smithsonian Institution Press, 1976.

FANTINI, GIROLAMO. *Modo per imparare a sonare di Tromba: A Modern Edition of Girolamo Fantini's Trumpet Method.* Boulder, Colo.: Empire Printing, 1977.

NAYLOR, TOM. L. *The Trumpet and Trombone in Graphic Arts, 1500–1800.* Nashville, Tenn.: Brass Press, 1979.

SMITHERS, DON. L. *The Music and History of the Baroque Trumpet Before 1721.* London: J.M. Dent, 1973.

TARR, EDWARD. *The Trumpet.* Portland, Ore.: Amadeus Press, 1988.

HORN

COAR, BIRCHARD. *A Critical Study of the Nineteenth-Century Horn Virtuosi in France.* DeKalb, Ill.: Coar, 1952.

COAR, BIRCHARD. *The French Horn.* DeKalb, Ill.: Coar, 1947.

JANETZKY, KURT, AND BERNHARD BRÜCHLE. *The Horn.* Portland, Ore.: Amadeus Press, 1988.

FITZPATRICK, HORACE. *The Horn and Horn-Playing and the Austro-Bohemian Tradition from 1680–1830.* London: Oxford University Press, 1970.

GREGORY, ROBIN. *The Horn : A Comprehensive Guide to the Modern Instrument and Its Music.* London: Faber & Faber, 1961.

MORLEY-PEGGE, REGINALD. *The French Horn.* London: Ernest Benn, 1973.

TUCKWELL, BARRY. *Horn.* New York: Schirmer Books, 1983.

TROMBONE

FISCHER, HENRY GEORGE. *The Renaissance Sackbut and Its Use Today.* New York: Metropolitan Museum of Art, 1984.

GREGORY, ROBIN. *The Trombone, the Instrument and Its Music.* New York: Praeger, 1973.

SMITH, DAVID. "Trombone Technique in the Early Seventeenth Century." D.M.A. thesis, Stanford University, 1981.

WIGNESS, C. ROBERT. *The Soloistic Use of the Trombone in Eighteenth-Century Vienna.* Nashville: Brass Press, 1978.

BARITONE, EUPHONIUM, AND TUBA

BEVAN, CLIFFORD. *The Tuba Family.* New York: Scribner's, 1978.

Trumpet and Cornet[1]	Horn	Trombone	Baritone, Euphonium, and Tuba
Antiquity			
Straight trumpets made of wood, bronze, and silver. Greek salpinx, Roman tuba, lituus, and buccina.	Scandinavian *lur* (bronze), Hebrew *schofar,* Roman cornu, and various animal horns.		
Middle Ages			
Trumpets reappeared during the crusades, probably derived from the Saracens. *Ca. 1300. Buisine, trumba, trombono, trombetta, trummet.* Medieval trumpeters played only on the lowest harmonics.			
Renaissance			
Ca. 1400–1413. The S-shaped trumpet was developed, followed by the folded trumpet and slide trumpet. The latter enabled the player to produce notes between the harmonics by sliding the instrument in and out on the mouthpipe.		*Ca. 1450.* The trombone developed from the slide trumpet. Both the exact date and identity of the originator of the movable slide are unknown. The connected double tubes of the slide represented a significant advance over the awkward slide trumpet and	

[1] The cornet is grouped with the trumpet in the interest of space. Actually, they have different origins. The cornet dates from ca. 1828, when Halary-Antoine added valves to the German post horn. Since the period of Arban (1869–1889), the evolution of cornet and trumpet playing has been intertwined.

Trumpet and Cornet	Horn	Trombone	Baritone, Euphonium, and Tuba
		reduced the distances between notes, greatly improving technique. The smaller slide movements also rendered tenor-range instruments practicable. These were known as the *saque-boute* or *trompone*.	
Ca. 1500. Corps of trumpeters were maintained by the large courts. Eventually, such large ensembles played in up to five parts (but with little harmonic variety). Players began to specialize in high and low ranges.	Two types of hunting horn were widely used: the curved horn and the helical horn. The latter was made of coiled metal and is the immediate predecessor of the *trompe de chasse*.	*Ca. 1540.* The earliest surviving instruments date from the mid-16th century. Three types were used in this period: an "ordinary" sackbut in B♭ (*gemeine-posaune*), an E♭ alto (*mittel-posaune*), and a bass (*grosse-posaune*), also known as *quart-* or *quint-posaune,* indicating its intervallic distance from the B♭ *gemeine-posaune.* Trombones in other keys were sometimes made, probably for transposition, and were also identified by interval from the "ordinary" in B♭.	

17th Century

Trumpet and Cornet	Horn	Trombone	Baritone, Euphonium, and Tuba
Ca. 1600. Instrument makers centered in Nuremberg produced improved natural trumpets designed to function well on the upper harmonics. The pitch was usually D or E♭ with terminal crooks added for lower keys. Lacking a tuning slide, natural trumpets were tuned by inserting small lengths of tubing to extend the mouthpipe.	Hunting horns were occasionally used on the stage in operas, usually depicting hunting scenes.	*Ca. 1600.* The same pattern continued during the 17th century with the addition of a contrabass instrument (*octav-posaune*), although it is unclear to what extent it was actually used. Sackbuts were regularly used in all types of ensemble, from large court bands to small mixed consorts where it could blend with the softest instruments. A "vocal" style was cultivated that was free of any influence from the trumpet. The capacity to blend with voices caused the sackbut to be widely used in church music. It was also common in municipal bands along with cornett and shawms, or in a consort of 2 cornetts and 3 sackbuts. Venetian composers such as Giovanni Gabrieli and Massaino wrote for the instrument regularly, occasionally calling for exceptionally large forces.	
Ca. 1600. Increasing use was made of trumpets in church music, often in combination with strings. Praetorius's *In dulci jubilo* (1618) calls for six trumpets.			
1620. Florid parts in the high register were written by Samuel Scheidt in his setting of *In dulci jubilo* and Heinrich Schütz's *Buccinate in neomenia Tuba* (1629).			
	Ca. 1660. The hoop-shaped *cor-* or *trompe de chasse* became a feature of hunting tradition in France.		

Trumpet and Cornet	Horn	Trombone	Baritone, Euphonium, and Tuba
Ca. 1665–1700. Beginning with Maurizio Cazzati, composers associated with the basilica of San Petronio in Bologna produced an important body of works for solo trumpet and strings. The style reached its apex near the end of the century in the solo concertos of Giuseppe Torelli, Domenico Gabrielli, and Giacomo Perti. These works are widely performed today.	*Ca. 1680.* A larger-wound *trompe de chasse* made its appearance in France. This instrument had a circumference large enough to fit over the body for carrying on horseback.		
Ca. 1680–1695. The trumpet was widely used as a solo instrument in central Europe by composers such as Heinrich Biber and Johann Schmelzer. In England, Henry Purcell and others made extensive use of the trumpet in stage works. Purcell's *Sonata in D for Trumpet and Strings* (1694) is an important solo piece.	*1680–1682.* Franz Anton, Count von Sporck of Bohemia, became interested in the *cor de chasse* during a visit to France. He had two of his servants, Wenzel Sweda and Peter Röllig, trained to play the instrument and established a tradition of horn playing in central Europe.	*Ca. 1685.* A small trombone pitched an octave above the tenor made its appearance in central Europe and was used mostly for playing chorale melodies in trombone ensembles.	

18th Century

Trumpet and Cornet	Horn	Trombone	Baritone, Euphonium, and Tuba
	Ca. 1700–1710. Viennese instrument maker Michael Leichnambschneider was probably the first to produce terminal crooks to put the horn into different keys. The crooks consisted of various lengths of coiled tubing that were inserted between the mouthpiece and instrument. For lower keys, the crooks could be coupled together, although the instrument become farther away from the player. Once the crook was in place, the horn was played in accordance with the natural harmonic series, which sounded in the chosen key.	Although there may have been diminished use of the trombone generally during the 18th century, the instrument continued to flourish in an important soloistic role (at least) at the Viennese Imperial Court. Following the pattern established in the 17th century by Antonio Bertali (1605–1669), composers such as Johann Joseph Fux (1660–1741), Marc Antonio Ziani (1653–1715), Franz Tuma (1704–1774), and Georg Reutter (1708–1772) used the trombone in virtuosic fashion in vocal and instrumental works. The style reached its peak in the concertos of Georg Christoph Wagenseil (1715–1777) and Johann Georg Albrechtsberger (1736–1809). Concertos were also written by Salzburg composers Michael Haydn (1737–1806) and Leopold Mozart (1719–1787). This interesting chapter in the trombone's history is described in detail in C. Robert Wigness's *The Soloistic Use of the Trombone in Eighteenth-Century Vienna*	
	1705. Two horns were used in the orchestra for the opera *Octavia* by Reinhard Keiser.		

Trumpet and Cornet	Horn	Trombone	Baritone, Euphonium, and Tuba

(Nashville, Tenn.: Brass Press, 1978).

Ca. 1716–1750. The Baroque trumpet reached its zenith in the works of Johann Sebastian Bach, who was well served by Leipzig trumpeter Gottfried Reiche. In his portrait, Reiche holds a coiled instrument known as a *jägertrompete,* probably by Nuremberg instrument maker J. W. Haas. Apparently, these were occasionally used in place of the more common long trumpet.

Ca. 1717. Handel's *Water Music,* which included parts for a pair of horns, was performed. During the Baroque era, horn parts focused on the upper portion of the harmonic series and were played without the hand in the bell.

Ca. 1750. Anton Joseph Hampel, a hornist of Dresden, developed the technique of filling in the spaces between the notes of the harmonic series by various degrees of handstopping, rendering the horn chromatic. The procedure is as follows:

Ca. 1755. Concerto by Georg Christoph Wagenseil (alto trombone).

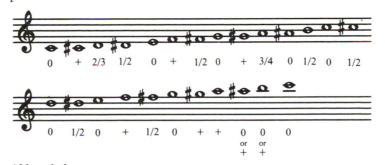

Although there was an unevenness of timbre between stopped and open tones, handstopping became the standard horn technique until well after the invention of valves. Placing the hand in the bell altered the tone, and a darker and softer timbre became accepted as traditional horn tone. To improve on the limitations of terminal crooks, Hampel invented a new structural format that incorporated a fixed mouthpipe and located the crook in the middle of the instrument. The new instrument, made by Johann Werner (Dresden), was known as the *inventionshorn.*

1762. Horn Concerto No. 1 by Franz Joseph Haydn.

Ca. 1760. The high clarino style of trumpet playing declined, not from lack of ability on the players' part, but as a function of broad changes in compositional style. Henceforth, trumpets played a supporting role in the orchestra, although there are two late concertos written in the earlier clarino style (Leopold Mozart, 1762; Michael Haydn, 1764).

Ca. 1762. Concerto by Leopold Mozart (alto trombone).

1763. Larghetto by Michael Haydn (alto trombone).

1764. Divertimento in D by Michael Haydn (alto trombone). [Solo movements also published under the title *Concerto*].

Trumpet and Cornet	Horn	Trombone	Baritone, Euphonium, and Tuba
	1750–1776. J. G. Haltenhof (Hanau am Main) developed the tuning slide that was applied to the *inventionshorn.*	*1769.* Concerto by Johann Georg Albrechtsberger (alto trombone).	
Ca. 1777. Handstopping, first used on the horn in 1750 and by this time normal practice, was applied to the trumpet by Michael Wöggerl. Notes of the harmonic series could be lowered a half or full tone by covering the bell with the hand, although a veiled tone resulted. Stop trumpets were curved or made quite short to increase the bell's accessibility; they followed the *inventionshorn* in locating the crook in the middle of the instrument, thereby eliminating terminal crooks.	*1780.* Parisian instrument makers Joseph and Lucien-Joseph Raoux brought out a structurally improved *inventionshorn,* calling their new model *cor solo.* Designed for solo playing, it had crooks only for the common solo keys: G, F, E, E♭, and D.	*Ca. 1780.* The trombone began to be used in opera to lend dramatic effect to certain scenes, as in Mozart's *Don Giovanni* and *Magic Flute.*	
1795. Trumpeter's and Kettledrummer's Art by Ernst Altenburg was published. This is an important source concerning the natural trumpet and clarino style (see translation by Edward Tarr [Nashville: Brass Press, 1974]).	*1781–1791.* Concertos for horn—Wolfgang Amadeus Mozart: *Rondo in E♭,* K.371, 1781; *Concerto in E♭,* K.417, 1783 (No. 2); *Concerto in E♭,* K.447, 1786 (No. 3); *Concerto in E♭* K.495, 1786 (No. 4); *Concerto in D,* K.412, 1791 (No. 1).		
1795. Viennese trumpeter Anton Weidinger gave solo appearances, performing on a keyed trumpet of his own design. Haydn's *Trumpet Concerto* (1796) was composed for him, as was the concerto by Hummel (1803).	*Ca. 1795.* Terminal crooks once again became popular with orchestral players, but with individual crooks for each key instead of the cumbersome practice of coupling crooks together for the lower keys. English players, however, continued to use the earlier system of terminal crooks and couplers; their instruments were fitted with tuning slides.		

Trumpet and Cornet	Horn	Trombone	Baritone, Euphonium, and Tuba
		19th Century	
Ca. 1800. The natural trumpet flourished in England later than elsewhere (through most of the 19th century) due to John Hyde's invention of a spring-slide mechanism that allowed the instrument's fundamental pitch to be lowered a half or whole tone without affecting the timbre. An active tradition of performing Handel's clarino parts on the natural trumpet was thereby maintained.	*1800. Horn Sonata*, Op. 17, by Ludwig van Beethoven. Written for virtuoso Giovanni Punto (Jan Václav Stich). *Ca. 1800.* Before the invention of valves, there were attempts to construct a chromatic horn. These included the keyed horn and omnitonic horn. Neither gained wide acceptance, and the hand horn continued as the primary orchestral and solo instrument, with players specializing in either high or low ranges. *1806. Concertino for Horn* by Carl Maria von Weber; revised 1815. The cadenza includes horn chords.	*Ca. 1800–1850.* During the early 19th century, composers increasingly called for 3 trombones in the orchestra. Parts were included in Beethoven's 5th and 9th symphonies. The normal trio of E♭ alto, B♭ tenor, and F bass began to give way as alto parts were often performed on the tenor. A large-bore trombone in B♭ was occasionally substituted for the bass in F. The alto trombone was retained (as it is today in central Europe) for parts requiring a high tessitura and light balances.	(The valved low brass have no direct predecessors. The instruments they replaced were the serpent [the bass of the conetto family and its more developed form, the bass horn] and the ophicleide, which was derived from the keyed bugle.)

The Development of Valves

In 1788, Charles Clagget was granted a patent for a "chromatic trumpet," which in fact consisted of two instruments, each with its own fundamental and a switching mechanism to direct the single mouthpiece to one side or the other. Although the invention was demonstrated, it failed to achieve any acceptance and should not, therefore, be considered a stage in the development of the valve.

The history of the valve begins with an article in the *Allgemeine musikalische Zeitung* of May 3, 1815, by G. B. Bierey, which reported on a new invention by horn player Heinrich Stölzel. Through the use of two "levers", a chromatic scale of almost three octaves could be obtained. The author described the timbre of the valve notes as "clear and strong," comparable to the natural tones. By 1818, Stölzel had joined the court orchestra in Berlin, when Friedrich Blühmel turned up claiming that the invention was his. A joint 10-year patent was granted to Stölzel and Blühmel; we will probably never know which of them was responsible for the original idea.

The joint patent of 1818 was for both a tubular and a square-shaped (box) valve. In the tubular valve (Stölzel's), the air column was directed downward through the valve tube and out the bottom. Valves of this type were popular during the first half of the century and were known as Stölzel valves. The square valve (Blühmel's) had the advantage of more direct windways, but was slower in action.[2]

In 1828, Stölzel and Blühmel were unsuccessful in obtaining patents for rotary valves. Of similar design, the valves were apparently developed quite early but, for some reason, Stölzel and Blühmel chose not to include them in the 1818 patent. Wieprecht stated that the rotary valve was immediately improved in Prague, a com-

[2] An important source of information on the early development of the valve is the account by Prussian bandmaster Wilhelm Wieprecht (1845), who knew both Stölzel and Blühmel. Relevant passages are translated in Anthony Baines, *Brass Instruments* (London, Faber & Faber, 1976), pp. 207–212. The most detailed study available is Herbert Heyde's series of articles, "Zur Frühgeschichte der Ventile und Ventilinstrumente in Deutschland (1814–1833)," *Brass Bulletin* 24 (1978), pp. 9–33; 25 (1979), pp. 41–50; 26 (1979), pp. 69–82; 27 (1979), pp. 51–59 (translations in English and French are included).

ment that lends credence to a story found in the papers of instrument maker Karl Nödel that credits hornist Joseph Kail with the invention of the rotary valve rather than Josef Riedl, who patented it in 1832.[3] According to Nödel, his father (also an instrument maker) and other old Viennese makers always maintained that Kail, a professor at the Prague Conservatory, invented the rotary valve in 1827, having gotten the idea from a beer tap. Kail apparently described his idea to Josef Riedl during a visit to Vienna and Riedl proceeded to manufacture the valves, eventually securing a patent.[4]

Another valve in use today (but only on the Vienna horn) is the double-piston valve, which was patented in 1830 by Viennese instrument maker Leopold Uhlmann as an improved version of an earlier design by Christian Friedrich Sattler of Leipzig. With attached twin pistons, the air column flows from the bottom of one piston (like the Stölzel valve) and, after going through the requisite length of tubing, reenters the bottom of the second piston. This action is believed to contribute to the exceptionally smooth slurs and free tone of the Vienna horn.

In 1835, Wilhelm Wieprecht and instrument maker J. G. Moritz introduced improved piston valves known as *Berliner-Pumpen*, which featured unconstricted airways. Although they had a rather slow action, they were widely used in military bands in Germany and northern Europe (particularly on low brass instruments) and continued to be made into the beginning of the present century.

There were other experiments, such as the transverse spring slide by John Shaw and disc-type valves by Halary-Antoine, Shaw, and Köhler, but these had no significant impact on the development of the valve.

The final stage of development was reached in 1839, when François Périnet, a Parisian instrument maker, brought the piston valve into the form we know today. Thus the three modern valves—piston, rotary, and Vienna—were developed in the 1830s and have come down to the present era essentially unchanged. A new invention is the valve developed by Orla Ed Thayer. This valve has proved effective as a change-valve for the F and other attachments on the trombone.

[3] Nödel's statement is reproduced in Bernhard Brüchle and Kurt Janetzky, *Kulturgeschichte des Horns* (Tutzing: Hans Schneider, 1976), pp. 252–253.

[4] Another source, T. Rode, writing in the *Neue Berliner Musikzeitung* in 1860, says that Kail improved the rotary valve in 1829. Whether there is any connection between the Stölzel and Blühmel rotary valve and the Kail valve or (if the Nödel story is true) is a case of independent conception remains unclear. Another early type of rotary valve was made by Nathan Adams of Boston, Mass., as early as 1825.

Trumpet and Cornet	Horn	Trombone	Baritone, Euphonium, and Tuba
19th Century			
Ca. 1826. Spontini brought a German valve trumpet to Paris where it gained acceptance and was copied. Berlioz was the first to use the new instrument in the overture *Les francs-juges* of the same year. During this period, valve trumpets were often used beside natural trumpets. As the valve trumpet developed during the 19th century, instruments were produced with Stölzel,	*Ca. 1825.* Although valve horns made their appearance, players preferred to use hand technique whenever possible on the new instruments. The valves were used to avoid the most obvious inequalities of timbre inherent in the hand horn technique. French instrument makers often produced horns with removable valves, and a third valve was considered unnecessary.	As trombones were being increasingly used in orchestras, several trombonists attained fame as soloists. The first of these was Friedrich August Belcke (1795–1874).	

Trumpet and Cornet	Horn	Trombone	Baritone, Euphonium, and Tuba
piston, rotary, and Vienna valves. The usual key was F or G, and crooks were added for lower keys.			

Trumpet and Cornet

Ca. 1828. Jean-Louis Antoine (Halary)[5] modified the (round) German post horn to become a valve instrument, calling it *cornet à pistons*. Two Stölzel valves were fitted, and it was wound (in B♭) so that the bell projected forward. The cornet gained rapid popularity as a solo instrument because of its chromatic agility, and it was often used (in a pair) along with trumpets in works by French composers.

Horn

1835. Halevy's *La juive* was the first score to call for valve horns. A pair of hand horns and a pair of valve horns was customary.

Trombone

Ca. 1828. The new valve trombone was introduced, and, while it received some acceptance in bands, it was little used in orchestras.

Following in the virtuoso tradition of Belcke were Karl Traugott Queisser (1800–1846) and Antoine Guillaume Dieppo (1808–1878). The latter taught at the Paris Conservatory and produced a *méthode complète* in 1840

1837. Concertino by Ferdinand David (1810–1873).

1839. C. F. Sattler of Leipzig introduced the first B♭–F trombone. The change to the F attachment was (as it is today) made by a rotary valve.

Baritone, Euphonium, and Tuba

Ca. 1828. Tenor- and baritone-range instruments with valves appeared in German military bands during the late 1820s. These may be considered the first versions of the modern German *tenorhorn* and *baryton.*

Ca. 1835. The first tuba, a five-valve (*Berliner-pumpen*) instrument in F, was invented by Berlin bandmaster Wilhelm Wieprecht and instrument maker Johann Gottfried Moritz.

1838. Moritz produced a tenor tuba in B♭.

1842–1845. Parisian inventor Adolphe Sax produced his complete family of saxhorns, receiving a patent in 1845. These ranged from the E♭ soprano to the B♭ contrabass. Aside from the quality of their construction, the saxhorns' success can be attributed to their adoption by the French Army and by the famous Distin family quintet (who popularized them in England, where they were taken up by the developing brass band movement). Modern low brass instruments with piston valves evolved from the saxhorn.

1843. The *Euphonion* was introduced by Sommer of Weimar. A similar instrument, identified as the *Sommerophone,* was exhibited in 1851 at the Crystal Palace in London.

---

[5] J.-L Antoine took over the Halary business and adopted the name. His son, Jules-Leon Antoine, later joined him as a partner.

Trumpet and Cornet	Horn	Trombone	Baritone, Euphonium, and Tuba

1845. Contrabass tubas in B♭ and C with rotary valves rather than *Berliner-pumpen* were manufactured by the Bohemian firm of Červený. The tuba was rapidly accepted in orchestras in Germany but the ophicleide maintained its place in France and England until late in the century. Tubas found acceptance in bands everywhere.

1848. Jules-Léon Antoine (Halary), hornist and son of instrument maker Jean-Louis Antoine (Halary), devised the ascending 3rd-valve system, still in some use in France and Belgium.

Ca. 1850–1890. Possibly due to the influence of the B♭ cornet, with its advantage of more widely spaced harmonics, trumpeters gradually moved away from the long F and G trumpets toward instruments built in B♭ or C. Stölzel valves declined in popularity, and instruments were made with 3 piston or rotary valves.

1849. Robert Schumann was an important early advocate for the valve horn. His *Adagio and Allegro* for solo horn and piano and *Konzertstück* for 4 horns and orchestra demand the full capacity of the valve instrument.

Ca. 1850. From the mid-19th century, German trombones became larger in bore and bell and took on their traditional wide-bow construction. French trombones of the Courtois type retained a smaller bore and bell taper. Large bass trombones in F or B♭/F became the rule in German sections. A smaller bass trombone in G was used in brass bands and orchestras in England for almost a century.

Ca. 1840–1880. Berlioz and Wagner were early champions of the tuba. The latter wrote for it in *The Flying Dutchman* (1843) and it was included in Berlioz's *Damnation of Faust,* composed three years later. The bass tuba in F was normally used, but the contrabass was occasionally specified, as in Wagner's *Ring.* In France, a small C tuba (pitched above the F bass) with 6 valves finally replaced the ophicleide.

1865. Trio for Violin, Horn, and Piano, op. 40, by Johannes Brahms.

1864. Jean-Baptiste Arban's *Grande méthode complète pour cornet à pistons et de saxhorn* was published in Paris. Arban's influence as performer and teacher had wide impact on both cornetists and trumpeters, which extends to the present. His method forms the basis of most modern teaching of the instruments.

Ca. 1865. During the second half of the 19th century, horns were typically built (in Germany) in F with three rotary valves and either terminal or slide crooks. Players preferred to use the high B♭, A, G, E, and E♭ crooks when in those keys in order to retain the timbre of the open tones and avoid awkward fingerings. Henri Kling, in his *Horn-Schule* (1865), cited examples for the use of crooks and disparaged the practice of trying to play everything on the F crook, which was now theoretically possible through the use of valves. In France, horns with terminal G crook and ascending 3rd valve (which put the horn in F) were preferred, and English players used French instruments with descending 3rd valve and F crook. Uhlmann's ca. 1830 Vienna horn with double piston

Trumpet and Cornet	Horn	Trombone	Baritone, Euphonium, and Tuba

valves and terminal crook was (and still is) the standard instrument of the Imperial (now State) Opera and Vienna Philharmonic.

1871. Julius Kosleck, Professor at the Berlin *Hoch-Schule,* gave a demonstration of clarino playing which aroused interest in reviving this art. Later, in 1884–1885, he caused a stir by performing the Bach parts on a 2-valve straight trumpet in A. English players had similar instruments made by G. Silvani. Teste, of the Paris Opera, performed the *Magnificat* on a 3-valve G trumpet (1885) made by Besson. Mahillion produced a successful D trumpet in 1892, and Alexander an F for the 2nd "Brandenburg" Concerto in 1894. The great Belgian trumpeter Théo Charlier performed the 2nd "Brandenburg" Concerto on April 17, 1889 in Anvers and on Nov. 17, 1901 in Liège. Charlier used a G trumpet made by Mahillon for these performances. The various high trumpets were often called Bach trumpets.

1876. A contrabass trombone in B♭ with double-tubed slide was constructed for Wagner's *Ring* (composed 1848–1874; performed Bayreuth, 1876).

1874. A compensating system (still in use) to correct intonation when valves are used in combination was invented by David Blaikley of Boosey and Co. This significantly improved low brass instruments used in England and is a contributing factor to the high quality of British brass bands.

Ca. 1880. Červený introduced a very large bore tuba known as a *Kaiserbass*. This became the prototype for most modern rotary valve orchestral tubas in C and B♭.

1882–1883. First Concerto for Horn, op. 11 by Richard Strauss.

Ca. 1890. The modern form of the orchestral trumpet became established. Piston valve trumpets were generally found in France, England, and the U.S.; rotary valve trumpets in Germany, Austria, and Italy. Instruments in C were favored by French and Viennese trumpeters, while the B♭ was common elsewhere. (The long F trumpet survived into the early 20th century in England.)

1897. Edmund Gumpert, in collaboration with the instrument firm of Eduard Kruspe, developed the first F-B♭ double horn, a compensating type that was soon followed by the full double. (The idea had been partially anticipated by Gautrot, who designed a compensating system to correct intonation in 1865.)

Ca. 1890–1920. During these years, small-bore Courtois-type trombones were popular in France, England, and in bands in the U.S. Players in American symphony orchestras preferred large-bore German instruments, and these influenced the development of the modern American symphonic trombone (which combines the best features of French and German instruments).

Trumpet and Cornet	Horn	Trombone	Baritone, Euphonium, and Tuba

20th Century

Ca. 1905. The Belgian firm of Mahillon constructed a piccolo B♭ trumpet intended for Bach's 2nd "Brandenburg" Concerto.

Ca. 1929. Larger-bore piston valve B♭ trumpets based on the Besson model replaced smaller-bore instruments in American orchestras. Through the influence of Georges Mager, principal trumpet of the Boston Symphony (1920–1950), the C trumpet became increasingly common. By the late 1940s, it had largely replaced the B♭ as the standard orchestral instrument.

Ca. 1959. Improved high trumpets were developed, bringing the Baroque literature into the sphere of regular orchestral players rather than specialists.

Ca. 1960. French virtuoso Maurice André brought the trumpet into a new era as a popular solo instrument through worldwide appearances and recordings.

Ca. 1961. Performances on natural trumpets were revived to lend an authentic timbre and style to Baroque music. The standard of performance has now risen to a very high level, and there are several internationally recognized soloists on natural trumpet. Replicas of Baroque instruments are readily available.

At the beginning of the century, single F, B♭ and double horns were in simultaneous use.

Ca. 1928. Hornist Louis Vuillermoz developed a compensating double horn (piston valve) based on the ascending 3rd-valve principle. This became the standard orchestral horn in France and parts of Belgium until ca. 1974.

1942. Second Concerto for Horn by Richard Strauss.

Ca. 1945–1950. In England, French-type piston valve horns were gradually replaced by German single B♭s, and doubles (a change regretted by many).

Ca. 1950–1957. English horn player Dennis Brain achieved world renown as a soloist, establishing the horn as a major solo instrument.

Ca. 1958. The first practical B♭F alto double descant horn was developed by Richard Merewether. Double descants are also made in F–F alto, B♭–E♭ alto, and B♭–B♭ soprano. Single descants are most commonly built in F or G alto and B♭ soprano.

1965. Richard Mereweather introduced the triple horn in F–B♭–F alto.

Ca. 1939. The trombone gained widespread popularity through the influence of bandleaders such as Tommy Dorsey and Glenn Miller and its use in jazz. Tommy Dorsey, in particular, left his mark on all trombonists for his remarkable control and smooth legato.

Ca. 1950. American-type orchestral trombones became standardized throughout the world, in some cases (as in England) displacing traditional small-bore instruments, in Germany and Austria, but German trombones continued their independent line of development.

Ca. 1952. Several American bass trombonists were frustrated by the limitations of the B♭–F instrument in producing good notes immediately above the pedal range. They experimented with an additional length of tubing connected to the F attachment by a second valve that lowered the pitch to E. This was later altered to E♭ or D, and the dependent double-trigger bass trombone soon became standardized.

Ca. 1965. Hans Kunitz invented the in-line independent double-valve large bass–contrabass trombone, tuned F/C–D–B♭.

Ca. 1970. Dr. B. P. Leonard independently invented the in-line design. From Leonard's patented design, tuned B♭/G–E–D. Other versions, tuned B♭/F–G–E♭ or B♭/F–G♭–D, were developed and produced commercially as bass trombones.

1900–present. German low-brass instruments continued in the 20th century essentially unchanged from their 19th-century counterparts. Band instruments such as the E♭ *althorn, tenorhorn,* and *baryton* (the latter two equivalent to the baritone and euphonium) were wrapped in an oval form with rotary valves and remain the same today. German tubas became accepted in many countries as the standard orchestral instrument. In England, an agile piston valve tuba in F (Ralph Vaughan Williams wrote his *Bass Tuba Concerto* [1954] for this instrument) was favored up to World War II. Since then, the brass band-type E♭ is standard, with occasional use of a B♭ contrabass for certain works. The small French C tuba was used for some years, but has now given way to more conventional instruments in Parisian orchestras, usually a German-type 6-valve F or contrabass. The C instrument is still used for high solos, as in Mussorgsky-Ravel's *Pictures at an Exhibition* and Stravinsky's *Petrouchka.* German tubas were widely used in American orchestras (though not in bands) from the late 19th century onward. Some large-bore piston valve tubas were made by domestic firms early in the century and are greatly prized today.

Trumpet and Cornet	Horn	Trombone	Baritone, Euphonium, and Tuba
Present. Trumpet sections composed of C trumpets are now standard in American orchestras, but the B♭ is used in certain repertoires. English and German players generally prefer the B♭, while C trumpets are widely used in France and Austria. Trumpets with piston valves are most common, but rotary valve instruments are the mainstay of orchestras in Germany and Austria, and have been adopted by American players for certain repertoire. B♭ cornets and trumpets are invariably used in bands. Baroque parts are now usually played on the piccolo B♭/A trumpet. Present-day trumpets are available in the following keys: B♭, C, D, E♭, E, F, G, (piccolo) A, B♭, C. Some are built in one key with slides for other keys, e.g. D/E♭, G/F/E, and piccolo B♭/A. German-type rotary valve trumpets follow the same format in keys.	*Present.* The F–B♭ full double is the standard orchestral instrument today. Exceptions are the single F horn used in the Vienna Philharmonic (there is renewed interest elsewhere in this horn) and the occasional single B♭ or triple horn. Double or triple descant horns are usually used for high-register work.	*Present.* Large-bore tenors with and without F attachment and in-line double-rotor bass trombones are used in orchestras and bands today. While small-bore trombones are rare, medium and medium-large bores are widely used by students and in the jazz and recording fields. Alto trombones are used for certain repertoire (particularly in Germany). Modern versions of traditional German trombones are preferred in Central Europe. The valve trombone is now only found in jazz, where it is an important solo instrument. Parts for contrabass trombone are usually played on the bass trombone, due to the increased capability of the in-line double-valve instrument, but there is increased use of modern forms of the contrabass instrument.	American tubists established the trend of using the C contrabass as the primary instrument, reserving the bass in F for high-register passages, and this pattern has been followed elsewhere (although the B♭ contrabass is preferred in some countries). At present, large-bore piston valve C tubas based on early 20th-century models have come into wide orchestral use and improved rotary valve instruments now offer a viable choice in instrument type. Orchestral-type rotary valve tubas are widely used in bands in the U.S. Marching bands use the Sousaphone. British-type Euphoniums are preferred in American concert bands, while traditional narrow-bore baritones and alto (tenor) horns are now used only in brass bands. At present, brass bands, modeled on the British tradition, are gaining popularity in America and Scandinavia. There is also some use of "American-bore" baritones (larger), usually as substitutes for the euphonium.

PART TWO

TECHNIQUE

CHAPTER 10

Tone Production

The most vital attribute a brass player can have is an effective and reliable production of sound. Not only is this the basis of one's ability to play, but it is also the cornerstone of a performer's confidence. Whether playing in the high or low ranges, loud or soft, notes must respond easily and dependably with a clear and resonant sound. Tone production consists of several elements that must be understood and brought together into a concept of how to play the instrument.

This is not a complex process in which each muscular function must be analyzed and consciously controlled. Rather, a practical concept of how to produce sound must first be developed and then transformed into a straightforward procedure that enables the player to achieve consistently good musical results. Brass students sometimes become obsessed with an analytical approach to playing. This often leads to what Adolph Herseth, principal trumpet of the Chicago Symphony Orchestra, calls "paralysis by analysis." The best approach is a natural, common-sense method that is based on sound principles and focused on musical results.

It should be recognized, however, that good brass players have different concepts and methods of playing; ultimately, a method of tone production must be judged on the basis of its results, and it has been amply demonstrated that brass players play successfully by differing means. Presented in this chapter is a method of playing as it is taught by the author. It is a proven method that works well for both beginners and advanced players.

Musical sound on brass instruments is created by pitch-vibration. Pitch-vibration is in turn made by the motion of the air stream, which sets the embouchure into vibration at specific frequencies. To these fundamental elements is added articulation. Because the air is the motive element in brass playing, how the air is moved by the respiratory system is considered first.

The Air

Before presenting a practical approach to moving the air in and out of the lungs as this applies to brass playing, it would be helpful to discuss respiration in a general way since misconceptions abound in musical circles. Air is moved in and out of the lungs by a process of expansion and reduction. This is accomplished by the respiratory muscles. Certain of these muscles work together to create various degrees of expansion to bring air into the lungs, and others bring about a reduction to expel air (under various levels of pressure) out of the lungs. The two procedures are called inspiration (taking in the air) and expiration (blowing the air out).

The lungs are contained in a flexible structure known as the rib cage. Within the lower ribs is a domed-shaped sheet of muscle called the diaphragm, which contracts

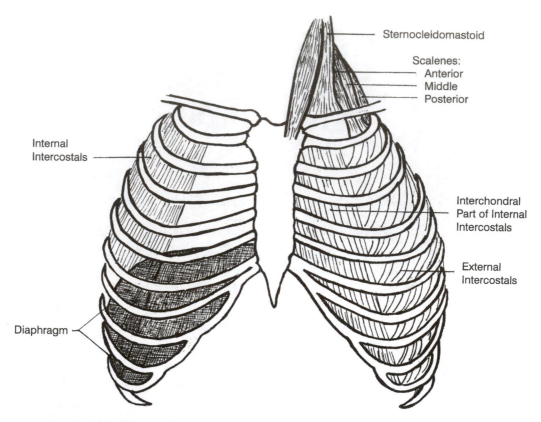

Figure 10.1. **Diagram based on Frank H. Netter, M.D., Atlas of Human Anatomy** *Summit, N.J.: CIBA–Geigy Corp., 1989.*

upon inspiration (the muscular action of the diaphragm applies only to inspiration, not expiration). When the diaphragm contracts upon breathing in, the dome descends, vertically increasing the size of the thoracic cavity (the part of the trunk between the head and abdomen). With the downward contraction of the diaphragm, the abdominal contents are forced downward and forward; this also elevates the lower ribs, thus increasing the diameter of the rib cage at that level. The actual movement of the diaphragm is about one centimeter in normal tidal (quiet) breathing. In active breathing (known as forced inspiration and expiration), the movement can be up to ten times greater.[1]

The other primary respiratory muscles that bring about expansion during inspiration are the external intercostal muscles and the interchondral part of the internal intercostals (see Figure 10.1). These muscles are attached between the ribs. The ribs slant downward and forward; when the intercostals contract upon inspiration, the ribs are pulled (rotated) upward and outward, increasing the diameter of the rib cage. In addition to the primary muscles of inspiration (diaphragm, external intercostals, and interchondral part of the internal intercostals), accessory muscles also participate in the three-dimensional process of expansion. Although these are little used in quiet breathing, they play an important role in the active breathing required in brass playing, as well as in vigorous exercise. The sternocleidomastoids elevate (raise) the sternum at the same time as the scalenes (anterior, middle, and posterior) lift the first two (uppermost) ribs. This serves to further increase the size of the thoracic cavity and, consequently, the volume of air inhaled.

[1] John B. West, *Respiratory Physiology—The Essentials,* 4th ed. (Baltimore: Williams & Wilkins, 1990).

Before inspiration, the pressure inside the lungs is equal to atmospheric pressure. As a result of the expansion created by the contraction of the muscles of inspiration, the intrathoracic pressure falls below atmospheric pressure and air flows into the lungs to equalize the pressure difference.

In quiet breathing, expiration is by passive recoil of the lungs and chest wall. The diaphragm and other muscles of inspiration relax, allowing the lungs and chest wall (through their natural elasticity) to return to their preinspiration position. Again, in the active respiration used when playing brass instruments, or in exercise, there are contractions in the muscles of expiration. The abdominal muscles (rectus abdominis, external oblique, internal oblique, and transversus abdominis) create pressure on the lower ribs and compress the abdominal contents; this pushes the released diaphragm upward toward its position before inspiration. It should be emphasized that this, like all of the muscular actions associated with respiration, are unconscious; by inspiring or expiring air, the respiratory musculature automatically becomes active in accordance with the demand placed on the respiratory system. Along with the contraction of the abdominal muscles, the internal intercostals (except for the interchondral part) contract, pulling the ribs down and in; this decreases the diameter of the rib cage and the volume of the thorax.

In light of the foregoing discussion of respiration, it would be well to dispel several common misconceptions. First among these is the notion that the upper part of the thorax should not be used in brass playing. What occurs in following this idea is a restriction of inspiratory expansion, thus reducing the quantities of air that are exchanged and compromising the effectiveness of the respiratory process. Although this may be reasonable in situations where low total volumes of air are required (such as singing), this approach does not produce a sufficient volume of air for modern brass playing.

The second misconception is that the shoulders should not be raised during inspiration. Although it is true that the shoulders should not consciously be raised, the normal elevation and expansion of the rib cage as the air is taken in causes the shoulders to rise somewhat. This should not be resisted. Only by decreasing the volume of air that is inhaled can this natural motion be eliminated.

The third problem is bringing the body into a state of rigid isometric tension to create support during expiration. The resultant buildup of muscular tension (which spreads to the neck and throat) obstructs the process of reduction in expiration and resists the outflow of air. Support should be seen as the concentrated outward motion and pressure of the air stream rather than static muscular tension.

Given this understanding of how the respiratory system works, we must devise a strategy for taking in and blowing out the air that is both effective and easy to use. The two starting points of effective respiration are posture and relaxation. In order for the expansion that occurs on inspiration to take place without encumbrance, the body must be upright. The body's respiratory system functions under the force of gravity; therefore, it must be balanced in an erect position and not bent in order to permit unimpeded expansion and reduction. When seated, it is essential to sit tall and not rest on the back of the chair. The latter obstructs the rotational motion of the ribs in expanding and elevating during inspiration. Of equal importance is that the body remain relaxed. Bodily tension inhibits the inflow and outflow of air and resists the respiratory system's natural movements.

The best way of bringing in a full volume of air is to visualize it as a *quantity* of air to be inhaled. Because air is essentially infinite, this is not easy to do. The way it can be done is to visualize a certain quantity of air as a finite form. Any common item of sufficient (or greater) size that represents the desired volume to be inhaled can be used for this purpose. A ball, balloon, or bag works well enough. This method of inspiration came to the author one day in teaching a lesson to a student who, although very talented, tended to take in air as little "sips." The author suggested that the student visualize a volume of air the size of a basketball and inhale that quantity of air into his lungs. The effect was dramatic and lasting. Of course, the volume of air contained in a basketball is greater than the actual volume of air the student needed to inhale, but the mental image caused the student to take in a full breath in exactly the right way. In using this procedure, it is not necessary to think about where the air is going in the lungs or how the respiratory system operates; if the player remains relaxed and does not resist the natural expansion, the volume of air that is inhaled will automatically go to the right places. The actual filling of the lungs is from the bottom upward. The important thing to remember is that the respiratory system knows how to take in air; by creating a mental image of a volume of air to be inhaled, the player allows his or her respiratory system to automatically accomplish that purpose in a natural way. It should be emphasized again that in following this concept of inspiration, the body must be relaxed.

There is an important relationship between the volume of air that has been inhaled and the effectiveness of the expiration. Expiration is most efficient when the lungs are full. This efficiency decreases as the volume of air in the lungs becomes smaller (or is small to begin with). When a full volume of air has been inhaled, a natural outward propulsion of the air is created by the recoil of the lungs and chest wall. This is the basis of the expiratory motion of the air; to this is added the (unconscious) contraction of the internal intercostal and abdominal muscles, which reduce under pressure the volume of the thoracic cavity, creating a more forceful outflow. As in inspiration, a conceptual means of bringing about the action of the respiratory system is the best way of approaching expiration.

Expiration as it is applied to brass playing should be conceived of as air in motion. It is the active motion of the air that creates stable pitch-vibration in the mouthpiece and produces a good quality of sound. This can be accomplished by thinking of moving the air as *wind*.[2] Wind, as we observe it in nature, is air in motion. If the player visualizes creating wind pressure when blowing the air outward, the respiratory system will respond to produce an appropriately forceful air stream. This type of air stream is needed for stable pitch-vibration of the embouchure.

There are two components of the expiratory outflow of air: volume (the quantity of the air) and pressure (the force of the air). Both are present in varying degrees, depending on the instrument and the range of the note being played. In general, low brass instruments require comparatively more volume and less pressure than the high brass, in which these proportions tend to be reversed. High notes require more wind pressure than low notes, which need a greater volume of air (dynamics also affect the ratio of pressure to volume). There is an optimum mixture of pressure and volume of air for each note; when this is achieved a sound that is full, on-pitch, and unforced will result. Therefore, the player should think of creating both wind pressure and air volume when blowing the air outward. Taking a note in the middle register as a base level of pressure and volume, both the pressure and volume should be raised in ascending to the upper register. In descending from the middle register

---

[2] The concept of moving air as wind in brass playing is one of a number of important pedagogical principles developed by the great tubist Arnold Jacobs. Mr. Jacobs's work has had wide-ranging influence on modern brass playing. See M. Dee Stewart, *Arnold Jacobs: The Legacy of a Master* (Northfield, Ill.: Instrumentalist Publishing Co., 1987); Kevin Kelly, Arnold Jacobs, and David Cugell, M.D., "The Dynamics of Breathing," *The Instrumentalist* (Dec. 1983), pp. 6–12; Bill Russo, "An Interview with Arnold Jacobs," *The Instrumentalist* (Feb. 1973); Arnold Jacobs, "Arnold Jacobs Master Class," *The Instrumentalist* (June 1991); Arnold Jacobs, "Mind Over Metal," *The Instrumentalist* (Oct. 1992); Brian Frederiksen, "Arnold Jacobs—A Bibliography," *ITG Journal* (May 1993); Brian Frederiksen, *Arnold Jacobs: Song and Wind* (Gurnee, Ill.: Windsong Press, 1996). The Kelly and Russo articles are reprinted in the Stewart book.

note to the lower register, the volume of air should be increased along with sufficient pressure to maintain an even dynamic level and stable sound. Some players approach this by visualizing varying speeds of air. The basic (middle register) speed should be considered fast wind. The wind speed should increase or decrease from this point (with suitable adjustments of air volume). The author's method is to think of producing the right wind pressure and quantity of air for each note to sound in tune with a full, resonant, unforced tone quality.

There are three basic approaches to blowing the air outward that are used by brass players today. It should be stressed that although they differ in means, the end is to create an effective air stream to vibrate the embouchure. Just as there are different technical approaches used by players in the same sport, each of the three methods seems to work better for certain individuals. The choice of one method over another may also be related to the degree of resistance in the instrument.

The first approach follows the natural action of the respiratory system described above. As the player thinks of creating wind pressure, the respiratory system automatically brings about the necessary reduction to propel the air outward. Because it is dependent on the recoil of the lungs and chest wall to a large extent, a full inspiration is particularly important for this method.

The second approach is like the first, but adds a conscious contraction of the abdominal muscles. As discussed earlier, there is an unconscious contraction of the abdominal muscles during expiration that returns the diaphragm to its original position. In the second method, this is supplemented by a conscious contraction (a feeling of pushing inward and upward, like a bellows). Sometimes this method is reserved for high or loud passages, rather than maintained as a constant effort.[3]

The third approach is often used when there is a feeling of resistance from the instrument. This method uses the diaphragm as a brake to balance the unconscious contraction of the abdominal muscles. As the abdominal contraction is gently resisted by the opposite force of the diaphragm, the reduction takes place first in the thorax, creating a higher level of air pressure, and then in the abdominal area.[4] Although it appears complex, this method is very simple to use. After inspiration, the player thinks of keeping the expanded area around the waist out while the air is blown outward. Players who use this method sometimes speak of lower body support.[5]

The Embouchure and the First Steps in Playing

Sound and pitch are created in the mouthpiece by the vibration of the embouchure. To generate pitch-vibration, the lips must be formed in such a way that they can be brought into oscillation by the motion of the air stream. The mouthpiece must be placed on the embouchure formation so that optimal vibration is encouraged and an air seal is formed. This isolates the oscillating parts of the lips from the facial musculature outside the mouthpiece; the latter support and regulate the formation inside the mouthpiece. An important step was taken in our understanding of what takes place in the mouthpiece with the development of the TRU-VU transparent

---

[3] The second approach is discussed in Frøydis Ree Wekre's excellent book, *Thoughts on Playing the Horn Well* (Oslo: Frøydis Ree Wekre, 1994).

[4] See Pip Eastop, "Some Ins and Outs of Breathing," *The Horn Magazine* (Winter 1996), pp. 30–32.

[5] There is a fourth (less common) method of expiration. In this approach, the inhaled air is compressed immediately before expiration. After inspiration, the player pulls the waist area inward (this pushes the diaphragm upward, compressing the air) just before beginning to blow outward. See Antonio Iervolino, "Breathing Technique," *The Horn Call* (Vol. 12, no. 2, April 1982), pp. 19–25.

Figure 10.2. **The TRU-VU transparent mouthpiece demonstrated by Peter Sullivan, trombonist with the Orchestre Symphonique de Montréal.** *Photo courtesy of L-S Music Innovations.*

mouthpiece.[6] (See Figure 10.2.) A videotape was made of professional brass players using transparent mouthpieces to play scales, intervals, and arpeggios while a strobe light isolated the actual vibratory motion of the lips. This motion was revealed to be an opening and closing of the embouchure for each complete oscillation. The number of oscillations corresponds to the frequency of the pitch played (for example, A = 440 oscillations per second).

To form an effective embouchure, bring the jaw forward so that the upper and lower teeth are more or less aligned. A small space should be made between the teeth for the air stream to pass through. Form the lips as if saying "poo." The "oo" formation that is created in pronouncing "poo" brings the lips into a slightly pursed configuration that creates a cushion for the mouthpiece to rest on. This not only protects the lips from mouthpiece pressure, but creates the conditions that cause the embouchure to vibrate in response to the motion of the air stream (see Figures 10.3 and 10.4). The "p" part of "poo" brings the center of the lips to the starting position for vibration and makes them responsive to the motion of the air. Although the sound can be started with a "poo" syllable for practice purposes, once the basic "poo" formation is established, another consonant such as "t" or "d" can be substituted for "p" ("too" or "doo"). To get the feeling of blowing outward through the lips and creating a stable air stream, hold a sheet of paper about a foot in front of the face. Blow a stream of air at the paper while saying "too" and observe the paper being blown backward. Keep the "oo" going while continuing to blow until the air runs out.[7]

---

[6] The TRU-VU transparent mouthpiece was developed by Ellis Wean, tubist of the Vancouver Symphony Orchestra. TRU-VU transparent mouthpieces and the videotape mentioned in the text are available from Ellis Music, 510.1333 Hornby St., Vancouver, BC V6Z 2C1 Canada.

[7] Blowing outward toward a piece of paper is suggested in Dale Clevenger, Mark McDunn, and Harold Rusch, *The Dale Clevenger French Horn Methods* (Park Ridge, Ill.: Neil A. Kjos, 1974).

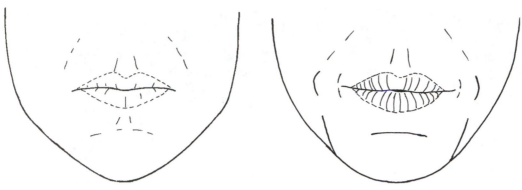

Figure 10.3. **Natural lip formation.**   Figure 10.4. **Embouchure formation.**

It is important in forming the embouchure that the corners of the mouth not be allowed to pull outward as in a smile. If this happens, the pursed "oo" formation becomes distorted and the embouchure cannot function effectively. Similarly, the cheeks must not be puffed out. This causes a similar problem as stretching the lips back into a smile, and the inflation prevents the facial musculature from supporting the embouchure formation inside the mouthpiece. The next step is to place the mouthpiece in the best position to promote pitch-vibration.

Mouthpiece placement is an important consideration because embouchure difficulties often stem from an improper placement. The mouthpiece rim should be centered horizontally on the embouchure. This is the preferred position, but it should be recognized that many successful players play slightly off-center due to variations in dental structure. The vertical placement is more critical, and this is usually described as proportions of upper and lower lip within the mouthpiece rim. These vary somewhat between instruments. An embouchure visualizer or transparent mouthpiece is helpful in checking the vertical placement. For the trumpet, an equal proportion of upper and lower lip in the mouthpiece is generally preferred, although some players use a slightly higher placement. In earlier periods, a one-third upper/two-thirds lower placement was often recommended, but this is generally not encouraged today, due to the possibility of the upper rim of the mouthpiece sliding down onto the upper lip and impeding vibration. For the horn, a two-thirds upper lip/one-third lower lip placement has always been used, and this continues to be favored today. This is necessary for the wide range covered by the horn and because of the depth of the horn mouthpiece. Most trombone, euphonium, and tuba players use a placement somewhat above half and half, but the latter is advocated by some trombonists. In addition to Figure 10.2, Figures 10.5 through 10.8 illustrate typical placements for each instrument.

After having practiced forming the embouchure and placing the mouthpiece a few times, the player is ready to produce the first sounds. This should be done first with the mouthpiece alone. In making sound on the mouthpiece, the same process is used as on the instrument. However, the mouthpiece does not provide any pitch centers; the player must create the pitch. Hold the mouthpiece at the bottom of the shank with two or three fingers and the thumb. Place the mouthpiece lightly on the embouchure. Inhale through the sides of the embouchure beyond the mouthpiece rim and blow the air out by creating wind while pronouncing "poo." Keep the "oo" going while blowing outward. A sound should result. If this does not occur the first time, keep trying. Sometimes placing a finger partially over the end of the shank or cupping the hands around the end of the shank will help to get the sound started by

Figure 10.5. **Peter Bond, Metropolitan Opera Orchestra.** *Photo: Robert Sutherland.*

increasing the resistance.[8] Alternatively, the lips can be buzzed alone by pronouncing "poo" and blowing air through them. When a reliable buzz has been achieved, go back to the mouthpiece.

Whatever pitch results, try to hold on to it. Control and stability will be gained by holding long tones through a full breath. Once notes can be played with some reliability on the mouthpiece, gradually focus on specific pitches in the middle register.[9] It is important that the pressure of the mouthpiece against the embouchure be no greater than that required to form an air seal. Excessive mouthpiece pressure thwarts the normal functioning of the embouchure and causes it to tire quickly.

A word should be said about breathing when the mouthpiece is in place on the embouchure. The most common way of doing this is to release the playing pressure of the mouthpiece against the embouchure while leaving the mouthpiece rim lightly touching the lips. Open the lips at each side of the mouthpiece and draw in the air. It is important that the embouchure not be distorted when taking in the air. Sometimes students stretch the lips backward to make an opening for the inflow of air. This alters the embouchure position within the mouthpiece so that when playing is resumed, the lips are out of position. A less common but also effective approach is to drop the jaw and bring the air in below the mouthpiece.

---

[8] Using a Buzz Extension and Resistance Piece (BERP) or Buzz Aid is often helpful to beginners in making their first sounds. The added resistance makes it easier to get the sound started. Once the player gains control over playing pitches on the mouthpiece, it is preferable to use the mouthpiece alone without any added resistance.

[9] Recommended starting pitches are given in Chapter 12, along with suggestions for teaching young beginners.

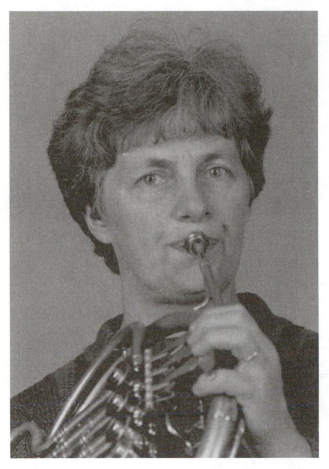

Figure 10.7. **SSgt. Steven Kellner, Principal Euphonium, United States Marine Band.** *Photo courtesy of "The President's Own" United States Marine Band, Washington, D.C.*

Figure 10.6. **Norwegian horn soloist Frøydis Ree Wekre.** *Photo courtesy of Frøydis Ree Wekre.*

Having gained some confidence in playing long tones on the mouthpiece, the next step is to learn to change pitch. This can be done on the mouthpiece by sliding back and forth from one note to another, beginning with the intervals of a major second or minor third. To change pitch on brass instruments, there are very subtle adjustments of embouchure firmness, jaw and tongue positions,[10] as well as variations in the air stream. These adjustments are too subtle and complex to control consciously. Fortunately, this is not necessary because the ability to change pitch can be learned on the mouthpiece and this will carry over to the instrument. Once the player can produce stable notes on the mouthpiece and change pitch, notes should be started with an attack (this can be done by changing the "p" to a "t" and pronouncing "too"); attack and tonguing are discussed later in this chapter. After some further practice with the mouthpiece, it is time to move to the instrument and begin

---

[10] Changes occur in the oral cavity when playing in different ranges. The rear part of the tongue rises when going from the low to the high register, thus reducing the oral cavity. The tongue flattens in returning to the low register, enlarging the oral cavity. This is usually brought about by using the syllables "ah" for the low register, "oo" for the middle, and "ee" for the high. Once the pattern is established, many brass players do not consciously think of forming syllables as they play and consider this part of an automatic process of centering the sound and pitch of various notes. Although this subject has been debated by brass players at various times, the variations in the oral cavity have been confirmed by X ray in the research of Bengt Belfrage, Mats Haverling, and Hans Bergstedt, *Practice Methods for Brass Players Based on Physiological Factors* (Stockholm: AB Nordiska Musikförlaget—Edition Wilhelm Hansen, 1982).

Figure 10.8. **Arnold Jacobs, Former Principal Tuba, Chicago Symphony Orchestra.** *Photo: Jim Steere.*

work with an elementary method or the exercises presented in Sections A and C of Chapter 12.

Attack and Tonguing

Sound commences when the embouchure vibrates in response to the motion of the air stream. After the basic "poo" formation of the embouchure is established, the tongue is used to contribute a clear and controlled beginning to the sound. It also creates different effects in how the beginnings of notes sound through the use of varied styles of attack. The way this is done is by pronouncing an "attack syllable" into the mouthpiece. "Too" ("tu") and "ta" are common syllables; these provide a clear, definite beginning to the sound. When a softer attack is desired, the syllables are pronounced less sharply, or the consonant is changed to a "d," as in "doo" ("du") or "da." The syllables can be modified from very hard to soft by pronouncing them with greater or lesser force. The sound of a musical passage is first visualized (or

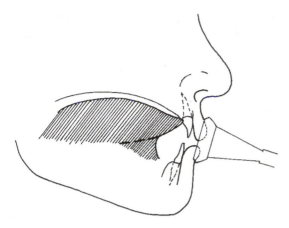

Figure 10.9. **Tongue placement.**

heard in the mind's ear) and the syllables are then pronounced with the appropriate degree of hardness. In tonguing various patterns within musical passages, a new syllable is pronounced for every tongued note.

The syllables "too" and "doo" are preferred because these syllables are related to "poo" and therefore create an effective embouchure formation as well as start the sound. However, some players find "ta" or "toe" to work better on their instruments. The best syllable for an individual to use can be determined only by trying different syllables.

It is best if inspiration, expiration, and attack are approached as a continuous action. Inspiration should flow smoothly into expiration with no stop at the changeover point. There should be no hesitation at the tongue before an attack is made. If either of these interruptions occurs, tension will probably build up in the throat and neck, impeding the free production of sound.

There is great variation between individual players in the placement of the tip of the tongue when starting attacks. So great is the variation that it is impossible to lay down firm guidelines for this aspect of tone production. Figure 10.9 illustrates a common tongue placement with the tip in the upper front corner of the mouth at the gum line of the front teeth. In actuality, however, players often place the tip of the tongue at the middle or bottom of the upper teeth or on the roof of the mouth. Some players do not think about tongue placement at all, and focus only on pronouncing the attack syllables.

To end a note, the basic procedure is to stop blowing. This is important; beginners often develop the habit of stopping the sound by replacing the tongue in its attack position with the note still sounding. This creates an unmusical and audible "thuk" sound at the end of the note. The player should listen to the end of the note carefully and end it without any sound or variation in pitch. The so-called tongued-release does have its place, however. Professional players often make use of it by pronouncing "tut" or a similar syllable in very staccato passages. This produces a shortness and crispness that can be obtained in no other way.

A very helpful practice technique for attack and tonguing that is advocated by the distinguished trumpet teacher Vincent Cichowicz is the use of "wind patterns."[11] This is done without the instrument by saying "too" on the rhythmic notation of the passage or piece. A full breath should be taken and the player should blow through

---

[11] Air patterns and other important techniques are described in Vincent Cichowicz, "Teaching the Concepts of Trumpet Playing," *The Instrumentalist* (Jan. 1996).

the notes in a sustained manner. No buzzing sound should be made, only the sound of the motion of the air in pronouncing "too." By practicing wind patterns, the player will get the feel of articulating the notes freely, without tension. This will carry over to the instrument. Wind patterns can do a lot to improve a player's attack and tonguing as well as promote a more relaxed and natural approach to the instrument.

Styles of Attack and Shaping Notes

The style or sound of the attack must be modified in accordance with the repertoire being performed. It is inconceivable to use a single style of attack throughout the repertoire. Similarly, the shape of the note must be varied to fit the stylistic characteristics of different composers. The style of attack and note shape can most easily be controlled and modified if a note is visualized as consisting of three parts: an attack, a middle portion, and a release. As has been discussed, different degrees of sharpness or smoothness can be imparted to the beginning of a note by pronouncing the attack syllable with greater or lesser force, or changing the consonant from a "t" to a "d." The middle part of the note can maintain a dynamic level that is equal to the attack, or increase or diminish after the attack, following a visualized contour that fits the musical context. The release can be abrupt, smooth, or tapered, depending on the desired effect.

To take a few examples: The style of attack and note shape used in Debussy is radically different from that used in Bruckner and Wagner. In French music (except where the composer indicates a different approach), a clear, bell-like attack should be sought, followed by an easing of the dynamic level of the middle of the note. In Bruckner and many other Germanic composers, a broader, less pronounced attack should continue into a sustained note and a tapered release. In the works of many other composers, a symmetrically shaped note is best; in this style of note, the volume remains even from the attack to the release. That is, the dynamic level of the attack, though clear, is not greater than the middle of the note or the release. This note shape should be cultivated as a player's normal approach to attacking and shaping notes. Once this is mastered, the player should carefully study representative performances of specific works and emulate the special note shapes and styles of attack used in pieces of individual composers.

Multiple Tonguing

When normal single tonguing cannot cope with the pace demanded by a passage or sounds labored, a special technique is required. By using the middle rear portion of the tongue for the second or third repetition, tonguing speed can be increased dramatically. The syllables "tu-ku," "ta-ka," "tu-tu-ku," and "ta-ta-ka" are most often recommended for this purpose.[12] The main difficulty in double and triple tonguing is achieving a quality of sound and evenness that compares favorably with single tonguing. The problem comes from less air being moved by the double and triple tonguing syllables, and a tendency to inequality caused by a certain weakness of the "k" syllable.

This can be remedied in two ways. By substituting the syllables, "da-ga" and "da-da-ga" for the usual syllables ("tu-ku," "ta-ka," etc.), the player will move more air and produce a stronger "k" syllable. The syllables should be pronounced as far to

---

[12] In certain passages, advanced players occasionally rearrange the order of triple tongue syllables to "tu-ku-tu," "ta-ka-ta," or "da-ga-da."

the front of the mouth as possible. If double and triple tonguing are practiced *slowly* and in direct comparison with single tonguing, the syllables will gain in control, clarity, and strength, promoting equality between the syllables.

Each measure or pattern in an exercise should first be single-tongued, then immediately repeated using double or triple syllables. The goal is to be unable to detect an important difference in the sound between the two procedures.

Another form of multiple tonguing is used by jazz players, especially trombonists. "Doodle" or "lah-dah" tonguing is a smoother, legato form of double tonguing. This form of articulation has been used by many jazz trombonists, and has been popularized on the trumpet by Clark Terry.[13]

Slurring

Slurring on brass instruments may be defined as moving between notes without the use of the tongue. This can be done on the harmonic series, known as a lip slur, or with the valves. The primary consideration in making a slur is that the connection between notes be smooth and without any break in the sound. It is essential to keep the air in motion between notes and it is helpful if the slur is approached as one sound going continuously into another.

Any interruption to the air flow or sound in the space between two slurred notes will ruin the quality of the slur. Valve slurs are particularly prone to this problem; care should be taken to move the air stream through the valve change. It is also important that the valve motion be quick. Slurring should first be learned on the mouthpiece. By sliding from one note to another, any break in the motion of the air or the vibration will be revealed. It is best to slide slowly between notes at first, gradually bringing the change up to the desired speed. Whenever problems with slurs occur, checking them on the mouthpiece in this way will correct the problem.

In order to obtain an even volume between slurred notes, it is necessary to increase the wind pressure when ascending to compensate for the slightly greater resistance that is encountered on the higher pitch. The air flow must also rise for descending notes to accommodate a more relaxed embouchure and lessened resistance. Sometimes it is useful (particularly in ascending) to crescendo on the lower note and let the momentum carry the sound to the higher note.

[13] Various jazz articulations and effects, including "doodle tonguing," are discussed in John McNeil, *The Art of Jazz Trumpet*, 2 vols. (Brooklyn, N.Y.: Gerard and Sarzin, 1993); Bill Watrous, *Trombonisms: An Extension of Standard Trombone Techniques and an Introduction to Some New Ones* (New York: Carl Fischer, 1983); and Jim Maxwell, *The First Trumpeter* (New York: Charles Colin, 1982).

Trombone Legato

Because the medium for changing notes is a movable slide, the subject of legato on the trombone must be treated separately. Actually, the only true slurs available on the trombone are the lip slur (moving between two different overtones of the harmonic series) and when the slide motion is opposite to the direction of the notes. The rest of the time the trombonist must depend on a refined legato tongue to create the effect of slurring. In practice, all three methods are used in one integrated technique.

What has been said concerning slurring in general applies to the trombone, particularly with lip slurs that take place in the same position. When the slide is moved, the problem of avoiding unwanted sound between notes becomes paramount. Quick slide motion is essential to avoid the slide's natural tendency to glissando.[14]

It is possible to achieve a clean slur between adjacent positions if the move involves a change from one series of harmonics to another. For example, a slur can be made from A at the top of the bass staff (second position, fourth harmonic of the series on A) to D above (first position , sixth harmonic of the series on G) without using the tongue if the slide motion is quick. Another approach is through the direction of the motion of the slide in relation to the direction of the notes. A smooth slur may be achieved if the notes move downward as the slide is brought inward. The reverse—notes ascending, outward slide motion—is effective only in the upper register.

For all other slurring, legato tonguing must be employed through the use of a soft syllable such as "du," "thu," or "loo." This is sometimes accompanied by moving the usual tongue placement to the roof of the mouth. To achieve a smooth legato it is vital to keep the air stream moving. Students sometimes hesitate with the air between notes to avoid a glissando, when the real problem is sluggish slide motion.[15] Some teachers advocate that the legato tongue should almost always be used in performance, and that natural slurs should be reserved for practice.

Range and Endurance

There is no magic secret for playing in the high register, and it does not involve a change in playing method. Rather, the high range should be viewed as the continuation of the upper middle register. It is important to remember that for each higher note added to the range, faster pitch-vibrations are required. To create progressively faster vibrations, the embouchure becomes more firm and tends to turn somewhat inward on itself, bringing the lips closer together (there are also subtle, unconscious adjustments of the jaw and oral cavity). To cause the more resistant embouchure to vibrate at the required frequency (and to overcome the acoustical megaphone effect described in Chapter 1), there must be a commensurate increase in the wind pressure and air volume. Each note requires an optimum balance of wind pressure and air volume in order to sound in tune with a free and unforced tone.[16] When this forms a basic part of one's playing method it is necessary only to continue upward, seeking the right levels of pressure and volume to create unforced pitch-vibration.

[14] Slide movement is discussed in Chapter 5.

[15] Several books of studies for trombone legato may be recommended: Joannes Rochut, *Melodious Etudes,* vols. 1–3 (Carl Fischer); André LaFosse, *Méthode Complète de Trombone à Coulisse* (Alphonse Leduc); Reginald H. Fink, *Studies in Legato for Trombone* (Carl Fischer); and Blazevich, *30 Legato Studies* (International).

[16] There is a subtle relationship in this process between wind pressure and air volume. Increasing the pressure without increasing the air volume creates tension in the throat and neck muscles. Every note requires the right balance of air quantity and outflow pressure.

Often, the increase in wind pressure and air quantity is insufficient to vibrate the more taut embouchure; this results in either no sound or a forced, bent note produced by a constricted, partial vibration. Another common upper register problem is that the embouchure overtightens for a specific pitch, resisting the air stream's effort to bring it into vibration. This is often accompanied by tension in the throat or excessive mouthpiece pressure. Sometimes, the embouchure formation is distorted by pulling back into a smile or some other contortion.

No progress in the upper register can be gained by trying to force the notes to sound.

The way to approach playing in the upper register is to integrate it into one's daily practice. The embouchure develops (along with expiratory strength) in response to the music and exercises that are played daily. Some of the regular daily exercise patterns should be continued upward to the top of the range. With each higher level, the wind pressure and air volume should be increased, allowing the embouchure to vibrate at the desired pitch without force. The goal is to produce a free, unconstricted sound. Playing the material first on the mouthpiece and then on the instrument is helpful. Each day, the exercise patterns should be taken as far upward as the notes can be played comfortably, without forcing. This should be part of a gradual program of development. If the notes are not forthcoming beyond a certain point, it is best to accept what has been accomplished for the current day and to return the next day. Over time, this approach will produce improvement in the upper range.

The player's choice of etudes and solos used in daily practice should also be integrated into a progressive plan designed to strengthen and maintain the embouchure and respiratory muscles. This is the foundation of endurance. The embouchure builds strength as it plays challenging material. The same is true of the muscles used in expiration. The great cornetist Herbert L. Clarke coined the term "wind power" in describing his method of playing. This is an excellent and fundamental concept, and it forms an underlying part of everything presented in this chapter. A player's wind power strengthens in proportion to the demands placed on it. In choosing the material to be played daily, consider the load placed on the embouchure and wind power. This should increase very gradually. If progress is forced, the embouchure will not be able to cope with it and residual fatigue will set in.

Residual fatigue occurs when the embouchure is overstressed by heavy playing. The embouchure cannot fully recover overnight and a residue of the previous day's fatigue is carried over into the next day. After several days of this, the embouchure will feel tired at the beginning of playing. When this occurs, the worst thing the player can do is to carry on with the normal routine (one hopes that this does not coincide with a performance). The second worst thing the player can do is not play at all. Both of these approaches usually make matters worse. The best thing a player can do is to practice, but limit the material played to a light workout. This allows the embouchure to regain its equilibrium, and the next day should see some recovery.

The way to good endurance is through well-chosen material arranged in a progressive program for the daily practice session.

Sustaining and Continuity

The related concepts of sustaining and continuity are underlying principles of all good brass playing. It is important that notes retain an evenness of volume. Any erosion of a note detracts from the tone and reflects a poor mastery of style. This creates ensemble problems with balance and intonation as well because it is difficult to balance notes that are uneven in volume.[17] Another very common error is to allow the note before a breath to decrease in volume (unless the musical context calls for a diminuendo). This creates an abrupt, unfinished end to one phrase and upsets the continuity between phrases. Care must be taken in practicing to develop the habit of sustaining up to the breathing point and then beginning the next phrase with a minimum of interruption. The beginnings and ends of phrases must be carefully shaped.

The concept of sustaining must be applied to phrases as well as individual notes. Brass players often speak of the need to blow through the notes. The air stream must remain constant through the phrase, with the player resisting any tendency to allow the air pressure to drop when notes are tongued or changed during a slur.

Continuity is a function of sustaining and is concerned with the coherence of the line or phrase. In legato and slurred passages, each new note should flow from the one before it without a break. This can be accomplished by approaching the phrase as one long tone. In his complete method, the nineteenth-century cornetist Saint-Jacome presented legato tonguing under the heading "Tonguing on the Sound."[18] This heading reflects a very clear concept of continuity: continuous sound uninterrupted by the tongue. Saint-Jacome's maxim might be diagrammed in the following way:

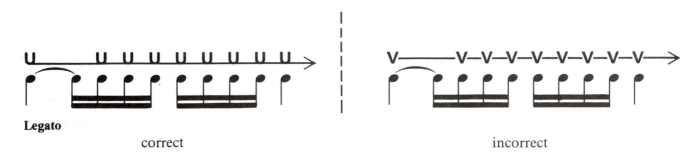

Tonguing on the sound.

Concept of Sound

A concept of sound is developed through careful listening. In the early stages, the teacher should lose no opportunity to play for and with the student. In this way elements of the teacher's tone will be transferred to the student. Although every great player has a unique and recognizable timbre and style of playing, many influences

---

[17] The importance of sustaining in ensembles is discussed in Chapter 8 under "Suggestions for Marching Band Directors" and in Chapter 14.

[18] Louis Antoine Saint-Jacome (1830–1898), *Grand Method for Trumpet or Cornet* (New York: Carl Fischer, 1894), p. 110.

have contributed to this individual quality. The process through which a personal sound is developed is by studying a variety of models. This will not only enrich a player's concept of sound, but will bring out its own special qualities.

It is inaccurate to think of sound as a single entity. Actually, the timbre must be modified according to the repertoire being performed. What may be appropriate in one context may not be in another. By meticulous observation of how representative players and brass sections approach specific works (via recordings, concerts, and broadcasts), an overall concept of sound and interpretive style can be formed.

Mental imagery plays a vital role in this process. By visualizing in the mind a clear image of the sound, the player guides the physical aspects of tone production to reproduce that sound.[19]

Vibrato

Vibrato should be viewed as a means of bringing added color to the sound. There are some contexts where it applies, and some where it does not. For example, in the author's view, the horn should never be played with vibrato because it adds nothing to the expressiveness of the timbre and robs the horn of its purity and natural beauty. With other members of the brass family, vibrato can add character and sensitivity when used in specific areas of the repertoire, but the majority of the literature should be played with a pure, vibratoless tone. It is important that a good sound be produced first without vibrato. With that as a basis from which to work, the player can add vibrato in specific works to lend expression and style without marring the essential quality of sound. Vibrato must be controlled and its speed should be varied within different musical contexts. In French music, for example, a light, quick vibrato gives the right color to the sound. In Russian works, a slightly slower, deeply expressive vibrato adds character to the music. The player should carefully study great performances of important works and consider what type of vibrato should be used, if any.

There are four types of vibrato currently in use: hand, diaphragm, slide, and lip/jaw.

Hand vibrato, which is effective only on the trumpet and cornet, is created by a gentle forward and backward movement of the right thumb resting on the bottom of the leadpipe. Because of its ease of control, it is the preferred means of vibrato on the cornet and trumpet.

Diaphragm vibrato consists of pulsations in the air stream (similar to that used on the flute). Although it can be effective, it tends to be difficult to control and consequently is rarely used on brass instruments.

Slide vibrato is commonly used by trombonists in the jazz and studio fields and it is also occasionally used by symphonic players. Less subtle than vibrato produced by the lip and jaw (which is more commonly used on the trombone), it is produced by moving the slide slightly inward and outward according to the desired speed.

Lip/jaw vibrato involves a subtle movement of the embouchure and jaw. It is the principal type of vibrato used on low brass instruments. Although it can

[19] See William H. Trusheim, "Mental Imagery and Musical Performance: An Inquiry into Imagery Use by Eminent Orchestral Brass Players" (Ed.D. dissertation, Rutgers University, 1987) and Dee Stewart, *Arnold Jacobs: The Legacy of a Master.* Another book that presents concepts of mental imagery is Paul Severson and Mark McDunn, *Brass Wind Artistry* (Athens, Ohio: Accura Music, 1983).

also be applied to the trumpet, it tends to be heavy and less easily controlled than hand vibrato. Symphonic trombonists generally prefer lip/jaw vibrato for most of their work, but have a perfected slide vibrato available when the repertoire calls for it.

Special Effects

Composers sometimes call upon brass players to produce specialized sounds. Two of the most common are the flutter tongue and the glissando. The flutter tongue is produced by thinking of rolling an "R" and allowing the tongue tip to vibrate as the air passes into the instrument. It is most effective in the middle range.

On valved brass instruments, when an obvious glissando effect is called for, lowering the valves halfway and sliding upward or downward usually gives the best results. Composers sometimes indicate when a valve glissando is to be used. Expressive glissandi of shorter duration can be rendered by elongating a slur or, if a less subtle effect is desired, by allowing the valves to come up with a deliberately slow action. Trombonists are often required to produce a slide glissando; this technique is discussed in Chapter 5.

New effects are occasionally found in the works of contemporary composers. These include singing or hissing through the instrument, playing with the water key open, and raising or lowering the pitch by the hand in the horn bell, among others.

How to Warm Up and Practice Effectively

The warm-up is an important element of brass playing. This is the time when all of the playing functions are brought into good condition before being applied to the demands of the literature. To plunge straight into a rehearsal or performance without adequate preparation is to invite difficulties. The warm-up should be extended, whenever time allows, to include basic exercises covering all phases of playing. These daily studies form both the basis of the player's progress and the maintenance of skills already developed.

There are two approaches to warming up. Some brass players favor a flexible warm-up, choosing material at random. Others (and the author falls in this group) base their daily warm-up on a series of exercises that have been designed to bring the player's tone production up to peak form gradually. The flexible approach allows the player to vary the material according to the condition of the embouchure and the time available, but this can also be done with the routine approach by having a variety of daily exercises available. A common point between the two approaches is to avoid forcing the embouchure through material when it is not up to it (due to heavy playing or a layoff). In such cases, it is better to work slowly and patiently, selecting the material in accordance with the condition of the embouchure. The goal is to try to bring the embouchure into condition gradually. It is important that the player plan the warm-up time carefully. If this involves traveling to a rehearsal or concert, one should arrive early enough to have a calm, unhurried time period in which to warm up. When there is too little time for this, the player often must begin the rehearsal or concert with a feeling of not being completely warmed up, a frame of mind not conducive to confidence.

At the beginning of the warm-up, some time should be devoted to playing on the mouthpiece alone. This helps center the pitch and stimulates a free production of sound. The mouthpiece might be played every so often as the warm-up and practice session develop. Fluency is encouraged if the first portion of the warm-up consists of slurred material. This should begin in the middle register and gradually work into the upper and lower ranges. After the instrument is responding easily and consistently, various tongued exercises may be added. By the end of the warm-up period, the entire compass should have been covered.

For those taking the flexible approach, warm-up material may be selected from various studies, melodies, intervals, scales, and arpeggios or it can be improvised. Those who take the routine approach usually write or excerpt special material that (while offering a selection) is organized in a progressive arrangement.[20] The goal of the warm-up is to get the wind moving freely and the notes responding easily throughout the range with a full, centered tone. This should be achieved with an overall feeling of relaxation in the production of sound.

Practice should be organized around a planned program of development. This should consist of daily work on basic skills, such as slurring, tonguing, multiple tonguing, scales and arpeggios, and flexibility, with any weak areas singled out for special attention. Those striving for orchestral careers should also incorporate transposition into their daily work. The second part of the practice session might be devoted to systematically working through important study literature for the instrument. There is immense value in etudes, many of which were written by great players of the past. The variety of technical and musical challenges presented will expand one's ability to play the instrument in a way no other literature can. The final portion of practice may include study of solo works, orchestral or band excerpts or parts, brass quintet or ensemble parts, and sight reading.

Flexibility is the key to successful practicing. The order of the practice session may be varied or portions omitted. Practice may be lengthened or shortened as necessary. At all times, the player should work patiently, stressing good tone production. Objectivity is needed to evaluate one's performance. Occasionally recording the practice session or segments of it can be helpful. Although areas needing improvement should be noted, it is also important in the interest of building confidence to acknowledge when something is played well. Accuracy can be developed only through repetition, but it is of no use to practice beyond the tiring point. The best results are achieved by working in a relaxed but thorough manner, always concentrating on establishing a solid foundation to one's playing while building confidence.

---

[20] Warm-up and daily study material can be excerpted from Max Schlossberg, *Daily Drills and Technical Studies* (M. Baron); Herbert L. Clarke, *Technical Studies* and *Clarke's Setting Up Drills* (Carl Fischer); Pierre Levet, *La technique journaliere du corniste* (Lemoine); Frøydis Ree Wekre, *Thoughts on Playing the Horn Well* (Wekre); Remington, *Warm-up Studies* (Accura); Bell, *William Bell Daily Routine for Tuba* (Encore); and Bobo, *Mastering the Tuba*, 3 vols. (Bim). With adjustments, many of the studies contained in the above books can be used with all brass instruments, or individual studies can be developed for specific instruments based on them.

CHAPTER 11

Playing Position

In the early stages of playing, the importance of the playing position is not always stressed or recognized. In actuality, however, how the body is positioned when playing a brass instrument is the starting point of good tone production.

Two vital factors must be considered. First, if there is to be free movement of the air during inhalation and exhalation, the body must be positioned in an upright posture so that the natural expansion and reduction of the thorax can take place without restriction. It is essential not to lean on the back of the chair when playing in a seated position because this obstructs the rotational elevation and expansion of the rib cage. Any forward curvature of the posture interferes with the breathing process and creates tension; this impedes the inflow of air on inspiration and reduces the quantity that can be inhaled. On exhalation such a curvature constricts the outward motion of the air. The second vital factor is the need for overall relaxation in both taking in and blowing out the air. An upright but relaxed posture is the first requirement in learning to play a brass instrument.

Carefully study the photographs of leading professional players in this chapter. All of the essentials of playing position are clearly revealed in these photographs. When playing, try to imitate the positions shown.

Trumpet and Cornet

The trumpet or cornet is supported by the left hand, which lightly grips the valve casings (see Figures 11.1 through 11.5). How the fingers are positioned around the valve casing varies among professional players, but in general the third or little finger should be placed in the ring on the third valve slide. Place the thumb in the ring on the first valve slide or around the trigger if one is present; otherwise, the thumb should wrap around the valve casing. Position the tips of the fingers of the right hand over and lightly touching the valve caps. In order to press the valves straight down, the fingers must be curved. Turn the right thumb upward and rest it on the bottom of the leadpipe; this helps to balance and support the instrument. Better valve action will be achieved if the little finger is kept free of the ring on the leadpipe, but many players do at least rest it on the ring.

The instrument should be held fairly straight or at a slight downward angle. Only the minimum effort necessary to hold the instrument should be used, and the arms must remain as relaxed as possible. Remember to always sit in an upright position and not lean against the back of the chair. Practice time should be divided between sitting and standing.

Young players often point the instrument directly into the music stand and attempt to read over the bell. Aside from the negative effect on the sound, this habit

Figure 11.1. **Playing position (trumpet): Charles Schlueter, Principal Trumpet, Boston Symphony Orchestra.** *Photo: Steven A. Emery.*

Figure 11.2. **Playing position (trumpet): British trumpeter Philip Jones.** *Photo courtesy of Decca Records International.*

tends to cause the trumpet to pull downward and the jaw to recede, affecting the embouchure. The solution is to place the stand slightly to the side or lower it so that it does not obstruct the radiation of sound from the bell.

Figure 11.3. **Playing position (trumpet): George Coble, First Trumpet, Syracuse Symphony Orchestra.** *Photo courtesy of George Coble.*

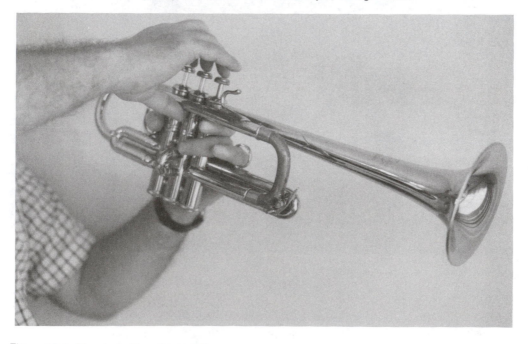

Figure 11.4. **Hand position (trumpet).**

Figure 11.5. **Playing position (trumpet): Peter Bond, Metropolitan Opera Orchestra.** *Photo: Robert Sutherland.*

Horn

Of all the brass, the horn is the most susceptible to poor playing positions. Due to the horn's unique rear-radiating shape, the bell can easily be blocked by the body, resulting in a dull, nonresonant timbre; with the bell resting on the thigh, there can be a tendency to slump over the horn, diminishing the player's air capacity and hindering efficient respiration.

There are two methods of holding the horn: keeping the body upright and holding the bell free, and resting the bell on the right thigh. The upright position has long been standard in Britain and European countries and is rapidly growing in the United States, notably in the Chicago Symphony Orchestra and other orchestras (Figures 11.6 through 11.8). This position has a definite advantage in that it allows the horn to be brought to the embouchure naturally and the body to maintain an

Figure 11.6. **Two views of playing position (horn): Dale Clevenger, Principal Horn, Chicago Symphony Orchestra.** *Photos: Jim Steere.*

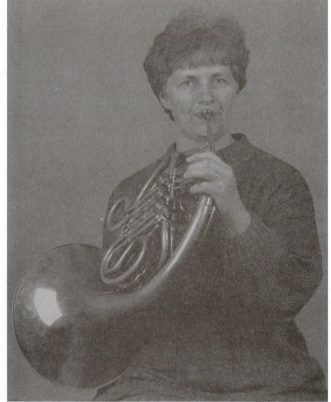

Figure 11.7. **Two views of playing position (horn): Norwegian soloist Frøydis Ree Wekre.** *Photos courtesy of Frøydis Ree Wekre.*

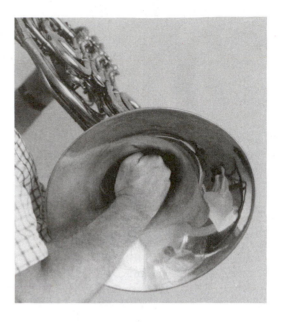

Figure 11.10. **Right hand position (horn).**
Photo: Joseph Hetman.

Figure 11.8. **Playing position (horn): soloist Barry Tuckwell.** *Photo: Fritz Curzon.*

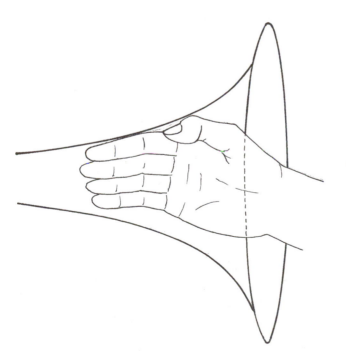

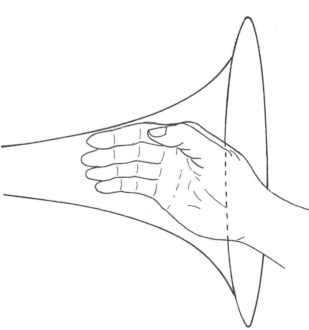

Figure 11.9. **Right hand positions (horn).**

upright posture. This allows the respiratory system to function optimally. The timbre retains all of its partials, thus producing color and resonance in the sound that projects well in the concert hall. By resting the bell on the right thigh, partials are absorbed; this damps some of the resonance of the sound, creating a more covered, blending quality.

In using either playing position, turn the chair slightly to the right. This enables the entire circumference of the bell to clear the body so that the sound can project rearward without obstruction. For those resting the bell, turning the chair allows the right leg to be brought back to a point where the bell rim can rest comfortably on top of the thigh.

The first three fingers of the left hand should be curved over the valve levers (the little finger may rest in the hook). The left thumb should rest on the B♭ valve lever on double horns, or in the ring on single F horns.

The right hand position is of critical importance in influencing response, tone, and intonation. The hand should be slightly cupped, with the thumb resting either on top of the fingers or alongside the index finger (see Figures 11.9 and 11.10). This seemingly small difference in the placement of the thumb actually makes an important difference in how the horn plays and sounds.

By moving the thumb from on top of the index finger to beside it, the hand goes slightly farther into the bell, darkening the tone somewhat and altering the pitch of some of the notes. Placing the thumb on top of the index finger makes sense acoustically because the purpose of the hand is to narrow and extend the bell throat. With the thumb on top, the hand forms a more effective wall within the bell throat. But it keeps the hand in a position farther out in the bell taper. This also affects intonation, response, and timbre. Due to the great variation in hand size and the different bell throats in use (medium, large, and extra large), no rule can be laid down for the position of the thumb. The player must try both thumb placements and determine which works best for his or her hand and the horn being used.

Sealing any space between the fingers (as in swimming), place the hand vertically into the bell. The back of the hand (where the knuckles are) must rest against the bell's far wall. The free space between the palm of the hand and the near wall can be closed down or opened to control intonation, as well as change the tone from a more covered quality to a brighter timbre. Opening the hand raises the pitch, and closing it lowers the pitch. A helpful way to find the right degree of "cover" is to close the bell so that the tone is somewhat muffled and gradually open it until a resonant, clear sound results. Then, go past this point until the tone becomes harsh and sharp. Finally, go gradually back to the best-sounding position; this procedure will define for the player the desirable degree of "cover" to be used.

There are several problems that often occur with horn students. Aside from incorrectly forming the right hand position, students often unconsciously allow the hand to shift away from the outer bell wall, causing a muffled tone. Another common problem is when the horn is held so that the mouthpipe approaches the embouchure at too straight an angle. On the horn, the mouthpiece and mouthpipe must assume a slightly downward angle (see Figure 11.6). By holding the horn so that the bell is perpendicular, or tilted only slightly backward, the player will automatically find the proper angle of the mouthpipe. Sometimes the horn is simply too large for a youngster to hold correctly. The only solution is to gradually perfect the position as the student grows, although it would be helpful if manufacturers constructed student instruments in a more compactly wrapped pattern.

It should be noted that horn players are expected to stand when playing a solo, as the tone can be projected more clearly and a better visual impression is created. It

Figure 11.11. **Two views of playing position (trombone): Jay Friedman, Principal Trombone, Chicago Symphony Orchestra.** *Photo: Jim Steere.*

is wise, therefore, to occasionally practice standing. In the standing position, care should be taken that the right hand position does not change.

Trombone

The full weight of the trombone must be supported by the left hand and arm so that the right arm is free of tension and able to move the slide quickly from position to position. Place the left index finger on the mouthpiece shank or receiver and form the remaining fingers around the inner slide brace and the cork barrel. The left thumb should grasp the bottom of the bell brace, or the rotary valve lever on instruments fitted with F attachments.

With the right hand, hold the outer slide brace between the thumb and first two fingers. Usually, the third and fourth fingers curl under the lower portion of the slide. The slide is controlled through a combination of finger, wrist, and forearm motion.

The most natural playing position for the trombonist is with the instrument held at a slight downward angle. Be careful not to lean the head to one side or the other.

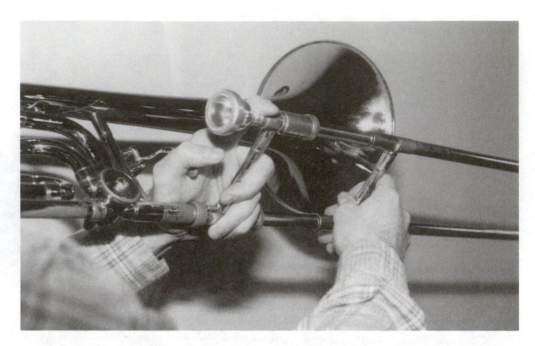

Figure 11.12. **Hand position (trombone).** *Photo: Joseph Hetman.*

Keep the head erect and bring the trombone to the embouchure rather than adapting the body to fit the instrument. (See Figures 11.11 and 11.12.)

Music stands often cause difficulties for trombonists. The best location for the player and the slide is to the left of the stand. The music can be read by looking to the right. The tone will project more resonantly with the bell clear of the stand.

SLIDE POSITIONS

The trombone slide has been compared to a violin string. It is continuously variable in pitch, so the exact placement of a position must be determined by careful listening. Some basic visual guidelines may be offered as a starting point, but these should not be taken as absolute because there are variations among instruments and individual players.

Some of the positions are more clearly defined on the slide than others. The first, third, fourth, and sixth positions are fairly easy to locate. Less obvious are the second, fifth, and seventh positions, which require even greater reliance on the ear to place them precisely. (See Figures 11.13 to 11.19.)

There is some tendency to place the second position high (sharp), particularly when it occurs on a leading tone. The fifth position is rather awkward and depends heavily on the ear to find its exact center. Intonation problems are sometimes encountered in ensemble playing with this position. A good way to locate it is to match the fifth-position B♭ to the first-position B♭. Advanced players usually play the notes produced by the sixth and seventh positions in first and (altered) second position on the F attachment. However, it is unwise for students to develop a dependency on the F attachment. Comparable ease and confidence should be sought on the longer positions as on the shorter ones.

Figure 11.13. **Trombone, first position: Slide fully in, lightly touching the corks or springs.**

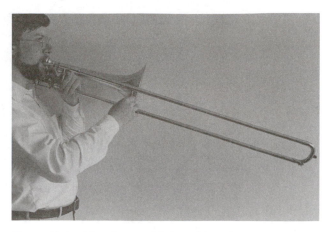

Figure 11.14. **Trombone, third position: brace slightly above the bell rim.**

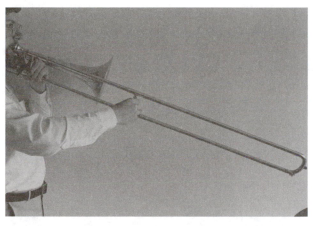

Figure 11.15. **Trombone, fourth position: top of outer slide below the bell rim.**

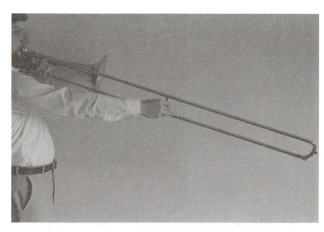

Figure 11.16. **Trombone, sixth position: a comfortable arm's length.**

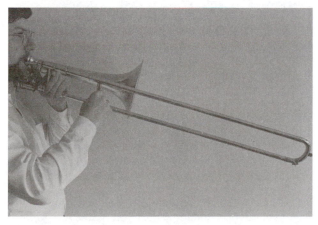

Figure 11.17. **Trombone, second position: approximately one-third the distance between first and third positions.**

Figure 11.18. **Trombone, fifth position: approximately halfway between fourth and sixth positions.**

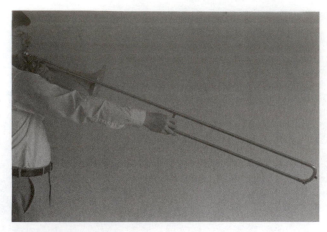

Figure 11.19. **Trombone, seventh position: a stretched arm's length, exposing the slide stocking (boot).**

Baritone and Euphonium

The baritone or euphonium should be held diagonally across the body with the lower bow pressed in to the waist to provide stability (Figures 11.20 and 11.21). It is important for the mouthpiece to be brought upward to the embouchure rather than

Figure 11.20. **Playing position (euphonium): Ssgt. Steven Kellner, Principal Euphonium, United States Marine Band.** *Photo courtesy of "The President's Own" United States Marine Band, Washington, D.C.*

Figure 11.21. **Playing position (euphonium): Brian Bowman, euphonium soloist, United States Air Force Band.** *Photo courtesy of Dr. Brian Bowman.*

Figure 11.22. **Two views of playing position (tuba): Arnold Jacobs, former Principal Tuba, Chicago Symphony Orchestra.** *Photo: Jim Steere.*

allowing the instrument to rest on the lap or chair. If the instrument is too low, the player must bend forward to reach the mouthpiece, thereby restricting breathing. If necessary, a pillow, folded towel, or specially made stand[1] should be used to bring the instrument to the correct height. Mouthpiece pressure must also be monitored to make certain that the embouchure is not being used to help support the instrument.

On instruments with three top-action valves, round the fingers of the right hand and place them over the valve caps beneath the upper bow. The left arm must reach across the lower bow and grip some of the tubing on the right side. When a compensating fourth valve is located on the side, use the left index or middle finger to depress the valve. It is important that the left hand completely support the weight of the instrument so that the fingers of the right hand are free to press the valves.

On top-action designs having four in-line valves, the player has the option of placing all four fingers over the valves or operating the fourth valve with the left index finger, as it is used in compensating models with the fourth valve at the side. The latter approach has an advantage, because coordination is less effective between the middle and little finger. By using the left index finger, fourth valve action is usually improved.

[1] The Stewart Stand is designed for this purpose. A model is available for both euphonium and tuba.

On euphoniums with side-action valves, bring the right arm to the front of the instrument and grip the left side of the top bow with the left hand. If rings are provided on the tuning or valve slides to adjust intonation, the left hand may rest on one of these.

Tuba

The tuba should rest on the lap or the front of the chair and be stabilized by the left arm and a gentle tension between the thighs (Fig. 11.22). On tubas with top-action valves, place the fingers of the right hand over the valve caps. The left hand should grasp any tubing that can be comfortably reached on the right front of the instrument.

The right arm must reach around to the front of rotary and side-action (front-action) piston tubas, where the fingers rest on the valve levers or caps. Place the thumb in the ring; it is important that no tension (resulting from weight) be felt at the thumb, hand, or arm in order to promote good finger dexterity. The left hand should grasp the first valve slide, which is moved in controlling intonation.

Some students have difficulty reaching the mouthpiece on larger tubas; in such cases, the player should use a cushion or some other means of bringing the embouchure and mouthpiece into alignment. There should be no tendency to lean back into the chair or curve the torso. Some tubists feel that leaning the instrument slightly forward assists the free movement of the air and provides a greater feeling of control, but this is debatable.

CHAPTER 12

Getting Started

Teaching Young Beginners

Before teaching begins, it is vital to make certain that students are provided with good-quality instruments and mouthpieces. Too often a youngster has to struggle with equipment that would present difficulties to an advanced player. At any level, brass players are dependent on their equipment. Mouthpieces, especially, are of concern, and those supplied with rental instruments are often less than satisfactory. This is particularly so with horn mouthpieces: Some commonly found examples actually make learning to play the horn more difficult. The teacher should specify the mouthpieces that are to be provided with rental instruments, and the school should, if necessary, purchase appropriate mouthpieces to be lent to students. It is also advisable to furnish parents with a list of recommended mouthpieces before they purchase an instrument (sometimes retailers will substitute a mouthpiece of the customer's choice for the one that normally comes with the instrument).

In selecting mouthpieces suitable for beginners, the main requirements are that the mouthpiece respond easily and that it produce a characteristic tone. Mouthpieces of medium cup diameter and depth are best for this purpose. Small or large mouthpieces should be avoided at this stage. A recommended list of suitable mouthpieces for young beginners is provided in Chapter 2, along with a discussion of the elements involved in selecting a mouthpiece.

After making sure that a workable mouthpiece is provided, check each instrument to determine whether it is of reasonable quality and in acceptable condition. The following is a checklist that the teacher may follow in making this assessment:

1. *Mouthpiece.* Is the mouthpiece among the recommended models? If not, is it suitable for a beginning student?

   The throat and backbore should be clean. Instructions for cleaning brass instruments are presented in Chapter 13.
   There should be no dents at the bottom of the shank.
   There should be no scrapes or gouges on the mouthpiece rim.
   The plating should be in good condition.
   The shank must fit the instrument's receiver.

2. *Valves.* The valves should be checked to see whether they move freely.

   If the instrument seems blocked up and does not play, check to see whether each piston is in the correct valve casing (this is discussed in Chapter 13).
   Valve casings should be free of dents.

If the instrument plays, but the response and tone are uneven, valve alignment should be checked. This is especially important on rotary valve instruments. Valve alignment is discussed in Chapter 13.

Frayed or broken strings on rotary valves should be replaced.

On horns, the height of rotary valve keys should be adjusted to fit the students' hands. See Chapter 13.

The left hand grip on the horn should not be too wide (from the little finger ring to the thumb ring or valve lever) for small hands. If necessary, the little finger ring can be moved by a repair technician.

The valves should be oiled.

3. *Slides.*

   Tuning and valve slides should move freely. All slides should be lubricated.

   The trombone slide should move smoothly without binding and be free of dents. The slide should be lubricated following the suggestions in Chapter 13.

4. *Dents.* There should be no dents in critical areas of the tubing such as the leadpipe.

5. *Water keys.* The water key spring and pad should be checked to be certain that an airtight seal is formed.

6. *Cases.* Instrument cases must provide adequate protection. Many dents are caused by the instrument not fitting tightly inside the case. Also, there must be a secure place for the mouthpiece and other accessories so that nothing is loose inside the case that could dent the instrument.

Above all, the teacher should play each instrument to evaluate both condition and quality. The first consideration is whether the instrument's air seal is acceptable. Excessive wear of the valves and slides will cause leaking, which affects the instrument's response and tone. This can usually be detected as the instrument is played. A sluggish response, particularly in the upper register, combined with a dull and uneven tone are indications that the instrument may be leaking (although faulty valve alignment or a deficient water key seal can also cause these symptoms). A leaking condition can be corrected, but it represents a major repair of considerable expense. If all of the previous criteria have been successfully met, the teacher should test intonation, response, tone quality, and evenness from register to register. Once the teacher is confident that the instruments to be used by the class are satisfactory, teaching should begin.

Elementary Brass Classes

Classes composed of the same instrument are generally more successful at the elementary level than classes of mixed instruments. The size of the class should be kept small because of the need for individual attention. In programs where private lessons can be offered as part of the regular curriculum, it is advisable to start students in pairs to take advantage of the positive motivation that results from the natural interaction between students.

Although some texts lay great stress on how students should be selected for instrumental classes, it is difficult to predict with accuracy whether a student will be successful on a particular brass instrument. Aside from reasonable pitch discrimination, the primary considerations are the type of lip structure and the teeth. Students who have a larger, thicker lip structures are usually better suited to the low brass rather than the horn or trumpet, but there are many exceptions. Perfectly even teeth are not essential, but protruding or missing teeth can cause problems. Far more important than physical factors are a student's interest and desire to learn combined with motivation to practice.

THE FIRST LESSON

No rigid plans should be set for the first few lessons. Better results are gained if the teacher is free to approach each lesson flexibly, responding to the needs of the students and following a personal teaching style. The chief goal of the first lesson is to get each student to produce sound. This should begin with the mouthpiece alone. The first step might be to explain that sound is created on brass instruments by pitch-vibration. Pitch-vibration is made by blowing air through the lips formed in an embouchure in the mouthpiece. The best way to convey embouchure formation is to ask the students to bring their upper and lower teeth into alignment, leaving a small space for the air. Form the lips as if saying "poo." To establish the feeling of blowing a stream of air outward, have each student hold a piece of paper about one foot in front of the lips and blow at the paper, causing it to bend outward, while forming the lips as if saying "too." Keep the "too" going until the air runs out. (The "oo" in "too" brings the facial musculature into the semi-puckered formation necessary for vibration and creates a cushion for the mouthpiece to rest on.) This little exercise also gets the students to blow a fast stream of air to an external point, thereby giving them the feeling of moving air as "wind." After experimenting with this exercise a few times, the teacher should show the students how to place the mouthpiece correctly for each instrument following the guidelines presented in Chapter 10. As the students practice placing the mouthpiece, the teacher should remind them to keep a small space between the teeth for the air to pass through, as they did in the paper exercise.

PRODUCING SOUND

With the mouthpiece, the teacher should demonstrate a buzz and have the students try to imitate that sound. By forming the lips as if saying "poo" and blowing wind into the mouthpiece, the students should be able to make a sound. It is not important what pitch is produced at this point, as long as some sound is made. The objective is to have students experience that sound is produced by vibration, and that vibration is caused by the motion of the air through the lips.[1] The next step is to try to lengthen the mouthpiece buzz, making a long, steady note. It is important to remind the students to blow the air freely outward, as they did when blowing the paper outward. Very gradually, the teacher should guide the buzzing toward the following middle-register pitches (holding them as long as possible):

[1] Some very useful advice on teaching beginning brass players was presented in two lectures by Arnold Jacobs at the Second International Brass Congress at Indiana University in 1984. Texts of the lectures appear in M. Dee Stewart, *Arnold Jacobs: The Legacy of a Master* (Northfield, Ill.: The Instrumentalist Publishing Co., 1987), pp. 127–143. Many of the ideas presented here are based on concepts of Mr. Jacobs.

Occasionally, a student is found who has difficulty making any sound on the mouthpiece. This is often caused by the lips being too far apart in the mouthpiece to vibrate. This can be corrected by having the student form the lips as if saying "poo" without the mouthpiece, and blow air through them, creating a buzzing sound. The teacher might demonstrate how to buzz the lips alone or into an embouchure visualizer (cutaway rim) and ask the student to imitate that sound. Once the student can make the lips buzz in some fashion, it should be possible to transfer the feeling of vibration to the mouthpiece. (In general, buzzing the lips without the mouthpiece should be limited to a few minutes a day because the lips function differently when the mouthpiece and instrument are used. Also, there can be a tendency for tension to develop in the throat when the lips are buzzed for long periods of time without the resistance of the mouthpiece or instrument.) There are ways of making mouthpiece buzzing easier in the early stages. Placing the tip of the index finger slightly over the end of the mouthpiece shank adds a little resistance that helps to stimulate a buzz; alternatively, a BERP or Buzz-Aid could be used.

CHANGING PITCH AND STARTING THE SOUND

Once there is some stability in the middle-register pitches, the teacher should show the students how to slide the buzzing sound upward and downward by a note or two with a glissando effect. Again, the students should try imitating the teacher's sound. Specific pitches are not important, but each student should experience the feeling of moving the pitch of the buzzing sound upward and downward.

This is an appropriate time to introduce the idea of starting the sound with the tongue, using a "too" syllable rather than "poo." In presenting this skill, however, it is important to emphasize that it is the air that starts the sound; the role of the tongue is to help give a clear beginning to the sound. The tongue should not be used to stop the sound because this makes an audible noise at the end of the note. The best way of ending a note is to stop blowing.

TRANSFERRING SOUND MAKING TO THE INSTRUMENT

The students should now be ready to transfer the sound making to the instrument. The teacher should first demonstrate how to assemble the instrument (instrument assembly is discussed below). Next, it is important to establish a good playing position with each student following the recommendations and observing the photographs in Chapter 11.

In making the first sounds on the instrument, it is best not to insist that students begin on predetermined pitches. Although the notes shown above are good starting tones and many students will have no difficulty carrying over the mouthpiece pitch to the instrument, if a student seems inclined to produce a higher or lower pitch, it is better to work with this note. Once some pitch is produced, the student can gradually be guided to one of the recommended starting tones. A good way of beginning the process is for the teacher to play a sound on the instrument and ask the students to try to imitate it. As before, each note should be held as long as possible. This portion of the lesson should be directed to having the students play as many long tones as possible.

If a transparent mouthpiece is available, it would be helpful to reinforce the concept of pitch-vibration by playing a note and allowing the students to observe the vibration taking place in the mouthpiece. This provides the student with a visual image of how sound is made on a brass instrument. An even greater impression will be made by asking the student to play on a transparent mouthpiece while looking into a mirror. This will help establish the concept of moving air to create vibration in the student's mind from the beginning of the student's playing experience.

AURAL IMAGERY

One of the most important processes involved with learning to play a brass instrument is the formation of aural images. Research on mental imagery and brass performance has shown that sound memory and imitation are powerful tools that guide the development of the player.[2] One of the most effective things the teacher can do, therefore, is to demonstrate a poor sound on the instrument and follow it with a good sound. This initiates a clear sound image in the mind of the student. This image will be recalled when the student attempts to produce sound. By imitating the teacher's sound, a student's mental sound image functions like a guidance system in directing the physical aspects of sound production. It is beneficial to use the technique of demonstration and imitation frequently in beginning classes. When the teacher creates both a satisfactory and an unsatisfactory sound, a more clearly defined picture of what to strive for is conveyed to students.

BREATHING

It is important right from the beginning to form the habit of working with sufficient air. With young beginners it is not necessary to explain the intricacies of how the respiratory system functions as it is applied to playing brass instruments. What is needed is a means of getting the student to take in a large volume of air and blow it out without tension or restriction. A very little explanation is helpful; for example, explain that respiration consists of expansion and reduction, that the rib cage is flexible and expands with the intake of air, and that the middle of the body also expands as the diaphragm contracts downward to create more space for the lungs to fill with air. But the best means to get the student to use the air effectively is to use a mental image of a quantity of air to be inhaled. An inflated balloon, a plastic bag, or a ball can be used to define a quantity of air. The author's image of a mass of air the size of a basketball works very well for teenagers and adults (see Chapter 11). A suitably smaller image should probably be used by youngsters, but it should be large enough to encourage them to take in a sufficient amount of air. By visualizing an external quantity of air as a finite form, students will be able to inhale a comparatively large amount of air in the most natural and effective way. It is of vital importance in this process for the body to be relaxed when the air is taken in.

Teachers often warn students not to raise their shoulders when breathing. Although students do sometimes make large chest and shoulder motions in inhaling without bringing in much air, there will be some upward motion of the shoulders if a large amount of air is taken in correctly (this is caused by the upward and outward rotation and expansion of the rib cage). If the emphasis is placed on taking in a mass of air that is determined by a visual image and the body is allowed to expand naturally, the resultant motion at the shoulders should be viewed as normal. It could also be mentioned that the lungs fill from the bottom upward; as the air fills the upper parts of the chest cavity, the shoulder areas will be elevated somewhat.

Natural means should also be used in blowing the air out. The body knows innately how to expel air from the lungs (this ability was called on in the blown-paper exercise). All that is necessary is to encourage the student to blow a fast stream of air as *wind* without holding back the outflow or creating tension by setting muscles in a rigid way. The focus should be to blow an abundant quantity of air and allow the body to accomplish this goal in its own natural way. (The various approaches to expiration can be explored once the student has reached a more advanced level.) It

---

[2] See William H. Trusheim, "Mental Imagery and Musical Performance: An Inquiry into Imagery Use by Eminent Orchestral Brass Players" (Ed.D. dissertation, Rutgers University, 1987).

might be helpful to again stress that respiration on brass instruments is composed of expansion to bring the air in and reduction to move the air out.

THE END OF THE FIRST LESSON

Toward the end of the lesson, some attention should be given to connecting the sounds being produced with their notation. After giving practice instructions and the assignment for the next lesson, the teacher should briefly review the basic fundamentals presented in the lesson. If these principles are summarized at the end of the lesson, the students will tend to keep them in mind during practice. The lesson might conclude by demonstrating the proper method of lubricating the valves or trombone slide (see Chapter 13), removing accumulated condensation, disassembling the instrument, and placing it correctly in the case.

THE SECOND LESSON

The second lesson should begin with a very brief review of the fundamentals covered in the first class. It is important to have the students play early in this lesson to take advantage of their natural eagerness to make sound. A main goal of the lesson is for the teacher to carefully observe the students to make certain that each individual is following the teacher's instructions and to watch for problems. Potential problems are as follows:

Incorrect mouthpiece placement

> *Beware especially of a too-low placement that causes the upper rim to rest on the red part of the upper lip. (Horn students, in particular, often start with the mouthpiece placed too low on the upper lip; it is essential to use the conventional two-third upper, one-third lower placement.)*

Stretched embouchure

> *Watch for students pulling the lips outward in forming the embouchure. Forming the embouchure as if saying "poo" or "too" will prevent this.*
> *Students sometimes stretch the embouchure when taking a breath.*

Puffed-out (inflated) cheeks

Poor playing position

Not taking a large enough breath

Excessive mouthpiece pressure

The objectives of the second lesson are to add more notes, to change pitch, and to begin to learn simple tunes. Using the technique of demonstration and imitation, the teacher should have the students play various notes on the mouthpiece, holding each note as long as possible. More middle-range notes should be added to those attempted in the first lesson. Next, the teacher should demonstrate changing pitch with the mouthpiece and ask the students to try to imitate this sound. Once the students are able to change pitch to some degree, simple tunes in the middle register can be introduced (although this may not be possible until subsequent lessons). Buzzing melodies on the mouthpiece is of great value; it brings together all of the factors involved in tone production in a framework that is first conceived in the mind. In this way, playing tunes on the mouthpiece stimulates the basic aural–mental process that is used in brass playing of visualizing a musical sound and then attempting to produce it. The practice of playing melodies on the mouthpiece should continue through the most advanced stages.

After spending some time with the mouthpiece, the class should move to the instruments and begin working on some basic progressive material for the remainder of the lesson. For this purpose, one of the elementary methods listed in Chapters 3 through 7 or a band method could be used. Alternatively, the teacher could create some original exercises or use the material presented in Sections A and C of this chapter. At the conclusion of the lesson, the teacher should observe how each student disassembles the instrument and places it in the case, offering any necessary corrections.

SUBSEQUENT LESSONS

Subsequent lessons should focus on establishing good tone production, exploring the instrument, developing the ability to read, and improving tone quality. Every lesson should contain some form of reinforcement of the basic concepts of tone production, perhaps using different words, and each student's progress should be carefully monitored by the teacher. Each individual should play alone at least once during the lesson to enable the teacher to observe what each student is doing. Sometimes, a student will play the notes of an exercise correctly, but with a poor approach to producing the sound. The teacher should be alert to this and place the emphasis on good tone production rather than on getting the notes. In tonguing, it is important to stress that the air must be kept moving between tongued notes, rather than being interrupted by the tongue. Brass players call this concept blowing through the notes. A sustained, linear approach to exercises and tunes should be the rule. As the students begin to move upward in range, it is important to encourage them to use fast air on the higher notes and slower air on the lower notes.

A good method is to play each tune or exercise first on the mouthpiece and then on the instrument, with the teacher demonstrating frequently. A good ear-training exercise (this could also be a short warm-up) is for the teacher to play random open tones in a musical manner and ask the students to imitate what the teacher plays. It is important to introduce new material at each lesson. Students will realize a greater feeling of accomplishment by progressing through a number of exercises and tunes that achieve similar things than by remaining on the same material from class to class. Motivation is intimately linked to a sense of accomplishment. Familiar melodies and folk tunes are especially important because students will unconsciously focus their thought patterns on the melodic sequence of the tune instead of on the mechanical aspects of producing sound. Melodic material should remain a part of a student's study routine throughout all levels. Melodies can be used to explore the instrument and develop a feel for different keys. It is also worthwhile to encourage students to try to play notes of the harmonic series of each valve or slide position as well as bugle-like melodies.

Method books should be worked through in a systematic way to ensure a steady line of development. Unfortunately, not all method books are organized in the most practical, progressive sequence, so it is often necessary to supplement the primary method with additional studies from other books or material written by the teacher. Teachers should adapt both the study material and their approach to the needs of individual students.

Above all, teachers should strive to develop a concept of sound in each student by playing and demonstrating whenever possible. It is also rewarding to play recordings of brass artists and ensembles for the class and occasionally bring in advanced students to perform. As early as possible, easy duets, trios, and quartets should be attempted to lay the foundation of a sense of ensemble.

One of the main reasons students give up their study of a brass instrument is a feeling of lack of progress. This is often the result of poor practice habits. In the early stages, progress must be made rapidly. As youngsters advance in their ability to play, a sense of pride in this special skill develops and their motivation increases. Discouragement sets in if the process seems to be standing still. This is why effective principles of tone production must be established from the beginning along with a purposeful practice routine. The importance of the latter cannot be overstressed. Gaining the support of parents is essential. All will go better if the teacher clearly explains to the parents what the student needs and what he or she is supposed to do. For example, a practice strategy should be developed:

> The student should, as far as possible, practice at the same time every day. In effect, this time should be reserved for practice.
>
> A music stand and a straight-backed chair need to be provided.
>
> Practice should take place in a well-lighted room that is free of distractions.
>
> A parent may need to help the student in the earlier phases.

Along with a practice strategy, there should be a systematic procedure for practicing the lesson:

> Spend the first 5 to 10 minutes buzzing on the mouthpiece. This could consist of tunes or buzzing exercises written by the teacher.

With the assigned lesson material:

> Say the note names in rhythm.
>
> Say the note names in rhythm and do the fingerings at the same time.
>
> Play the exercise or tune on the mouthpiece.
>
> Play the exercise or tune on the instrument.

A well-organized course of study should be developed that, along with bringing in new material to stimulate interest, is designed to ensure progress over a specified period of time. This should include regular evaluations to make certain that each student is progressing at a prescribed rate.

Despite their best efforts, however, students sometimes encounter problems with specific instruments. In such cases, the teacher might consider recommending a change to a different instrument. There are many successful professional players who began their study of music on one instrument and later switched to another.

After a certain level has been reached, it is of great benefit for students to have an opportunity to play in an elementary band or orchestra in addition to their weekly lessons. Membership in such a group offers a wealth of positive experiences, boosts motivation, and provides an opportunity to learn new skills.

Surviving While Playing a Brass Instrument with Braces

Students need a great deal of patience, support, and encouragement while trying to play with braces. There is a period of adjustment when the braces are put on. Aside from the different feel to playing, the braces tend to cut into the inside of the lips under normal mouthpiece pressure. It is essential, therefore, that the embouchure formation create a cushion for the mouthpiece. This will be accomplished naturally if the lips are formed as if saying "poo" or "too." Various means have been devised to protect the inner lips from the braces. Brace Guard and wax are often used for this purpose. One of the most practical and effective shields can be made by cutting a rectangular piece of chamois skin to the right size and inserting it between the braces and the lips. Because it is very thin and made from animal membrane, it tends to interfere less with the embouchure while offering good protection. When the braces are taken off, there is another (although shorter) period of adjustment during which the student needs similar support and encouragement.

Assembling Brass Instruments

The following procedures should be followed in assembling brass instruments. The mouthpiece should be carefully inserted into the receiver and given a very slight turn to lock it in position. It must never be forced or tapped into the receiver. In assembling the trombone, the slide should remain locked to prevent it from accidentally falling out and becoming dented. While the left hand holds the bell section securely, the right hand should grasp the slide by both braces and insert the end into the bell lock receiver. The slide should be rotated so that an angle of 90 degrees (or slightly less) is formed and the lock nut tightened. Particular care must be taken in removing trombones from their cases because the slide rests in the case lid. The case should be laid flat and the lid opened evenly from end to end to avoid twisting the slide. With all brass instruments, it is important to remember to pull the main tuning slide out a half inch or so before beginning to play. From this position, the slide can be moved to conform to a tuning pitch.

Removing Condensation

Condensation forms as warm breath is blown into the instrument. If this is not removed every so often, a gurgling sound results. The water can be removed almost silently by forming the lower lip around the mouthpiece rim and blowing lightly with the water key open. One or more of the valve slides may require clearing as well, and these should be removed as necessary.

Removing water from the horn is slightly more involved. With the instrument resting on the left leg and held vertically so that the valves are downward, the horn should be rotated to the right, allowing any accumulated water to collect in the main tuning slide. The tuning slide should then be removed and the water poured out. Next, the horn should be returned to the inverted position so that water in the valve slides runs downward to the valves. The valves should be depressed to allow the water to enter the valves. With the third valve depressed, the horn should again be rotated to the right to direct the water into the third valve slide, which should be removed and emptied. Draining the valve slides is easier if the water is poured in the opposite direction from the loop (Figure 12.1).

The same procedure can be applied to the double horn, except that the F tuning slide must also be emptied. In clearing the valves, it is worth acquiring the knack of grasping both the F and B♭ third valve slides and emptying them together.

The College Brass Techniques (Methods) Course

The study of secondary instruments is obviously one of the most essential aspects of a prospective instrumental teacher's preparation. To be successful today, teachers need to have extensive knowledge of all the instruments and be able to convey ef-

Figure 12.1. **Removing water from the horn is slightly more involved.**

fective principles of playing technique to their students. Considering the highly specialized and developed nature of brass playing today, greater demands are now placed on the college brass techniques or methods course than ever before.

There are two fundamental goals of the course:

- To provide detailed knowledge of the brass instruments and contemporary brass playing
- To prepare students to teach brass effectively by giving them a firm grasp of correct tone production and technique, both in concept and in practice

The present text has been designed to meet both of these needs. In achieving the first objective, the content of the course can be enriched by incorporating information from the first nine chapters of this book. This will spur students' interest in the subject and provide the depth of knowledge that today's brass teachers need to be effective. The chapters on tone production and playing position and the studies and ensembles found in Sections A, B, and C of this chapter work together to develop a clear and practical concept of how to play brass instruments. Students should be encouraged to view the time and effort they spend in gaining knowledge and in learning to play as an investment in the future.

In the class material that follows, Section A consists of progressive studies to be played in unison, with some easy ensembles added at various points. The instructor should move at whatever pace seems appropriate to the class and remain on any material as long as it seems necessary. The choice of tempos is also totally at the discretion of the instructor; these will undoubtedly vary according to the ability level of each class. Typical classes are made up of both brass players learning the other brass instruments and students new to brass instruments. The brass-playing students will obviously develop at a faster rate, so the instructor must attempt to balance the pace between the two groups. My purpose has been to provide enough material so that both groups will feel challenged; the brass-playing students can go forward on their own and take advantage of the more advanced material. At the same time, a comfortable rate of progress for both brass players and non–brass players has been built into the studies so that by playing together in class, all will develop at a reasonable pace.

Many of the studies should be played first with the mouthpiece alone, and then on the instrument. In this way, students learn to center pitches accurately and their advancement will be faster. The great orchestral trombonist Denis Wick aptly referred to mouthpiece playing as lip solfège. In general, the horn should play the lower notation where possible because playing in the middle and lower range is beneficial in the development of tone. When necessary, however, exercises can be played up an octave. Beginning with exercise 89, common alternate positions are noted in the trombone part where appropriate. In learning fingerings and positions, it is helpful if students mentally practice the main fingering and position charts contained in Appendix D on a daily basis, with the goal of memorizing them. Although sixteenth notes often appear in the notation after exercise 129, the tempo should be very slow and can be subdivided as necessary.

Section B presents a series of ensembles that progress from easy to medium levels of difficulty. The instructor may wish to integrate these into Section A, or work through this section as a unit if time allows. There is great value in playing ensembles at any level. All ensembles appearing in this book have been scored for maximum flexibility of instrumentation so that they may be easily used in any brass class. The part number (1–4 or 1–5) of each line is shown as the circled number at the left. Trumpets are divided into two parts. The horn part usually doubles either the second trumpet or the trombone/euphonium line. Trombones and euphoniums may be used interchangeably. The bottom part is played by the tuba(s), but, in the event that no tuba is present in the class, this part has also been notated at the octave so that it can be played by a euphonium or trombone.

Section C is made up of 50 individual exercises for each instrument. These are intended to supplement the unison studies and ensembles used in class and to provide some additional material for the student to practice at home. This material has been found to be particularly effective in moving the student's playing ability ahead in the shortest time period and establishing good tone production. Students should be encouraged to make a daily project of starting at the beginning or some other point and working down a page or two of these studies. In order to be able to include more exercises, an abbreviation has been used in notating some of the studies. In such cases, the study should be repeated by starting on the (stemless) note shown and playing in that key. (See, for example, number 28 for trumpet and cornet.) This procedure has the benefit of challenging the student to explore the instrument. This process develops control, technique, and confidence in a way that no other exercise can. The author was trained in this manner as a student and can attest to its effectiveness as a pedagogical procedure. The studies contained in Section C also serve as excellent warm-ups for players on any level. In using these studies as warm-ups, players should start after the first few lines, where the exercises become more flowing in style. The patterns may be extended upward or downward throughout the range. More keys may be included as well.

In addition to providing learning material for the college brass techniques (methods) course, the studies and ensembles presented in Sections A, B, and C can be used on the elementary and secondary levels, where they should also prove of value. The ensembles, in particular, are well-suited to junior and senior high school brass ensembles.

Unison Studies and Easy Ensembles for Class Use

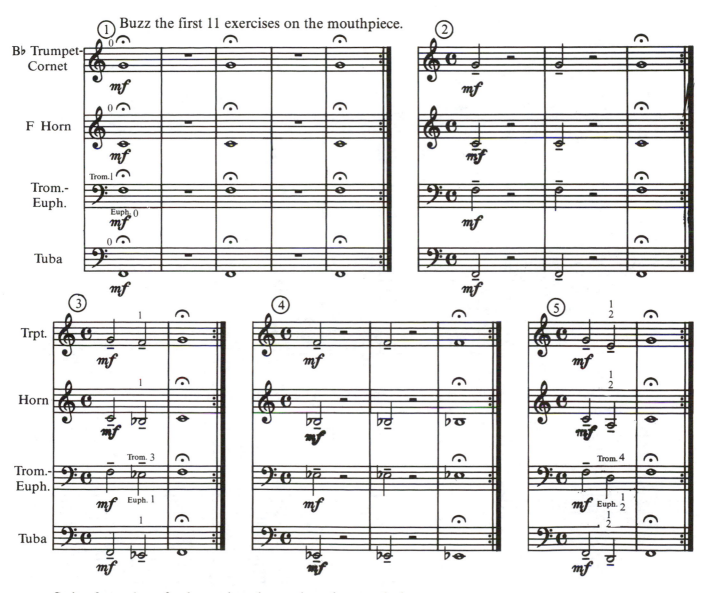

Strive for a clear, freely produced sound on the mouthpiece.
Concentrate on in-tune pitches.

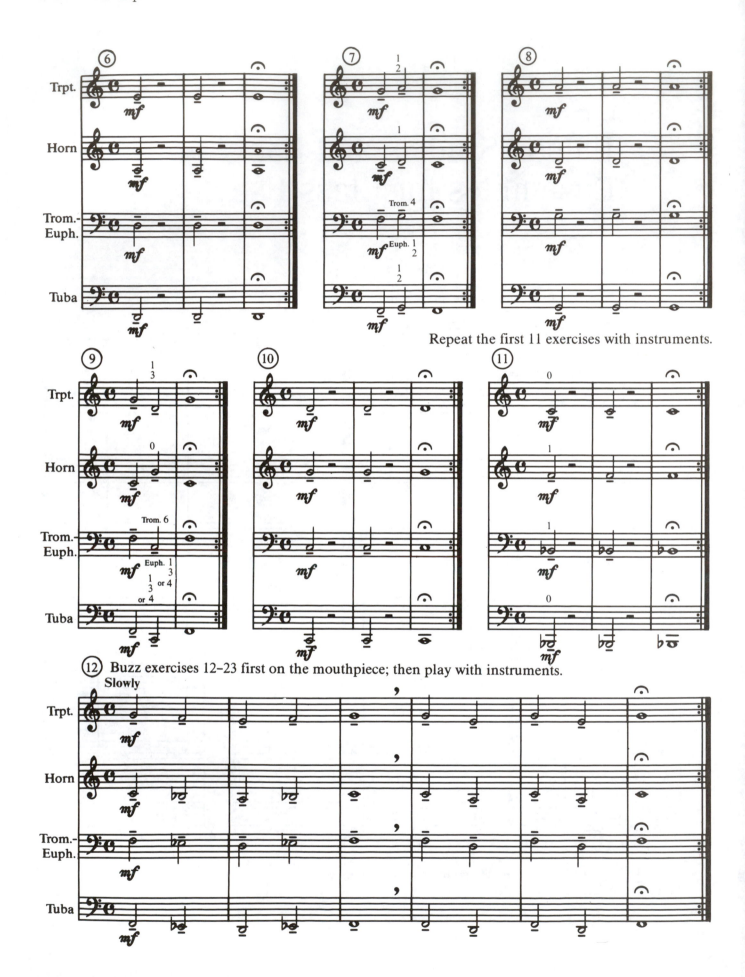

Repeat the first 11 exercises with instruments.

Buzz exercises 12–23 first on the mouthpiece; then play with instruments.

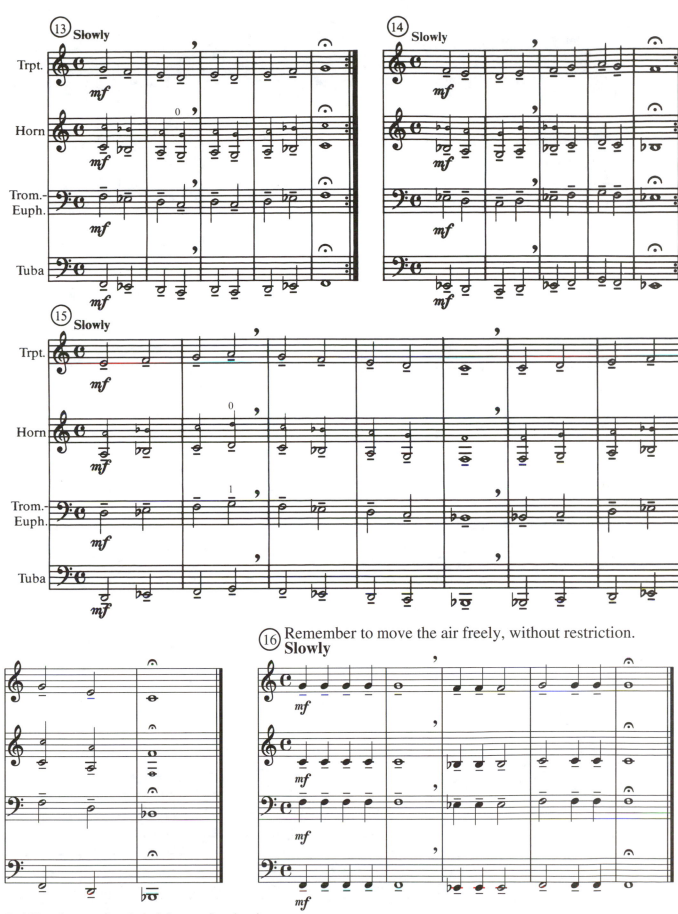

Stabilize the sound and pitch by moving the air.

Remember to sustain the sound and blow through the notes.

20 Hymn: *Abide with Me*
Legato

21 *The Prince of Denmark's March* Jeremiah Clarke (ca. 1674–1707)

25 *Chester* William Billings (1746–1800)

Andante

Think of creating *wind* in moving the air outward.

26 Scale

*To perform No. 27 as a round, parts should be identified as 1, 2, 3, or 4.
To develop independence, parts should be changed.

(36) From the *Ninth Symphony* Ludwig van Beethoven (1770–1827)

From the *Third Symphony* Ludwig van Beethoven (1770–1827)

Lip Slurs   Use the syllables ee-ah or oo-ah in descending,
and ah-ee or ah-oo in ascending. (See Chapter 10.)

Trombone Legato. In addition to the lip slur, a slur can be made when changing from one set of partials to another: Position:

The positions must be adjacent, however.   Partial number:

Trombone legato is discussed in Chapter 10.
(See also the harmonic fingering/position charts in Appendix D.)

A slur can also be made when the slide motion is opposite to the direction of the notes. For example:

Slide motion *inward,* direction of notes *downward:*

                    or

Slide motion *outward,* direction of notes *upward:*
    (This is more effective in the upper register.)

In all other instances, the trombonist must use an exceptionally smooth legato tongue to create the illusion of a true slur:

thu
loo
roo } Use whichever syllable produces the smoothest sound.
du

thu   thu   thu   loo   loo   loo   roo   roo   roo   du   du   du

Trombone Legato Studies

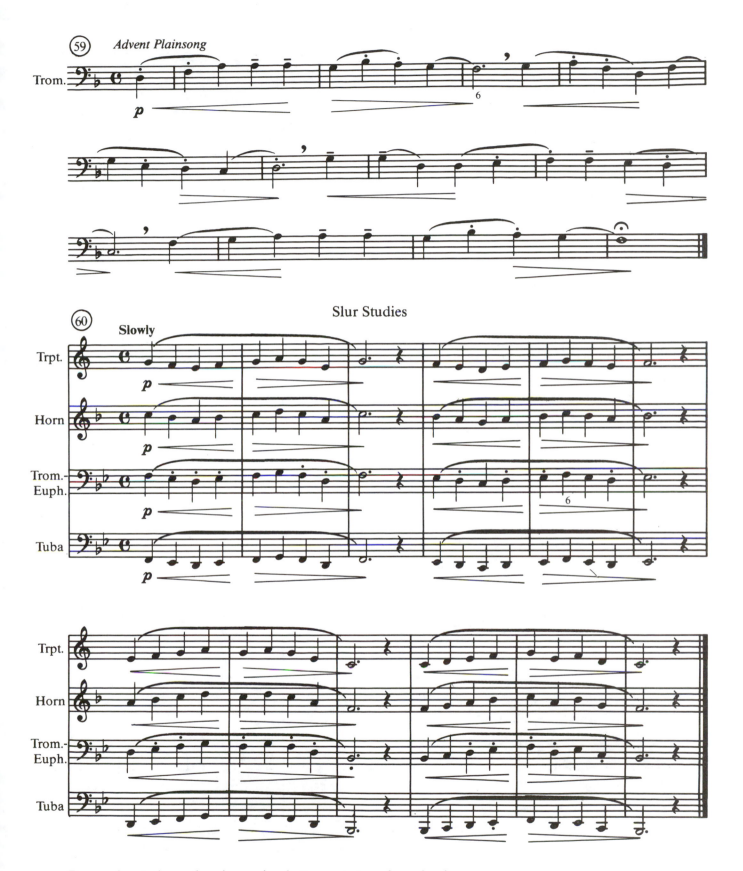

Remember to keep the air moving between notes when slurring.

Welsh Folk Song: *All Through the Night*
Andante

English Folk Song: *Early in the Morning*

Largo from the *New World Symphony (No. 9)* Antonín Dvořák (1841–1904)

From number ⑥⑥ onward, all exercises should be taken in four as slowly as necessary.
As the ability of the class develops, these exercises should be repeated in a faster four or ¢

A Also play No. 67 with these articulations:

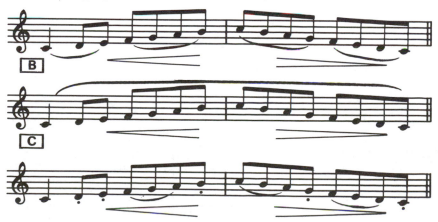

68 Pilgrim's Chorus from *Tannhäuser* Richard Wagner (1813–1883)

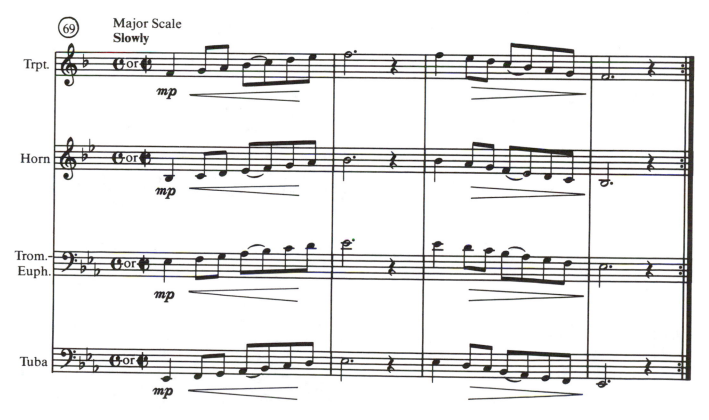

71 Scottish Folk Song: *Ye Banks and Braes*
Sadly (slowly in 6)

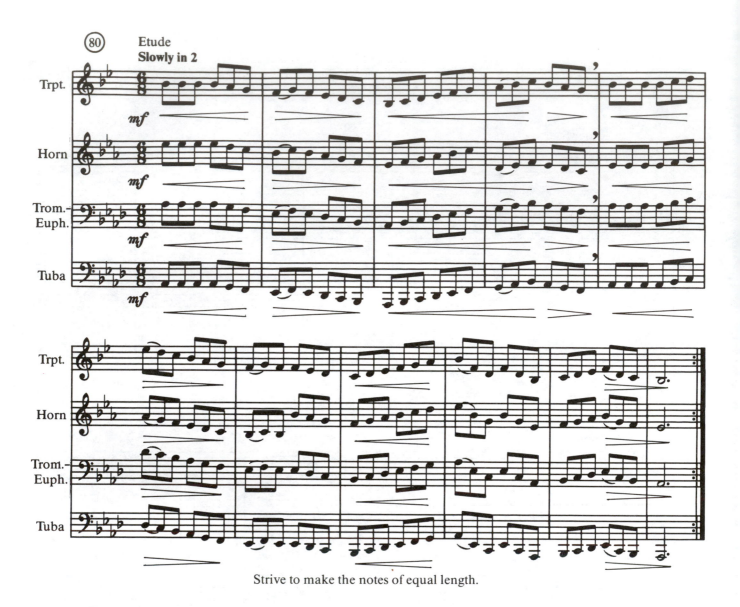

Strive to make the notes of equal length.

86 Arpeggio Study—Major
Moderately
Repeat tongued

Trpt.

Horn

Trom.-
Euph.

Tuba

87 Arpeggio Study—Minor
Moderately
Repeat tongued

Trpt.

Horn

Trom.-
Euph.

Tuba

Part
*① Trumpet 1   88 Four-part chorale: *Christus, der ist mein Leben* J. S. Bach (1685–1750)
② Trumpet 2   Moderately

② Horn

③ Trombone or
   euphonium

④ Trombone or
   euphonium
④ Tuba

*In all ensembles the part number is shown by the circled numeral next to the instrument designation.

Alternate Positions for Trombone

Try to achieve an equality of sound between the normal and altered position.

Maintain the direction of slide motion where
possible by substituting alternate positions. (See Chapter 5.)

97 Arpeggio Study—Minor
Slowly

Repeat: **A**   **B**

98 Etude *In the style of a minuet*
In 3, but with a feeling of one

99 Agnus Dei from *L'Arlesienne* (adapted) Georges Bizet (1838–1875)

Lip Slur Study

(104) Slowly

Now is the Month of Maying (adapted) Thomas Morley (1557–1602)

Since First I Saw Your Face (Abridged) Thomas Ford (d. 1648)

Studies in Staccato

Remember to keep the air moving in staccato playing.

Sea Chanty: *The Drunken Sailor*

Studies in Marcato

Sea Chanty: *Haul Away, Joe*
Slowly in 2

Welsh Folk Song: *Men of Harlech*

Studies in Legato Tonguing

English Folk Song: *The Wraggle–Taggle Gipseys*

(128) French Christmas Carol
Slowly in 2

Sea Chanty: *Rio Grande*

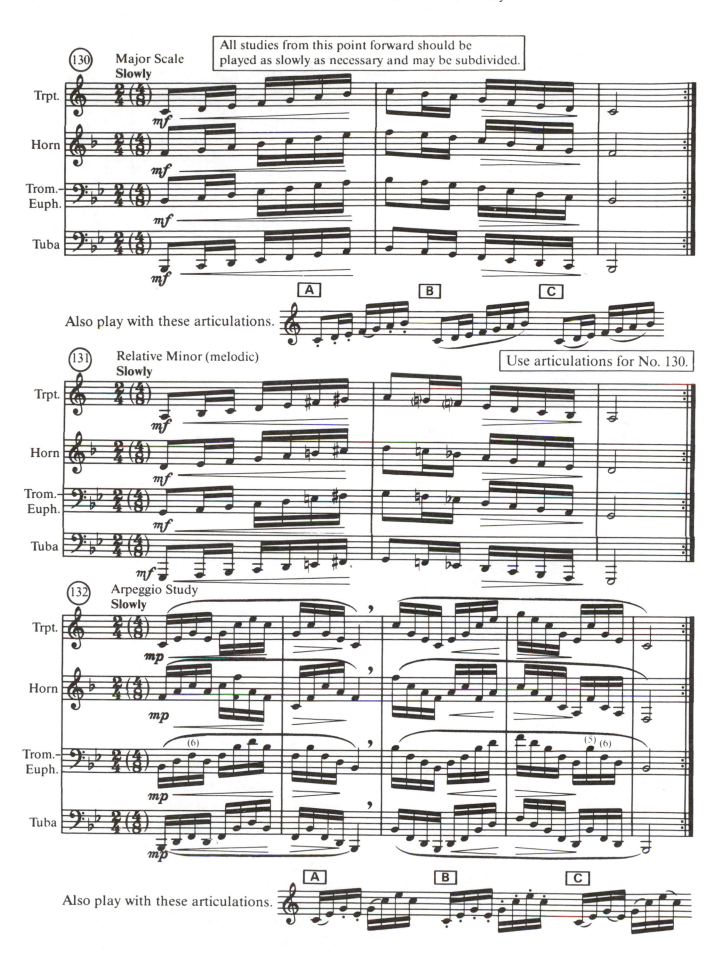

All studies from this point forward should be played as slowly as necessary and may be subdivided.

(130) Major Scale
Slowly

Also play with these articulations.

(131) Relative Minor (melodic)
Slowly

Use articulations for No. 130.

(132) Arpeggio Study
Slowly

Also play with these articulations.

Also play with these articulations:

All studies may be subdivided as necessary.

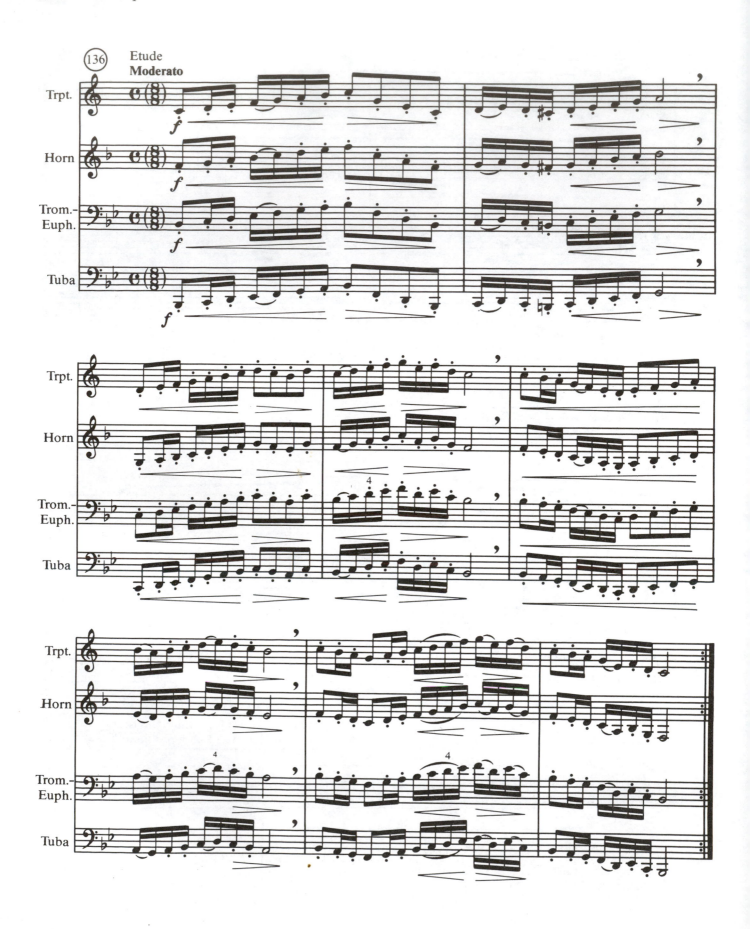

Exercises for double and triple tounging may also be practiced single-tongued.

(143) **Interval Study**

Trpt.

Horn

Trom.
Euph.

Tuba

(144) **Lip Slur Study**

Trpt.

Trom.
Euph.

Tuba

Repeat in all valve combinations

F Horn

Repeat in all valve combinations (omit 1–2–3).

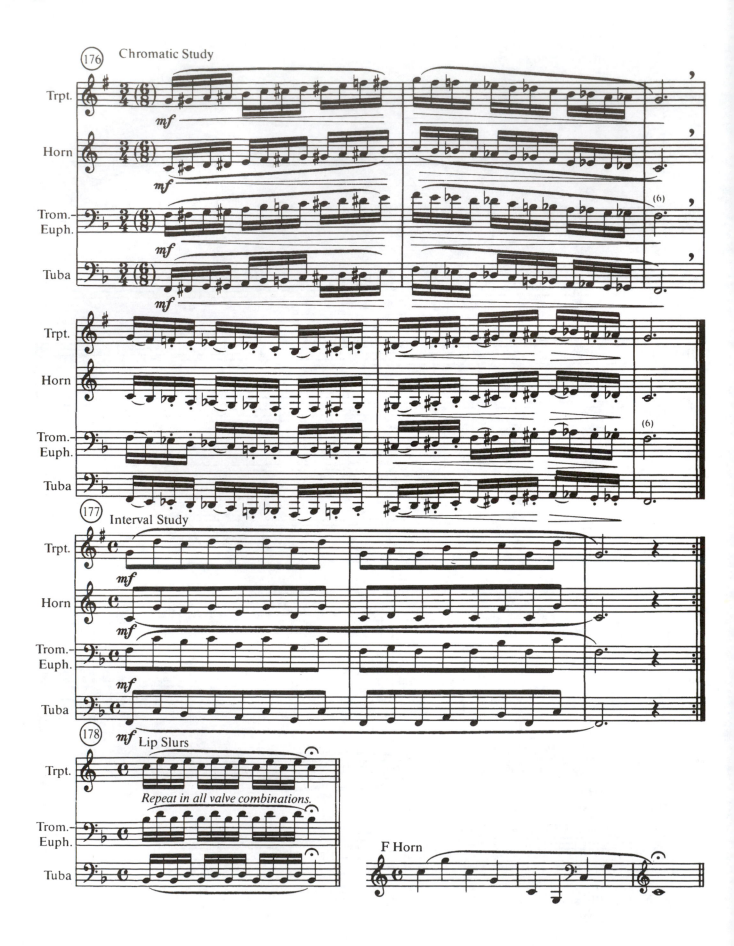

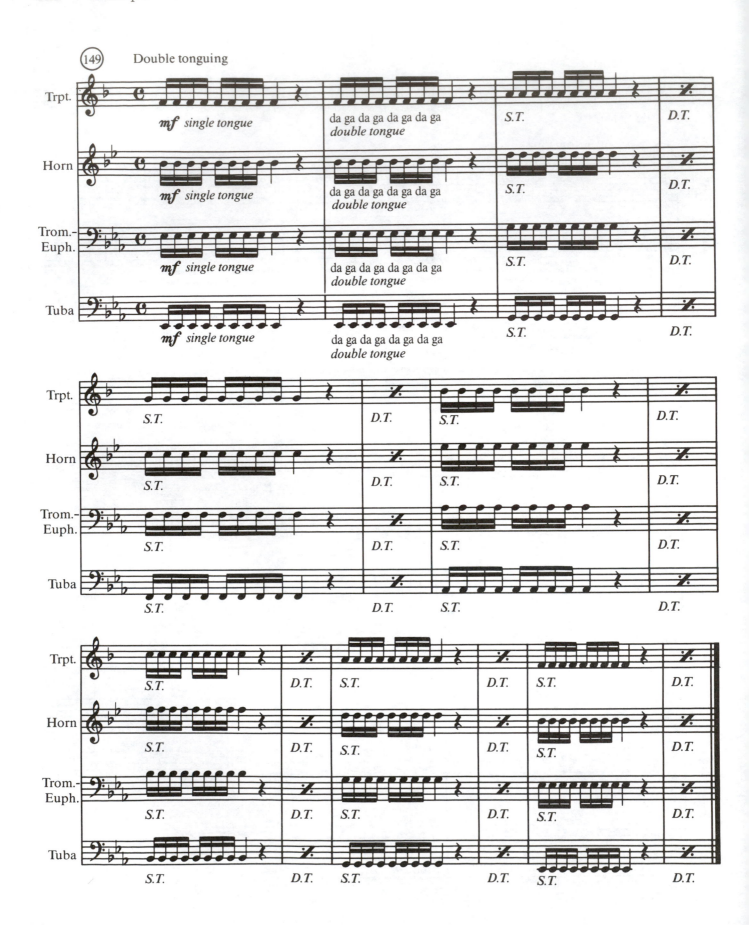

Exercises for double and triple tonguing may also be practiced single-tongued.

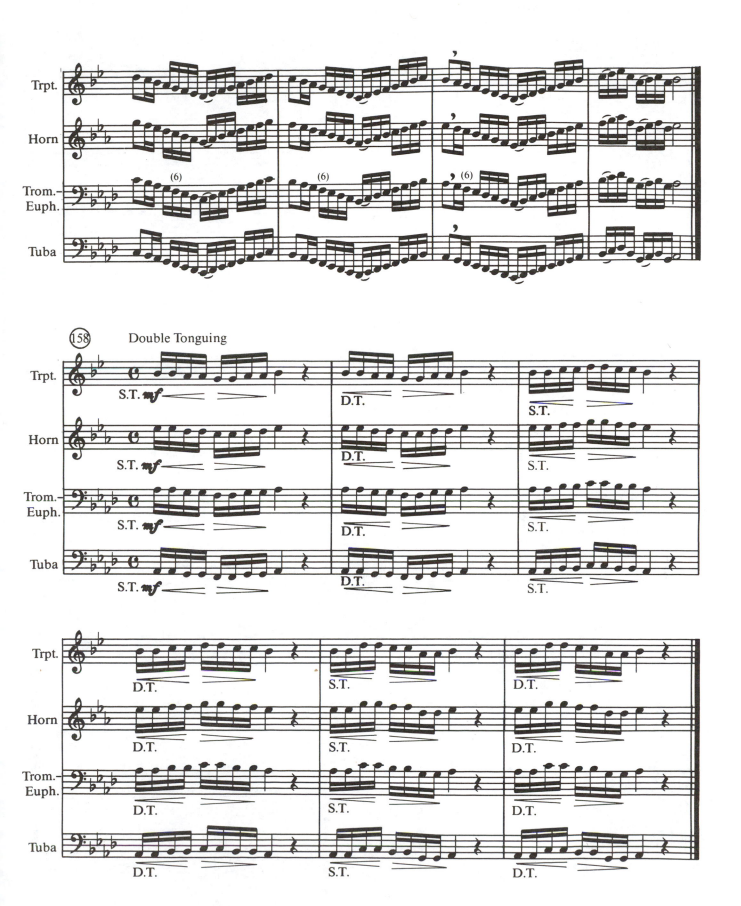

(160) *Rondeau* Jean Joseph Mouret (1682–1738)

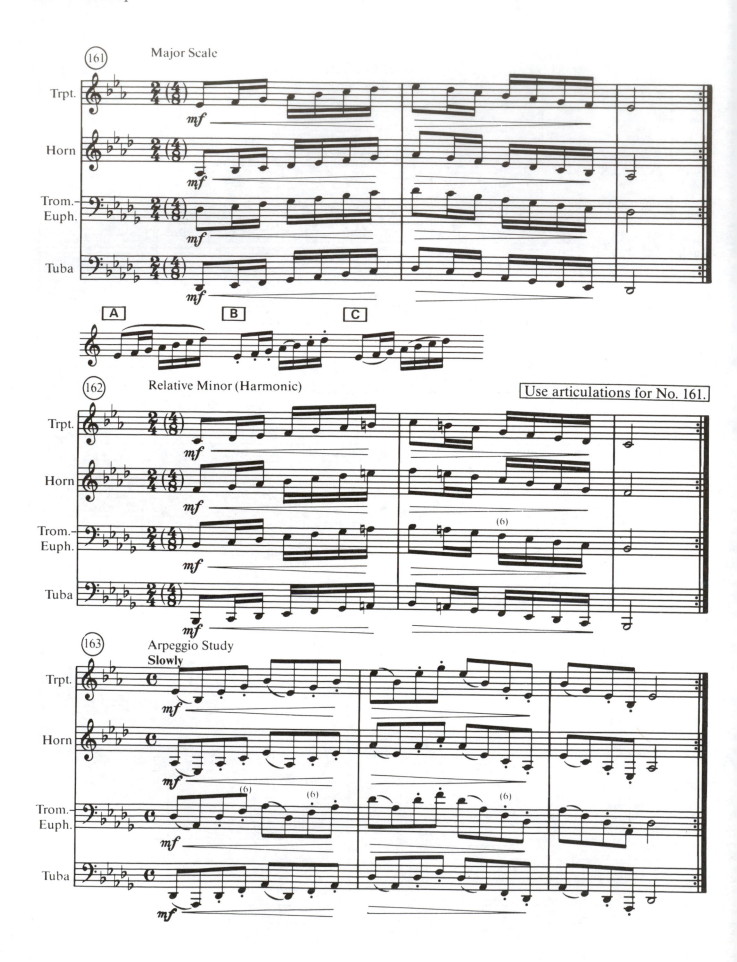

Exercises for double and triple tonguing may also be practiced single-tongued.

Nos. 173 and 174: Use articulations for No. 161.

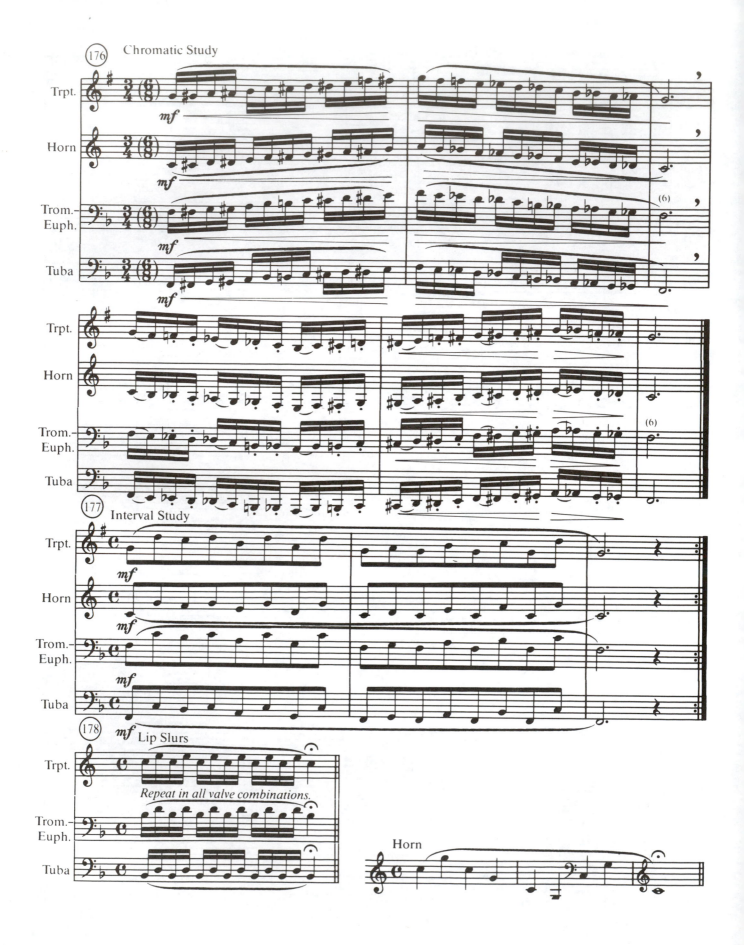

180 *Trumpet Tune* Henry Purcell (ca. 1659–1695)
Moderately

181 Double Tonguing

184 Relative Minor (Melodic)

Use articulations for No. 161.

185 Arpeggio (also slur)

186 Chromatic

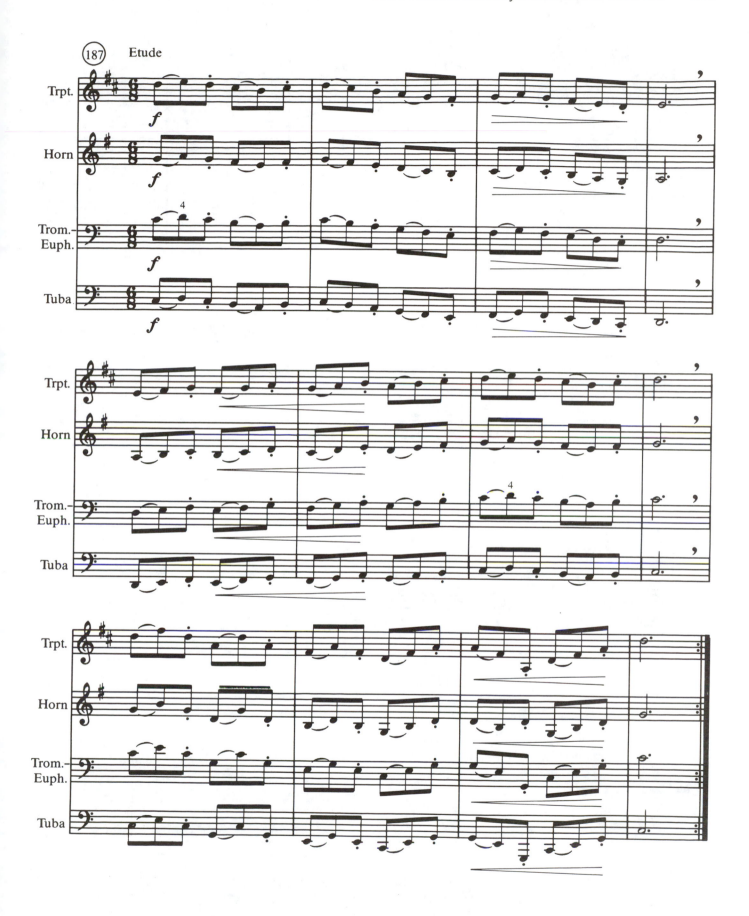

188 Irish Folksong: *The Minstrel Boy*
Slowly

Rall. last time
Fine

first time only

D.C. al Fine

rall.

189 Major Scale

190 Relative Minor (Harmonic)

Use articulations for No. 161

Use articulations for No. 161

Nos. 193 and 194: Use articulations for No. 161.

196 British Sailing Song: *Portsmouth*
     Moderately

Nos. 197–200 may be omitted.

Additional Scales

197 Major

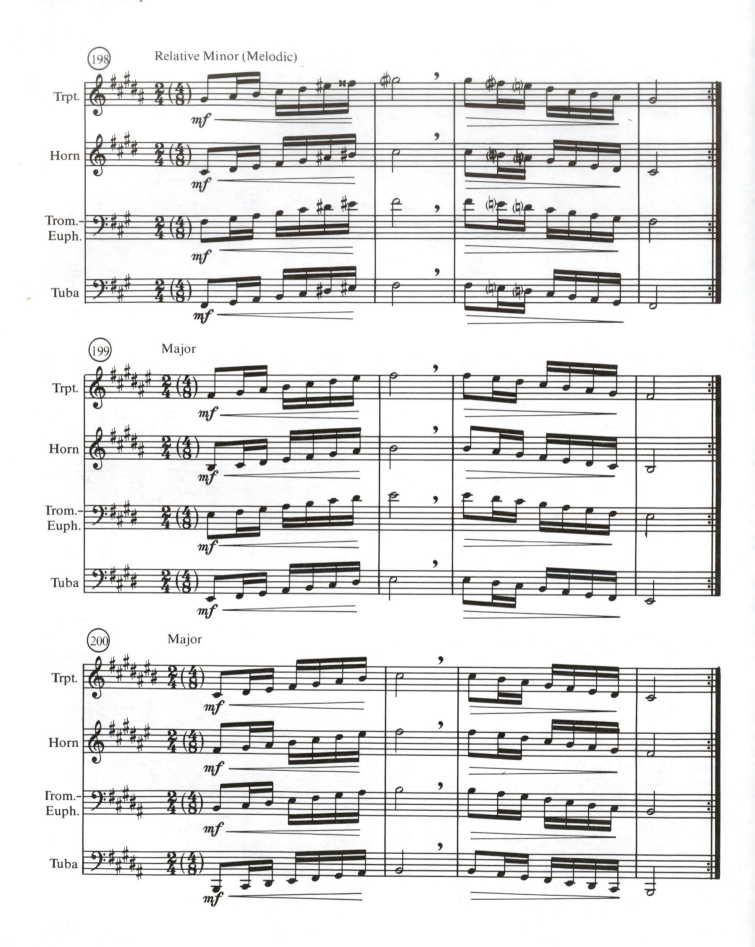

Progressive Ensembles

The Queen's Funeral March Henry Purcell (ca. 1659–1695)

* Parts are indicated by the circled number adjacent to the instrument designation.

Pavanne d'Angleterre Claude Gervaise (fl. 1540–1560)

La Mourisque Tylman Susato (ca. 1500–1561)

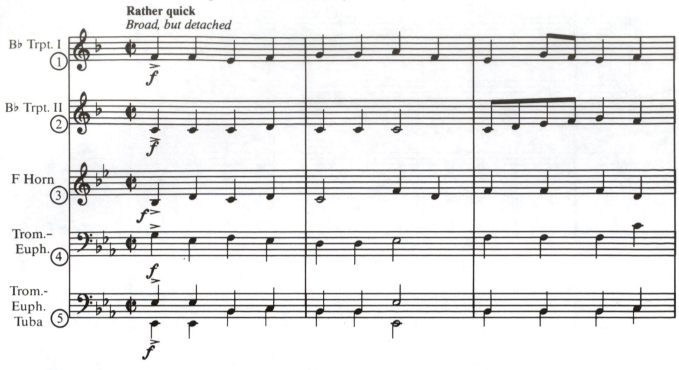

L'arboscello ballo Furlano (1578) Giorgio Mainerio (fl. 16th cent.)
Moderato *broad, but not legato*

Danse du Roy Tylman Susato (ca. 1500–ca. 1561)

Courtly Masquing Ayre John Adson (ca. 1585–1640)

Tourdion (1547) Pierre Attaingnant (ca. 1494–ca. 1552)

Canzona (from the *Queen's Funeral Music*) Henry Purcell (ca. 1659–1695)

Courtly Masquing Ayre John Adson (ca. 1585–1640)

Ballet Michael Praetorius (1571–1621)

Galliard Anthony Holborne (1584–1602)

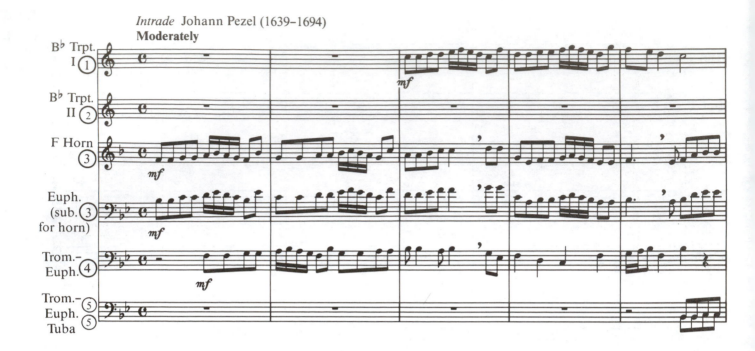

Intrade Johann Pezel (1639–1694)

Intrade (cont.)

The tuba should play the upper octave if possible.

Bransle Simple Claude Gervaise (fl. 1540–1560)

Studies for Individual Practice
Trumpet and Cornet

Play all exercises on mouthpiece before playing on instrument.
Repeat often

Play on each of the previous notes.

Stay on each exercise as long as necessary before moving on.

28 Exercises should also be played in the keys of the notes indicated.

30 Exercises from 30 onward are more advanced.

slur and tongue

Horn

Play all exercises on the mouthpiece first.
All F Horn

29 Exercises should also be played in the keys of the notes indicated.

Exercises from 30 onward are more advanced.

30 Use double horn as desired.

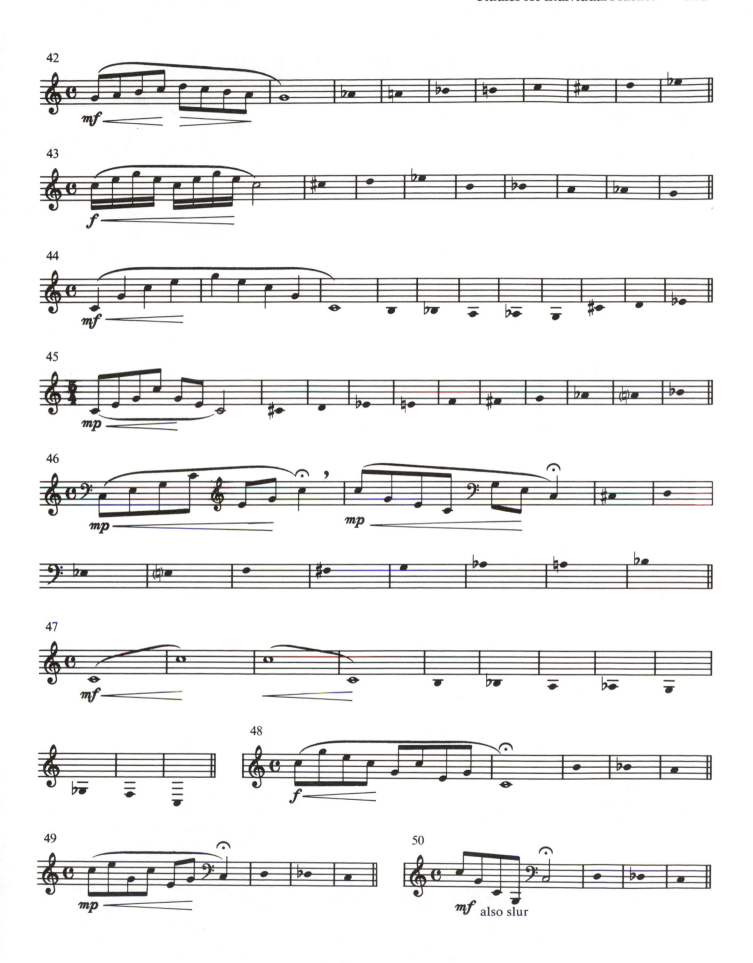

Trombone and Euphonium

Play all exercises on the mouthpiece first.

Euphonium players should also play the exercises for trumpet and cornet.

mf Play often.

Stay on each exercise as long as necessary before moving on.

Exercises should also be played in the keys of the notes indicated.

Tuba

Play all exercises on the mouthpiece first.

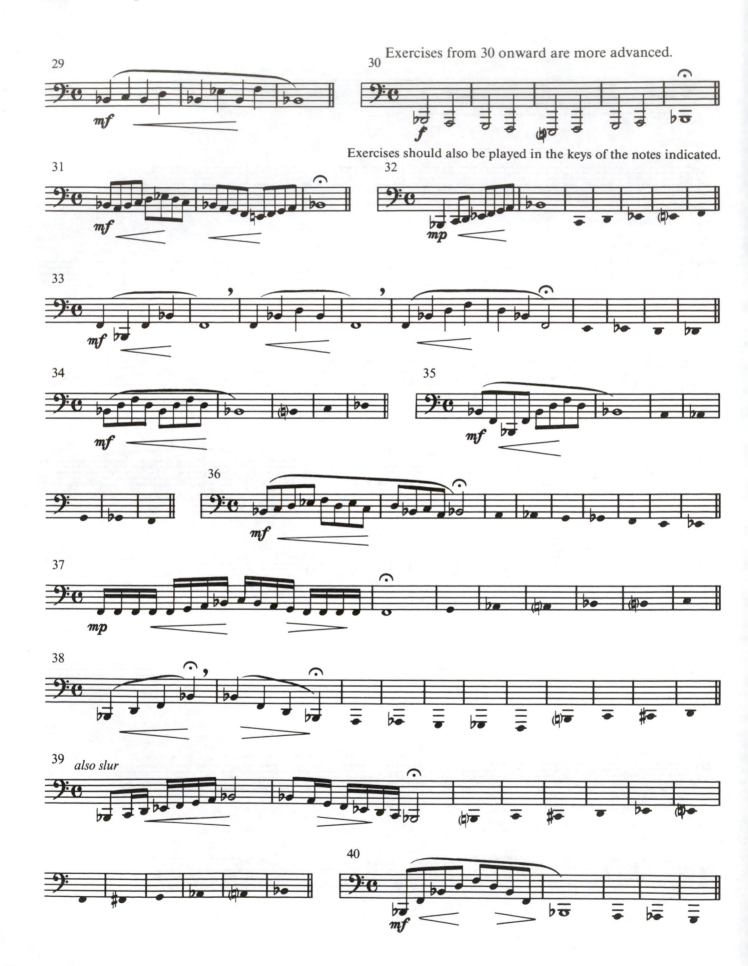

29

30   Exercises from 30 onward are more advanced.

Exercises should also be played in the keys of the notes indicated.

31

32

33

34

35

36

37

38

39   *also slur*

40

Instrument Care

Why Good Care Is Important

Brass instruments are complex acoustical devices and the process that takes place inside the tubing will function optimally only so long as the instrument remains in good condition. Most critical are the conical portions of the tubing, which must maintain an exact taper. As shown in Chapter 1, it is the instrument's taper that determines the pitch placement of many notes of the harmonic series. Equally important is its effect on response and tone quality. If any of the internal proportions of the tubing become altered because of grime or dents, the instrument's internal acoustical operation may be affected. It is also of prime importance that all moving parts work freely. Premature wear of valves and slides due to inadequate lubrication ultimately leads to a deterioration of the air seal and a subsequent decline in the instrument's playing quality. Dents on the trombone slide create high spots that accelerate wear and destroy the smooth motion of the slide. Given adequate care, brass instruments will last for many years. A number of professional players have used a single instrument (with regular service and repair) for a good portion of their careers.

Cleaning

Grime collects most often in the instrument's mouthpiece and leadpipe; these should be cleaned regularly at two- or three-week intervals. A tapered mouthpiece brush should be used to clean the mouthpiece after running water through it. Silver plating can be shined with ordinary silver polish. It is best not to polish gold plating too often (perhaps twice a year). For regular cleaning, gold plating can be brightened by lightly rubbing it with liquid soap under warm water. Nickel silver mouthpieces present a problem in finding an effective cleaner. The author has only been able to find one polish that works well.[1]

The best way of cleaning the leadpipe and the instrument's other tubing is to flush it with water under strong pressure. To do this, the player needs to make up a special cleaning tube. First, obtain a length (about 2 and a half feet) of plastic tubing that will fit inside the instrument's tubing. Plastic tubing of this type and an appropriate fitting that will attach it to a faucet are available at hardware stores. A laundry tub, large sink, or bathtub should be used for cleaning. To prevent dents, towels or foam rubber can be placed where the instrument might come in contact with the tub or sink. After inserting the plastic tube slightly into the leadpipe (large end) or other

---

[1] Happich Simichrome Polish, a German product, can be found in some hardware and home improvement stores. The Vermont Company Store, P.O. Box 3000, Manchester Center, Vt. 05255–3000 (802-362-2400) regularly stocks this product. The importer is Competition Chemicals, Inc., Iowa Falls, Iowa 50126.

tubing, lukewarm water should be forced through the tubing at high pressure. Any collected grime will be washed out with no danger to the soldered joints in the tubing. When done regularly, perhaps every three weeks, or once a month, this method of cleaning will prevent a buildup of grime.

Alternatively (especially when the instrument has not been cleaned for a long time), a flexible brush (snake) can be pushed through the tubing. However, there is some risk with this method of damaging the soldered joints. It is important in using a flexible brush that the tubing first be flushed with water and the brush end softened by soaking. Some flexible brushes come with a protective plastic coating, and this is to be preferred.

For a thorough cleaning, the pistons and slides should be removed (rotary valve instruments may be cleaned with the valves in place) and lukewarm water forced through all subsections of tubing as well as the tuning and valve slides. It is important that the temperature of the water not exceed lukewarm or the lacquer might be damaged. The interior of the valve casings of piston valve instruments can be wiped with a cleaning rod covered with a lint-free cloth (the rod must be completely covered to avoid damage to the valve casings). There are special cleaners available for this purpose. Otherwise, some valve oil added to the cloth will act as a solvent. All parts should be thoroughly rinsed and dried with a soft cloth.

Trombone slides require special handling to avoid damage. After separating the slides, the outer slide may be cleaned in the manner described above. The real danger is to the inner slide tubes. Smooth motion of the slide is dependent on the inner slide tubes being parallel; any jolt or pressure may distort their alignment. To be safe, the inner slide should be held by the side being cleaned. The water pressure method can be used to clean the interior of the tubes. Alternatively, a long cloth attached to a string and weight (a fishing line and sinker work well) can be pulled from the stocking end toward the cork barrel. The inner slide tube's exteriors should be carefully wiped with a solvent or special cleaner. Old slide lubricant tends to collect in the cork or spring barrel and this can be removed with a small brush.

Lubrication

The vulnerable point of every valved brass instrument is the air seal maintained by the valves. The problem is made more complex by the need for the valves to move freely and quickly. Inherent in these two parameters is a conflict. The degree of contact of the surfaces of the piston or rotor and its casing must be sufficient to be airtight, yet loose enough for fast motion of the valve. A balance is created between these opposing qualities when the instrument is made. This is accomplished by lapping the valve piston or rotor into its casing with an abrasive compound until a specific clearance between the surfaces has been achieved. The degree of clearance is chosen as the best compromise between quick action and an effective air seal within the valve. The problem for the player is to try to prevent this clearance from increasing through wear (which causes air leakage) as the valves are used under playing conditions. When one considers how many times the valves go up and down or rotate in a typical day of playing, the difficulty of preventing deterioration of the instrument's air seal by wear over a period of time is obvious.

The only means of protecting the valves against wear is to use the best lubricants available. A valve lubricant works by creating a protective barrier between the piston or rotor surfaces and those of the casing. The viscosity of the lubricant must be determined with great accuracy by the manufacturer. If it is too high, the valve will not move quickly enough; if it is too low, the barrier will be insufficient to protect the valve, or the barrier will break down. There are a number of formulations on the market. Some are synthetic,[2] while others use petroleum as a base. Thin kerosene-based lubricants generally do not provide the level of protection necessary, although they offer fast action. The player should study the lubricant manufacturer's literature carefully and choose wisely. Above all, premature valve wear can only be prevented by lubricating the valves every day.

To lubricate the valves, the following procedures may be used.

PISTON VALVES

Piston valves should first be cleaned using one of the special cleaners available or wiped with a soft cloth moistened with valve oil to remove any residue. After a light coat of valve lubricant is applied, the piston may be inserted into the casing following the alignment of the valve guides. The valve guides fit into the grooves on the side of the casings. The valve should not be turned or the piston surface will be scratched. The pistons are stamped with the appropriate number to avoid inserting them into the wrong casing.

ROTARY VALVES

In lubricating rotary valves, it is important to use lubricants that have been specifically formulated for this type of valve. Piston valve oil is too light and does not adequately protect the valve. In order to lubricate rotary valves, it is best if the containers have tubes (needle oilers) to apply the lubricant; this makes reaching the places where the lubricant must be applied much easier. Two viscosities of lubricant must be used with rotary valves: a lighter viscosity for the rotor and casing surfaces and a heavier viscosity on the bearings and linkages. With the instrument laid flat, the valve caps can be removed and a drop of the heavier lubricant placed on the end of each rotor shaft. The valves should be moved to encourage the lubricant to seep down between the shaft and the bearing plate to the bearing. After the caps are replaced, the instrument should be turned over and some lubricant applied to the gap between the stop-arm hubs and the lower bearing plates (this is the most critical area to lubricate). Again, the valves should be rotated several times. Next, each moving part of the valve activating linkage should receive some lubricant. The valve levers turn on a rocker shaft; some lubricant should be applied to the shaft and at the ends of each lever through the springs. (See Figure 13.1.)

To maintain a quick action, it is occasionally necessary to apply lubricant directly to the rotors and the casings. The lighter-viscosity lubricant should be used for this purpose. Lubricating the rotors must be done through the valve slides, so care must be taken to prevent slide grease (the valve lubricant acts as a solvent) from washing down into the valves, slowing their action. The horn should be held with the bell upward and the valve slides removed. The tube on the lubricant bottle or a long eye-dropper should be inserted into the open tubes and several drops of lubricant placed on the rotors. The slides should be replaced and the instrument turned to various positions while rapidly depressing the valves to spread the lubricant.

THE TROMBONE SLIDE

One of the silicone lubricants intended for this purpose should be used on the trombone slide. The inner slide should be cleaned before applying new lubricant. After cleaning, small spots of lubricant should be placed along the slide, including the stockings, and then spread evenly over the slide surface. Next, the slide should be gently wiped so that only a light film remains. A fine mist of water can be periodi-

---

[2] The author has found Hetman synthetic lubricants to offer good protection and a fast, smooth action.

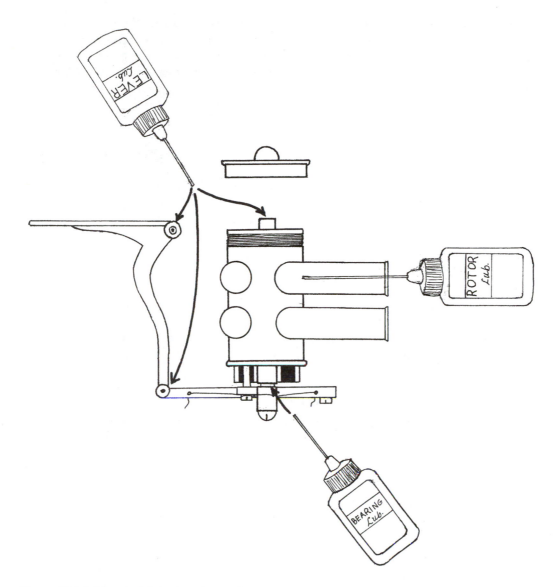

Figure 13.01. **How to lubricate rotary valves**

cally sprayed on the slide surface to maintain good action (plastic sprayers of the type available at garden stores may be used for this purpose).

TUNING AND VALVE SLIDES

Because the instrument's air seal is maintained by these slides as well as the valves, it is important to prevent wear by keeping them well lubricated. New products have appeared recently, and these should be tried to see whether they offer any improvements over anhydrous lanolin, which has been used for a number of years for this purpose. Anhydrous lanolin can be purchased at pharmacies, although now it usually must be specially ordered. Petroleum jelly and gun grease have also been used, but they tend to break down at a much faster rate than lanolin. For slides that must be moved often in playing, such as trumpet third-valve slides, one of the new low-viscosity synthetic lubricants or ordinary petroleum jelly should be used in place of pure lanolin, which is usually too heavy for this purpose.

On older instruments, slides tend to become worn and lose their air seal. These should be tightened by a repair technician. This requires special equipment that internally expands the inner slide tube to fit the outer tube. In severe cases, the slides can be replated, but, like valve replating, this should be attempted only by a very skilled craftsperson. In a complete overhaul, it is advisable to have both valves and slides replated to reestablish the instrument's original air seal.

Before lubricating, the slide must be wiped with a clean cloth to remove any residue. A light coating of lanolin should be applied completely around each inner slide tube about an inch from the end. The slide should be replaced and moved inward and outward several times; this spreads the lubricant evenly without forming a buildup at the end of the tube. Any excess lubricant should be wiped off. The valves should be depressed when inserting or withdrawing valve slides.

Miscellaneous

REMOVING STUCK MOUTHPIECES AND SLIDES

Jammed mouthpieces are common in school bands, so it is advisable to have a mouthpiece puller available. This is an inexpensive tool that removes the mouthpiece quickly and safely. The leadpipe or receiver can be damaged if any other method of removal is attempted. Frozen slides should generally be referred to a repair technician.

PISTON AND ROTARY VALVE ALIGNMENT

The valve ports of the piston must remain in correct alignment with those of the casing in order to minimize disturbance to the vibrating air column as it passes through the valves. On piston valve instruments, both vertical and radial alignment must be considered. The latter is maintained by the valve guides, which keep the piston from turning within the casing. Radial misalignment can occur only if the guides or keyways become worn.

The vertical alignment of piston valves is dependent on the thickness of the cork and felt bumpers. These become compressed with use and must be replaced periodically. Usually there is a mark on the valve stem that indicates the correct height of the bumpers. If no mark can be found, or in cases of radial misalignment, the instrument should be sent to a repair technician.

Rotary valve alignment is maintained by the neoprene or cork bumpers located on the cork stop plate. To check this, the upper valve cap should be removed and the bearing plate inspected to see whether one of the marks on the end of the rotor shaft lines up with the mark on the flange of the bearing plate with the valve at rest (closed). With the valve depressed (open), the other mark on the shaft should align with the mark on the bearing plate. If this is not the case, the bumpers must be replaced (or trimmed, if a high bumper is found). New neoprene or cork bumpers should be pressed into the cork stops and trimmed as necessary with a razor.

REMOVING ROTARY VALVES

Sometimes corrosion and accumulated grease from the slides slow the action of rotary valves to the point that lubrication does not help. The first corrective step is to flush the valves with lukewarm water under high pressure (as described above under *Cleaning*) and relubricate the valves, including the valve rotors. In most instances, this restores crisp action to the valve. In severe cases, the rotors must be removed and both the inside of the casings and the rotors must be cleaned and lubricated. In general, because there is a risk of damaging the valves in the removal process, this work should be left to a specialist. If this is not possible, the following procedure may be used: After taking off the strings or disconnecting the mechanical linkage, the upper valve cap should be removed and the instrument inverted so that the stop-arm hub and screw are upward. The stop-arm screw should be turned outward several times. While keeping the palm of the hand underneath the upper bearing plate (to catch it when it falls), tap the head of the screw lightly with a leather or wooden hammer (alternatively, a block of wood could be placed on the screw and gently tapped with a metal hammer). The instrument should be supported with the arm to absorb any shock. As the rotor is forced downward, the upper bearing plate will drop into the hand; the stop-arm screw and hub can then be taken off and the rotor removed. The interior of the casing and the rotor may be cleaned with one of the new cleaners for valves or a solvent and a soft cloth. After the rotor and casing are lubricated, the rotor may be replaced. The next step is critical: The mark on the upper bearing plate must be aligned with the mark on the casing. The plate may then be started into the casing (be certain that it goes in straight) and the raised flange at the center should be carefully tapped until the plate is fully seated. The rotor should be checked for free rotation. If the plate is tilted even slightly, the rotor will bind. (If binding occurs, the bearing plate must be removed and started again.) If all is well, the stop arm can then be replaced and the screw tightened.

RESTRINGING ROTARY VALVES

The restringing procedure can be seen in Figure 13.2. It is best to begin with the middle valve to make the adjustment of the valve keys easier. Special cord designed for the purpose should be used. If this is unavailable, 20- to 27-pound test fishing line may be substituted (linen or dacron line is preferable to that made from nylon). One end of a 6-inch length should be knotted and threaded in a figure-8 pattern. Once the string is correctly threaded, it should be pulled taut and set-screw number 1 tightened. To adjust the height of the valve keys, the key should be pressed to the desired position and set-screw number 2 secured. To change the height, it is necessary to loosen only set-screw number 2. The height of the other valve keys should be adjusted to match the middle valve. Special stringing jigs are available that make adjusting the height of the valve levers easier.

WATER KEYS

Periodically, water keys should be checked to make certain that the spring has not weakened and the cork makes an adequate air seal. Worn corks and springs should be replaced. A new cork of the exact size should be pressed into the water key cup (a slightly irregular cork can be secured with a drop of glue). It is a good idea for

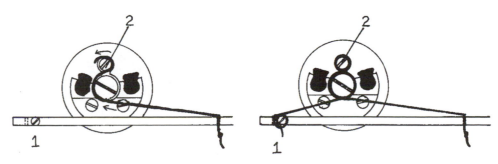

Figure 13.2. **Restringing rotary valves**

schools to maintain a supply of the correct springs and corks for each instrument. In an emergency, a worn cork can be turned upside down to form a temporary seal.

USING PISTON VALVES

On piston valve instruments, it is important that the valves be pushed straight down with the fingertips. If the middle part of the finger is used, pressure tends to be exerted on one side of the valve casing, causing it to go out of round and accelerating wear to that side of the piston.

DENTS

Dents are a constant concern. Tubing dents can cause poor response, affect the instrument's intonation, and cause other problems. Dents in a valve casing affect valve action and seriously damage the piston or rotor. Aside from careless handling, many dents occur in the case. Loose mouthpieces and other items moving inside the case are particularly destructive. It is essential that well-designed hard cases be provided with every instrument. The fit of the instrument within the case should be inspected to make certain that the instrument cannot shift, causing dents as the case is transported. During rehearsal breaks, instruments must never be left on chairs, but returned to their cases. Trombonists and trumpeters who use more than one trumpet should purchase one of the purpose-designed stands for instruments to rest on when not in use. The trombone slide, in particular, is extremely vulnerable to being knocked over and dented.

ADVICE ON REPAIRS

A less-than-competent repair technician can do more harm than good to a brass instrument. Every effort should be made to locate a skilled craftsperson. Professional players can usually recommend such a person, but if none can be found locally, it might be advisable to send the instrument to a specialist. Also, some manufacturers take their own instruments in for service. Repairs vary in complexity; valve replating, problems with trombone slides, and dent removal that entails taking the instrument apart should be attempted only by an expert. Horns, in particular, require special skills and equipment that are often beyond those of the average repair technician.

CHAPTER 14

Notes for Conductors

How the Brass Section Is Organized

The brass section is organized around a group of principal players who have the responsibility of directing all aspects of their sections' performance. Because full rehearsals offer little opportunity for concentrated work on intonation, balance, precision, and uniformity of style, a prime duty of the principal is to oversee sectional rehearsals to develop these qualities. The principal is responsible to the conductor for the overall performance of the section. It is important that principals communicate with each other to promote better ensemble playing in the brass section as a whole.

In orchestras, the third or fourth trumpeter usually also serves as an assistant or associate first, playing the first part on less important works on the program and providing relief to the principal. In some orchestras there is a co-principal, which usually means that the first parts are divided equally between two players or split on a 60%–40% basis. In British orchestras, players other than the principal or co-principal are identified as sub-principals. There are usually three cornet and two trumpet parts in bands, although the present trend among composers is to write for a single section of trumpets (or cornets) identified as first, second, third, etc., following the standard orchestral practice. In the traditional band format, the first cornet part includes most of the solo work, so this should go to the principal. The trumpets often perform independently of the cornets, and the first trumpet and first cornet parts are often doubled. For this reason, the player next in ability after the principal should be assigned the first trumpet part, with the remaining players filling out the lower parts. In scores that specify three or four trumpets in place of cornets, the first cornetist and first trumpeter should take the two highest parts.

Band conductors should review the scoring of each composition in order to assign parts to best advantage. The use of both trumpets and cornets was intended to create a contrast of sound and playing style within the band. This is also a feature of some orchestral works by French composers (Berlioz, Franck, and Debussy). Naturally, the intended contrast is lost when all of the parts are played on trumpets. Whenever possible, the conductor should try to have cornet parts played on cornets and should become familiar with the differences in timbre and playing style between the two instruments. If the conductor can bring out these differences, the work (whether for band or orchestra) will take on an entirely new character. (The cornet is discussed in Chapter 3.)

In horn sections, the two players of highest ability should be assigned the first and third parts. This is because horn sections are composed of two pairs of high and low players, and horn writing follows that pattern of notation. The pairs are sometimes called on to perform separately and solos may occur in both first and third parts. At other times, the third may be written so as to double the first. When all four play together, the usual voicing from upper to lower is 1–3–2–4. A similar pattern is followed in bands. Often, a fifth player is designated as an assistant first, whose duties include playing some of the tutti passages, thereby providing some rest for the principal. Occasionally, there is a co-principal.

Professional players usually specialize as high or low players, and this is normally reflected in the material used for auditions. Fourth horn players, in particular, must develop a strong low range and cannot be expected to perform in the upper register in the same manner as a first or third player.

The third trombone part is conceived specifically for the bass trombone, a much larger instrument than the two tenors, with extended low range. Bass trombone parts often diverge from the other two parts and the instrument should be treated more or less as a solo voice. Because the bass trombone and tuba often double or play in octaves, two contrasting opinions have arisen as to what the bass trombone timbre should be. One concept is that the bass trombone must blend with the tuba; this has led to ever-larger mouthpieces and instruments in the quest to darken the sound by reducing the presence of upper partials in the timbre. The other point of view is that the blend and balance of the three-part trombone section is sacrificed if the bass trombone timbre moves too far in the direction of the tuba. In effect, the bass trombone sound seems to drop from the trombone section down into a two-part tuba and bass trombone section. In the second concept, when the bass trombone doubles the tuba, the resultant sound should be a mixture, not a blend, of the two individual timbres. Both approaches have their advocates, and it is important for conductors to consider this question and articulate their wishes to the players.

Achieving a Good Brass Sound

The best results are achieved if the conductor approaches the brass section as a brass ensemble within the orchestra or band, rather than as autonomous sections. Balance is of prime importance because it strongly influences the quality of the sound produced by the section. A sense of balance is also critical in developing good intonation. Intonation and balance go hand in hand. When good balance is the norm, the players can hear irregularities of intonation more clearly, making correction easier.

Each player must develop the habit of listening to the highest voice and matching its dynamic level precisely. When individual sections perform alone, players on the lower parts should adjust to the principal. The first trumpet sets the volume level when the entire brass section plays together. When the low brass play alone, all should match the principal trombone. In a good brass section, there is an equality of sound from top to bottom.

Volume level is another factor that affects intonation. There is a far greater margin of error at high volumes, where faults in intonation tend to be covered up by the mass of sound, than at lower levels. When a passage sounds out of tune, a good corrective procedure is to repeat it slowly at a *mezzo forte* level. This affords the players both an opportunity to hear more clearly and sufficient time to make corrections. It is also a good practice to single out any chords needing correction. In extreme cases, the root might be played, and then the fifth and third added.

Another conceptual element that strongly influences the quality of sound is a sustained and linear style of playing, as opposed to one that tends to be vertical. This contributes continuity and direction to musical lines and encourages a refined and balanced sound. Attention must also be given to making certain that the length and shape of notes, attacks, and releases are uniform. (These concepts are discussed in Chapter 10.)

To ensure that the full resonance of the brass section is heard by the audience, trumpeters and trombonists should hold their instruments so that the bells are clear of the music stands. The music stand blocks the sound and absorbs partials when the sound is directed into it, destroying the clarity, balance, and tone quality of the brass section.

Seating Problems

Unfortunately, in many ensembles little thought seems to be given to the best way of seating brass players so that they can adequately hear themselves and each other. Playing in such groups is unpleasant and unrewarding. Among the worst and most common problems is placing the trumpets in front of the trombones. The first trumpeter can hear very little other than the sound radiating from the trombone bell in back of his or her head, and the first trombonist, who must balance and tune with the first trumpet, has difficulty in hearing this part. Even worse is to position the horns in front of trumpets or trombones.

The poorest location for the horns is in the center of the ensemble, another common placement. The horn bell is low and to the side of the player, where its rear-directed sound is absorbed by the clothing and bodies of the players seated behind. In such a setup, horn players can barely hear their own sounds and their ability to judge volume and intonation accurately is severely impaired. The most satisfactory position for the horns is at the rear or side of the ensemble, where their sound is unimpeded and can be reflected by one of the stage walls. If they must be placed in the center, it is better to place only percussion behind them.

Because the horn bell goes to the player's right, it is customary for the principal to be seated on the left end of the section so that the players to the right can hear the principal's sound clearly.[1] This arrangement is not universal, however. Some prefer the greater sense of support from the lower parts that is gained by sitting to the section's right. In this arrangement, the principal also has an advantage in projection because the sound can be bounced off a reflective wall without any absorption from an adjacent player. This is the standard formation of the horn section in the Vienna Philharmonic Orchestra and it was favored by the great English horn players Aubrey and Dennis Brain. A third approach is to place the third and fourth horns immediately behind the first and second; this plan works well and affords a viable alternative when a lateral layout is impractical.

The trombone section requires similar consideration. The principal trombonist normally sits on the right side of the section so that the bell (rather than the slide) is closest to the second player to the left. In this way, the principal's sound can be heard across the section. The bass trombonist should be next to the tuba to facilitate playing parts that are doubled.

Suggested seating plans for various types of ensemble are shown in Figures 14.1 through 14.6. Following these plans will allow members of the brass section to hear each other with reasonable clarity and project a well-balanced and vibrant brass sound to the audience.

---

[1] All suggestions for lateral placement refer to stage left or right; that is, from the players' perspective, looking outward from the stage toward the conductor and audience.

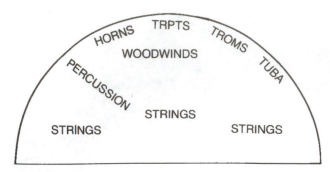

Figure 14.1. **Seating chart: orchestra.**

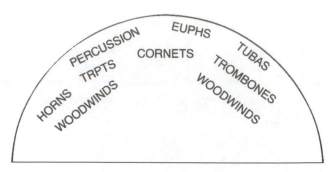

Figure 14.2. **Seating chart: band.**

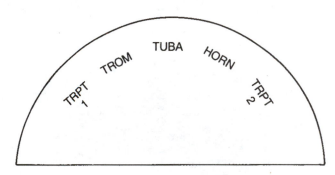

Figure 14.3. **Seating chart: brass quintet.**

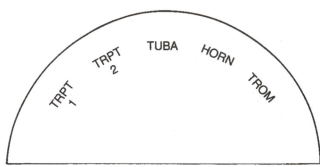

Figure 14.4. **Seating chart: brass quintet (alternate).**

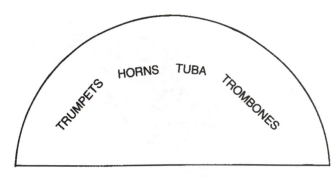

Figure 14.5. **Seating chart: brass ensemble.**

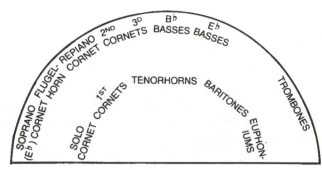

Figure 14.6. **Seating chart: brass band.**

Conducting Brass Players

A basic problem for the conductor is securing the arrival of sound from various distances at the point when the beat is felt. Given experience, brass players usually develop the knack of focusing their sound to the conductor's beat while compensating for any lags caused by distance. This process is aided if the conductor refuses to accept late attacks and provides feedback to guide the players. To avoid ragged attacks, it is helpful if the conductor gains eye contact with the brass before the entrance and breathes on the preparation beat.

Inexperienced conductors often create difficulties by demanding excessively soft dynamics. There is a minimum volume necessary for tone and security on brass instruments, and notes may fail to respond if this point is passed. High passages, in particular, require a certain effort and are placed at risk if too low a dynamic is demanded by the conductor. Also, it should be recognized that even the very best brass players miss notes occasionally. It does no good to make a public issue out of a missed note.

Brass players respond positively to conductors who are knowledgeable about their instruments and ask for more than the notes. By attempting to bring out varied stylistic and tonal concepts of brass playing as they apply to the literature, the conductor generates interest and commitment that carry over into the performance. To take two obvious examples, a more brilliant timbre and sharper attack should be used in Berlioz than in Brahms, which requires a dark, round tone and broad attack. Similarly, the full, sonorous sound one strives for in Bruckner is totally wrong in the works of Stravinsky.

The question of vibrato must also be carefully considered by the conductor. In general, a clear, pure, sound without any vibrato gives greater resonance and color to many brass passages, especially in chordal textures. However, certain compositions, such as works by Debussy, Ravel, and other French composers, require the use of a light, quick vibrato to give these pieces their special color and style. There are other instances in the literature where the use of vibrato enhances the expressive and stylistic effect of a composition. The speed of vibrato should be controlled and variable to create these contrasting sounds. (Vibrato is discussed in Chapter 10.)

The choice of instruments can also contribute to the effectiveness of a performance. Rotary valve trumpets lend a broader, rounder sonority to works by Wagner, Bruckner, and other Germanic composers. The use of cornets in *Le Carnaval Romaine* and *Symphonie fantastique* is essential if the contrast (to the trumpets) Berlioz intended is to be realized.

To gain an understanding of the various concepts and styles of brass playing, the conductor should make a study of representative recordings and seek out live performances, carefully analyzing the approach of each brass section to specific areas of the literature.

The World of Brass

Figure A.1. **Chicago Symphony Orchestra: trumpets, trombones, horns (note the use of rotary valve trumpets and an alto trombone).** *Photo courtesy of the Chicago Symphony Orchestra.*

Figure A.2. **London Symphony Orchestra: trumpets and trombones.** *Photo courtesy of the London Symphony Orchestra.*

Figure A.3. **Vienna Philharmonic: trumpets and horns (note the use of rotary valve trumpets and single F Vienna horns).** *Photo: Vivianne Purdom.*

Figure A.4. **Vienna Philharmonic: trombones and tuba (the two trombonists nearest the tuba are using traditional German trombones).** *Photo: Vivianne Purdom.*

Figure A.5. **Orchestre symphonique de Montréal: trumpets, trombones, tuba.** *Photo: Reproduction authorized by the Orchestre Symphonique de Montréal.*

Figure A.6. **Royal Philharmonic Orchestra, London: horns.** *Photo courtesy of the Royal Philharmonic Orchestra.*

Figure A.7. **Philip Jones Brass Ensemble (quintet).** *Photo courtesy of Philip Jones.*

Figure A.8. **Chicago Chamber Brass. Photo courtesy of Chicago Chamber Brass.**

Figure A.9. **Stockholm Chamber Brass.** *Photo courtesy of Svensk Konsertdirektion, Gothenburg, Sweden.*

Figure A.10. **Philip Jones Brass Ensemble (large ensemble).** *Photo courtesy of Philip Jones.*

Figure A.11. **Black Dyke Mills Band.** *Photo courtesy of Mike Heywood.*

Figure A.12. **The United States Marine Band, "The President's Own": director, Colonel John R. Bourgeois.** *Photo courtesy of "The President's Own" United States Marine Band, Washington, D.C.*

Figure A.13. **The Central band of Her Majesty's Royal Air Force: principal director of music, Wing Commander Eric Banks, M.B.E., F.L.C.M., L.R.a.m., L.G.S.M., R.A.F.** *Photo: Crown Copyright—Ministry of Defense.*

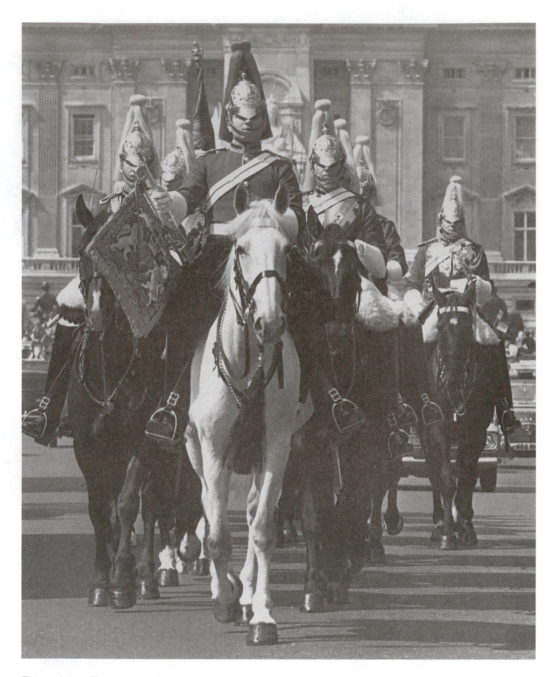

Figure A.14. **Trumpeters from the Household Cavalry, Buckingham Palace, London.** *Photo courtesy British Tourist Authority.*

Figure A.15. **Trumpeters from the Household Cavalry, Buckingham Palace, London.** *Photo courtesy British Tourist Authority.*

Selected Brass Recordings

All recordings in this listing are in the compact disc format, unless otherwise stated. For additional listings, see the Schwann Opus and TAP Music Sales[1] catalogs.

Solo Trumpet

MAURICE ANDRÉ

EMI 69152, Trumpet Concertos
Erato 45062, Italian Baroque Concertos
Erato 92861, *Ultimate Trumpet Collection*
Angel 47311, Haydn, Telemann, Torelli
Erato 88007, Hummel, Neruda
DG 413256, Telemann, Bach, Handel, Vivaldi

OLE EDVARD ANTONSEN

EMI 54897, Haydn, Hummel, Neruda, Tartini
Simax PSC1041, *Music for Trumpet and Piano*

GRAHAM ASHTON

Virgin Classics 45003, *Contemporary Trumpet Music*

ERIC AUBIER

Adda 590027, Tomasi, Desenclos, Jolivet

THIERRY CAENS

Pierre Verany 788092, *Wind Music from a Golden Age*

EDWARD CARROLL

Newport 60038, *Sound the Trumpet*

TIMOFEI DOKSHITSER

Marcophon 904, Brandt, Gliere
Marcophon 914, *Scherzo Virtuoso*
Marcophon 915, *Arabesque*

REINHOLD FRIEDRICH

Capriccio 10436, Classical Trumpet Concertos

ARMANDO GHITALLA

Premier 1027, *Trumpet Concertos of Three Centuries*

LUDWIG GÜTTLER

Capriccio 10016, *Chamber Music for Trumpet*

Berlin Classics 1036, Haydn, Telemann, Leopold Mozart

WOLFGANG HANNES AND BERNHARD LÄUBIN

DG 431817, Telemann, Albinoni, Franceschini

HAKAN HARDENBERGER

Philips 420954, Telemann Trumpet Concertos
Philips 420203, Hummel, Haydn
Bis 287, *Virtuoso Trumpet*

ADOLPH HERSETH

DG 41504, Haydn Concerto

DAVID HICKMAN

Summit 118, Telemann, Hertel
Crystal 668, Halsey Stevens, Kent Kennan

MIROSLAV KEJMAR   (Czech Philharmonic)

Supraphon CO-72511, Vejvanovsky Sonatas

HARRY KVEBÆK

Simax 1088, Trumpet and Organ

MICHAEL LAIRD

Argo 433 415 2, Purcell, Clarke, Charpentier (with Peter Hurford, organ)

WYNTON MARSALIS

Sony 42137, *Carnaval*
Sony 47193, Honegger, Halsey Stevens, Bozza
Columbia 44726, Hummel, Jolivet, Levy

RAYMOND MASE

Summit 148, *Trumpet in Our Time*
Summit 185, *Trumpet Vocalise*

MAURICE MURPHY   (London Symphony)

Collins 30082, Haydn, Hummel, Arutunian

ANTHONY PLOG

Summit 108, *Colors of the Baroque*
Centaur 2068, Corelli, Hertel, Scarlatti

[1] TAP Music Sales, 1992 Hunter Ave., Newton, Iowa 50208, USA, 800–554–7628, is a specialist in brass recordings of all labels.

CHARLES SCHLUETER

Vox 7513, *Bravura Trumpet*

PHILIP SMITH

Summit 144, Orchestral Excerpts

BERNARD SOUSTROT

Pierre Verany 788011, Hummel, Arutunian, Jolivet
Denon 7544, Michael Haydn, Albinoni
Angel 47140, Baroque Works

CRISPIAN STEELE-PERKINS

Innovative 821, Haydn, Neruda, Torelli
MCA MCAD-5844 and IMP Masters, Trumpet
   Concertos
ASV Quicksilva QS 6081, Baroque Trumpet Concertos
Priory 189, *The King's Trumpeter*

THOMAS STEVENS

Crystal 665, *Sonatas*

ALAN STRINGER

London Serenata 430633, Haydn Concerto

EDWARD TARR

Christophorus 74559, Fasch, Telemann, Handel

GUY TOUVRON

RCA 60858, Haydn, Hummel, Neruda
RCA 61200, Molter Concertos

JOHN WALLACE

Nimbus 5065, Hummel, Neruda
Nimbus 5010, Haydn
Nimbus 7012, Corelli, Torelli, Vivaldi, Purcell

HELMUT WOBISCH

Vanguard Classics OVC 2008, *The Virtuoso Trumpet*

Solo Cornet

MAURICE ANDRÉ

Erato 99091, *La Belle époque* Cornet Solos

PHILIP MCCANN

Chandos 4501, *The World's Most Beautiful Melodies*
Chandos 4502, *More of the World's Most Beautiful
   Melodies*
Chandos 4503, *The World's Most Beautiful Melodies,*
   vol. 3

Solo Horn

HERMANN BAUMANN

Philips 416380, Gliere Concerto and other works
Teldec 94525, *Virtuoso Horn*
Philips 422346, Haydn Concertos

DENNIS BRAIN

Andromeda 2512, Beethoven Sonata, Schumann
   Adagio and Allegro
EMI 761013, Mozart Concertos
EMI 747834, Strauss Concertos, Hindemith Concerto

CLAIRE BRIGGS   (City of Birmingham Symphony
   Orchestra)

Classics for Pleasure 4589, Mozart Concertos

JEFFERY BRYANT   (Royal Philharmonic)

Tring TRP047, Mozart Concertos

GREGORY CASS   (Orchestre de la Suisse Romande)

Gallo 741, Cherubini, Schumann, Rossini, Maxwell
   Davies

ALAN CIVIL

Philips 420709, Mozart Concertos

DALE CLEVENGER

Sony 44906, Mozart Concertos
Teldec 8.42960 Haydn Concertos
DG 415104, Mozart Concerto No. 3

PHILIP FARKAS

Coronet 1293, Bozza, Schumann, Gallay (cassette)
Summit 176, *Shared Reflections: The Legacy of Philip
   Farkas*

NORBERT HAUPTMANN   (Berlin Philharmonic)

Sony SK 53267, Strauss Concerto No. 2

IFOR JAMES

EBS 6052, Haydn Concertos, Neruda Concerto
EBS 6063, Strauss Concertos
EBS 6040, Miscellaneous program
EBS 6062, Mozart Concertos
AVM AVZ-3034, Beethoven Sonata, Cherubini, Danzi
EBS 6040, *Meditations*

ANDREW JOY

Capriccio 10 443, Othmar Schoeck Concerto

DAVID KREHBIEL

Summit 141, Orchestral Excerpts

FRANK LLOYD

Chandos 9150, Mozart Concertos
Merlin MRFD 92092, *The Virtuoso Horn*

MARIE-LUISE NEUNECKER

Novalis 150030, Mozart Concertos
Koch Schwann 3–1357, Gliere Concerto

FRANCIS ORVAL

Astoria DP 87012, Mozart Concertos

JOHN PIGNEGUY

Hyperion 66172, Malcolm Arnold, *Fantasy for Horn*

DAVID PYATT

EMI Eminence EMX 2238, Strauss Concertos

Bruno Schneider   (Orchestre de la Suisse Romande)

Claves 50–9010, Strauss Concerto No. 2

Gerd Seifert   (Berlin Philharmonic)

DG 419057, Mozart Concertos
Sony 45800, Strauss Concerto No. 1

Stephen Stirling and Tim Caister

Naxos 8.553204, Vivaldi Concertos for Two Horns

Michael Thompson

Nimbus 5010, Haydn Concertos
Nimbus 5018, Concertos by Vivaldi, Rosetti, Leopold
Mozart
BBC 600, Mozart Concertos
EMI 5 55452, Tippett Sonata for 4 Horns (with Jeffery
Bryant, Richard Watkins, and Hugh Seenan)

Barry Tuckwell

Etcetera 1121, Horn Music of Czerny
Etcetera 1135, Dukas, Poulenc, Bozza
EMI 769569, Mozart Concertos
Philips 30370, Strauss Concertos
London 417406, Baroque Concertos
ASV 716, Music of Koechlin

Radovan Vlatkovich

EMI 764851, Mozart Concertos

Richard Watkins

IMP Classics 865, Mozart Concertos
Conifer 75605–51228–2, Malcolm Arnold Concerto
No. 1
Conifer 172, Malcolm Arnold Concerto No. 2
Chandos 9379, Gliere Concerto
Marco Polo 8.223513, Ernest Tomlinson's Rhapsody
and Rondo

Frøydis Ree Wekre

Crystal 377, Schumann, Tomasi, Cherubini
Simax 1100, Norwegian Horn Concertos

Gail Williams

Summit 139, Nelhybel, Reynolds, Musgrave, Wilder

Jonathan Williams

ASV COE-805, Mozart Concertos

Zbigniew Zuk

Zuk 071088, Schoeck, Hindemith, Rosetti

Solo Trombone

Joseph Alessi

Summit 130, *Slide Area*

Ronald Barron

Boston Brass 1002, *Hindemith on Trombone*
Boston Brass 1001, *Le Trombone Française*

Michel Becquet

Koch Schwann 311127, Leopold Mozart Concerto
Koch Schwann 313342, Miscellaneous program

Ronald Borror

MHS 512214, Seventeenth-Century Italian
Sonatas

Ian Bousfield

Doyen 014, *Versatile Virtuoso*

Pia Bucher

Marcophon 901, Wagenseil, Caldara, Pergolesi

Abbie Conant

Audite 97410, Guilmant, Marcello, Handel

Vinko Globokar

Harmonia 905214, *Globokar by Globokar*

John Kitzman

Crystal 386, Creston, Hindemith, Pryor

Christian Lindberg

Bis 568, Concertos by Rimski-Korsakov, Tomasi
Bis 658, Concertos by Jacob, Howarth, Bourgeois
Bis 378, David, Grondahl, Guilmant
Bis 388, Berio, Xenakis, Kagel, Eliasson, others
Bis 638, Martin, Bloch, Serocki
Bis 628, Creston, Zwilich, Walker, Schuller

Jacques Mauger

Doyen 027 Concertos by Bourgeois and Grafe, other
works

Jeffery Reynolds and Michael Mulcahy

Summit 158, Orchestral Excerpts for Bass Trombone,
Bass Trumpet, and Tenor Tuba

Ralph Sauer

Summit 143, Orchestral Excerpts

Branimir Slokar

Claves 8407, Wagenseil, Martin, David, Tomasi
Claves 922, Leopold Mozart, Albrechtsberger, Bellini
Marcophon 913, Rimsky-Korsakov, others

Benny Sluchin

Adda 581087, *Contemporary Trombone*

Solo Euphonium

Roger Behrend

Coronet 400, *Elegance*

Brian Bowman

Crystal 393, Ross, Capuzzi, Boda, Adler (cassette)

Jean-Pierre Chevailler

Albany 201, *The Classical Euphonium*

BOB AND NICK CHILDS

　　Doyen 001, *Childs Play*
　　Doyen 002, *Euphonium Music*
　　Doyen 022, *Welsh Wizards*

MICHAEL COLBURN

　　Summit 150, *Golden Age of Brass*

NEAL CORWELL

　　Nicolai 119, *Distant Images*

FRED DART

　　Coronet 1054, Euphonium Solos (cassette)

PAUL DROSTE

　　Coronet 3026, Euphonium Solos (cassette)

Solo Tuba

OYSTEIN BAADSVIK

　　Simax 1101, *Music for Tuba*

ROGER BOBO

　　Crystal 125, *Bobissimo*
　　Crystal 392, *BoTuba* (cassette)
　　Crystal 690, *Tuba Libera*

FLOYD COOLEY

　　Crystal 120, *Romantic Tuba*

EUGENE DOWLING

　　Pro Arte 595, Vaughan Williams, Arnold, Jacob, Handel

JOHN FLETCHER

　　RCA Gold Seal 60586, Vaughan Williams Concerto
　　Chandos 4526, Gregson Concerto for Tuba and Brass Band

JAMES GOURLAY

　　Doyen 028, *Gourlay Plays Tuba*

PATRICK HARRILD

　　Chandos 8740, Vaughan Williams Concerto

TOMMY JOHNSON

　　Summit 152, *Tubby the Tuba*

MICHAEL LIND

　　Four Leaf 102, Arban, Gregson, Jacob

MARK NELSON

　　Crystal 691, Miscellaneous

DANIEL PERANTONI

　　Summit 163, Penderecki, McBeth, Arban

HARVEY PHILLIPS

　　GM 3017, Music by Peaslee

SAM PILAFIAN

　　Telarc 80281, *Travelin' Light*

GENE POKORNY

　　Summit 129, *Tuba Tracks*
　　Summit 142, Orchestral Excerpts

MELVYN POORE

　　Random Acoustics 005, *Groundwork*

DAVID RANDOLPH

　　ACA 20018, *Contrasts in Contemporary Music*
　　ACA 20025, *Tuba Suites and Other Sweets*

JIM SELF

　　Summit 132, *Changing Colors*

JOHN TURK

　　Dana 4, *Low Blows*

Performances on Historical Instruments

TIMOTHY BROWN

　　Virgin Classics 90845, Mozart Horn Concertos (natural horn)
　　L'Oiseau Lyre 417610, Haydn Horn Concerto No. 1 (natural horn)

CALLIOPE

　　Summit 112, Renaissance music (cornetts and sackbuts)
　　Elektra/Nonesuch 79039, *A Renaissance Revel* (cornetts and sackbuts)
　　Elektra/Nonesuch 79069, *An Italian Renaissance Revel* (cornetts and sackbuts)

GABRIELE CASSONE

　　Nuova Era 7128, *Trumpet in San Petronio* (natural trumpet)
　　Giulia 201008, Telemann Concerto in D (natural trumpet)

BRUCE DICKEY

　　Accent 9173, *Virtuoso Solo Music for Cornetto*

GABRIELI CONSORT AND PLAYERS
　　Virgin Classics 7590062, *A Venetian Coronation, 1595* (cornetts and sackbuts)

GOTTFRIED REICHE CONSORT
　　Ambitus 97865, *English Renaissance and Baroque Music* (cornetts and sackbuts; natural trumpets)

LOWELL GREER

　　Harmonia Mundi 907037, Beethoven Sonata (natural horn)
　　Harmonia Mundi 907012, Mozart Concertos (natural horn)
　　Harmonia Mundi 907059, Mozart Quintet (natural horn)

HAARLEM TRUMPET CONSORT

Teldec 8.42977, Works for Natural Trumpets

ANTHONY HALSTEAD

Nimbus 5190, Haydn Horn Concertos (natural horn)
Nimbus 5104, Mozart Horn Concertos (natural horn)
Nimbus 5180, Weber Concertino (natural horn)

HIS MAJESTY'S SAGBUTTS AND CORNETTS

Meridian 84233, Holborne, Adson, Locke
ASV 122, *Venice Preserved*
Meridian 84096, Music from Seventeenth-Century Germany

FRIEDEMANN IMMER

L'Oiseau Lyre 417610, Haydn Concerto (keyed trumpet)
Teldec 8.43673, Leopold Mozart Concerto (natural trumpet)
MD&G L 3271, *Trompetenkonzerte des Barock* (natural trumpet)
Deutsche Harmonia Mundi 77027, *Baroque Trumpet Music* (natural trumpets)

MICHAEL LAIRD

DG (Archiv) 410500, Bach "Brandenburg" Concerto No. 2, with English Concert (natural trumpet)

NEW LONDON CONSORT, PHILIP PICKETT, DIRECTOR

L'Oiseau-Lyre D103561, *Tielman Susato: Dansereye, 1551* (cornetts, sackbuts, natural trumpet)
L'Oiseau-Lyre 414633, *Praetorius: Dances from Terpsichore, 1612* (cornetts, sackbuts, natural trumpet)

PAUL PLUNKETT

Move 3127, Baroque Trumpet Music (natural trumpet)

CRISPIAN STEELE-PERKINS

EMI 476642, *Shore's Trumpet* (natural trumpet)
Hyperion A 66145, Biber Sonatas (natural trumpet)
Sony Vivarte SK533695, Stradella, Telemann, Albinoni (natural trumpet)

CRISPIAN STEELE-PERKINS AND STEPHAN KEAVY

Hyperion 66255, *Italian Baroque Trumpet Music* (natural trumpets)

EDWARD TARR

Christophorus 77168, Nineteenth-Century Trumpet Music (nineteenth-century valve trumpet)

MICHAEL THOMPSON

L'Oiseau Lyre 421429, Mozart Quintet (natural horn)

Brass Ensembles

AMERICAN BRASS QUINTET

Summit 133, Ewazen, Sampson, Snow
Summit 181, *Consort Music of 1600*

Delos 3003, Bach, Gabrieli, Scheidt, Holborne
New World 312–2, *The Yankee Brass Band*

AMERICAN HORN QUARTET

EBS 6008, Miscellaneous
Nonesuch 101660, Works by Turner
EBS 6038, Turner, Perkins, Bernstein, Hindemith

ARCTIC BRASS QUINTET

Simax 1074, Hindemith, Arutunian, Plagge

ATLANTIC BRASS QUINTET

Summit 119, *A Musical Voyage*
Music Masters 67142, Mussorgsky, Liszt, Bizet

BAYREUTH FESTIVAL HORNS

Acanta 43800, Music of Wagner
Acanta 43469, Hunting Music

BELGIAN BRASS SOLOISTS

Marcophon 923, Miscellaneous program

BERLIN PHILHARMONIC HORN QUARTET

Koch-Schwann 311021, Schumann Konzertstück and other works

BRASS OF AQUITAINE AND LONDON

ASV 870, Copland, Lully, Adson, Gabrieli, Purcell

CANADIAN BRASS

RCA 4733, *Greatest Hits*
Columbia 44031, Gabrieli, Monteverdi
RCA 14574, *High, Bright, Light & Clear*

CHICAGO CHAMBER BRASS

Pro Arte 805, *Fireworks for Brass*

LES CUIVRES FRANÇAISE

Pierre Verany 793041, Poulenc Trio, Gabaye Récréation, Solos

DETMOLD HORN QUARTET

MD + G 3098, Miscellaneous program
MD + G 3324, Bozza, Artôt, Wunderer

EASTERN BRASS QUINTET

Klavier 11025, *Classical Brass*

EASTMAN BRASS QUINTET

Allegretto 8154, *Renaissance Brass Music*

EMPIRE BRASS QUINTET

Telarc 80218, Organ and Brass
Telarc 80204, Gabrieli, Banchieri
Telarc 80220, *Class Brass*

ENGLISH BRASS ENSEMBLE

ASV 629, *Russian Brass*
ASV 740, Bach, Elgar, Widor

ENSEMBLE DE TROMPETTES DE PARIS

Arion ARN 68196, *Récital*

EQUALE BRASS

>   Nimbus 5004, Music by Arnold, Warlock, Poulenc, Bartók

EUROPEAN BRASS QUINTET

>   Pavane 7294, *Brass Meets Brass*

GALLIARD BRASS ENSEMBLE

>   ASV 6035, *Carols for Brass*

GERMAN BRASS

>   Audite 361401, Miscellaneous program
>   Angel 47430, *Bach 300*
>   Angel 49170, *Tribute to the Americas*
>   EMI 7 47692, Music of Samuel Scheidt
>   EMI S 55274, *Spirit of Brass*

HR BRASS   (Brass Ensemble of the Frankfurt Radio Orchestra)

>   Capriccio 10 361, Bach, Barber, Copland, Handel

LOCKE BRASS CONSORT

>   Chandos 6573, *Fanfare*
>   Chandos 8419, Brass Music of Richard Strauss
>   CRD 3402, *Symphonic Marches for Concert Brass*

LONDON BRASS

>   Electrola 46442, *Modern Times*
>   Electrola 44136, Praetorius, Bartók, Shostakovich
>   Teldec 9031–77604, Music by Baroque Composers
>   Teldec 2292–46443, *Christmas with London Brass*
>   Teldec 90856, *Gabrieli in Venice*

LONDON COLLEGIATE BRASS

>   CRD 3444, Walton, Tippett, Britten, Ireland
>   CRD 3434, Elgar, Vaughan Williams, Holst

LONDON GABRIELI BRASS ENSEMBLE

>   Hyperion 66517, *From the Steeples and the Mountains*
>   Hyperion 66470, Nineteenth-Century Brass Music
>   ASV-QS 6013, *Splendor of Baroque Brass*

LONDON SYMPHONY BRASS

>   Collins 13332, *Cathedral Brass*
>   Collins 12882, Copland, Bernstein, Cowell, Barber

MERIDIAN ARTS ENSEMBLE

>   Channel 2191, Lutoslawski, Arutunian, Jan Bach
>   Channel 6594, *Visions of the Renaissance*

MILLAR BRASS ENSEMBLE

>   Koss Classics 1011, *A Chicago Tradition*
>   Delos 3171, *Brass Surround*

PHILLIP JONES BRASS ENSEMBLE

>   London (Serenata) 425 727, *Baroque Brass*
>   London (Weekend Classics) 421 633, Clarke, Susato, Handel, Scheidt
>   Marcophon 928, *Divertimento*
>   Marcophon 929, *Easy Winners*
>   Marcophon 927, *Fanfare*

>   Marcophon 926, *Festive Brass*
>   Claves 600, *In Switzerland*
>   Marcophon 930, *La Battaglia*
>   Claves 8503, *Lollipops*
>   Chandos 6560, *Jubilate: Music for the Kings and Queens of England*
>   Chandos 8490, *PJBE Finale*
>   Marcophon 925, *Music for the Courts of Europe*

SAM PILAFIAN   (tuba ensemble)

>   Angel 54729, Tuba Sextets

PRINCE OF WALES BRASS

>   ASV WHL 2092, *Brass Around the World*
>   ASV WHL 2083, *Christmas Fanfare*

QUATTROMBONI

>   Marcophon 921, Music for Four Trombones

RHEINLAND PHILHARMONIC ORCHESTRA TROMBONE QUARTET

>   Bayer 100234, Music for Four Trombones

SAINT LOUIS BRASS QUINTET

>   Summit 120, *Baroque Brass*

SLOKAR TROMBONE QUARTET

>   Claves 8402, German Baroque Music

STOCKHOLM CHAMBER BRASS

>   Bis 544, *Heavy Metal*
>   Bis 613, *Sounds of St. Petersburg* (Music of Viktor Ewald)

STOCKHOLM PHILHARMONIC BRASS

>   Bis 223, Miscellaneous program

SUMMIT BRASS

>   Summit 127, *American Tribute*
>   Summit 138, *Delights*
>   Summit 115, Music of Hindemith
>   Summit 171, *Paving the Way*
>   Summit 101, Bach, Gabrieli

WESTPHALIAN TROMBONE QUARTET

>   MDG 3295, Miscellaneous

WIENER WALDHORN VEREIN

>   Aricord CDA 29408, *Makart Fanfares*

Brass Bands

BESSES O' TH' BARN

>   Chandos 4529, *Hymns and Things*
>   Chandos 6571, *Around the World*
>   Chandos 4526, *Concertos for Brass* with Ifor James (horn) and John Fletcher (tuba)
>   Chandos (Collect): 6571/72, Miscellaneous

BLACK DYKE MILLS

>   Chandos 8635, *Famous Marches*
>   Chandos 4516, *Celebrate 150 Years*

ASV 2039, *Walton—A Muse of Fire*
Chandos 6565, *World Famous Marches*
Chandos 4524, *The Great British Tradition*

BRITANNIA BUILDING SOCIETY

Doyen 004, *Rule Britannia*
Doyen 021, *Year of the Dragon*

BRITISH BANDSMAN CONCERT

Chandos 4513, Miscellaneous

CWS GLASGOW

Doyen 005, *Flower of Scotland*

GRIMETHORPE COLLIERY

Doyen 015, Miscellaneous
Doyen 013, *A Night at the Opera*

SELLERS ENGINEERING

Chandos 4531, *Legend in Brass*
Chandos 4511, *The World of Brass*

SOVEREIGN SOLOISTS

Doyen 012, Miscellaneous

Historic Brass Performances Recorded Before 1950 (Reissued on Compact Disc)

AUBREY BRAIN

EMI 64198, Mozart Horn Concerto No. 3 (recorded 1940)
EMI Classics CHS 764047, Bach "Brandenburg" Concerto No. 1 (recorded 1935)
EMI Classics CDH64495 and Testament SBT 1001, Brahms Horn Trio (recorded 1933)

HERBERT L. CLARKE

Crystal 450, Cornet Solos (cassette) (recorded 1904–1921)

CORNET SOLOS BY PIONEER AMERICAN RECORDING ARTISTS MADE BEFORE 1906

ITG 004 (International Trumpet Guild), Liberati, Rogers, Levy, Clarke, and others

GEORGE ESKDALE

EMI Classics CHS 764047, First recording (1935) of Bach's "Brandenburg" Concerto No. 2

HARRY GLANTZ, TRUMPET

RCA 09026–60929, Strauss's *Ein Heldenleben* with New York Philharmonic, conducted by Mengelberg (recorded 1928); also included is Strauss's *Don Quixote* conducted by Beecham (recorded 1932)

BRUNO JAENICKE, HORN

RCA 09026–60929, Strauss's *Ein Heldenleben* with New York Philharmonic, conducted by Mengelberg (recorded 1928); also included is Strauss's *Don Quixote*, conducted by Beecham (recorded 1932)

GEORGES MAGER, TRUMPET

RCA 09026–60929, First recording of Strauss's *Also Sprach Zarathustra* with Boston Symphony, conducted by Koussevitzky (recorded 1935)
Pearl Gemm 9487, Prokofiev's *Lt. Kijé* with Boston Symphony, conducted by Koussevitzky (recorded 1937) with Willem Valkenier, horn
Pearl Gemm 9492, Roy Harris's Symphony No. 3 and other American works with Boston Symphony, conducted by Koussevitzky (recorded 1939) with Willem Valkenier, horn
Pearl Gemm 9408, Sibelius's Symphony No. 2 and No. 5 with Boston Symphony, conducted by Koussevitzky (recorded 1935 and 1936)
RCA 09026–61392, First recording of Mussorgsky-Ravel, *Pictures at an Exhibition* with Boston Symphony, conducted by Koussevitzky (recorded 1930); also includes Ravel's *Daphnis et Chloé* (recorded 1944–1945)
Pearl PEA 9090, Debussy's *La Mer* with Boston Symphony, conducted by Koussevitzky (recorded 1938).
RCA 09026–61657–2, Prokofiev's Symphony No. 5 (recorded 1946) and *Romeo and Juliet*, Suite No. 2 (recorded 1945) with Boston Symphony, conducted by Koussevitzky.

ARTHUR PRYOR

Crystal 451, *Trombone Solos with the Sousa Band* (cassette)

KARL STIEGLER, GOTTFRIED VON FREIBERG, HANS BERGER

Pizka 04, *Great Hornists*

APPENDIX C

Sources

Instrument Manufacturers[1]

ADACI: Gerwigstrasse 29, D-7500 Karlsruhe 1, Germany (trumpets)

ALEXANDER: D-55116 Mainz, Bahnhofstrasse 9, Postfach 55001, Germany (horns and tubas)

AMATI: Geneva International Corp., 29 Hintz Rd., Wheeling, IL 60090 (tubas)

AMREIN: Im Gleisdreieck 31, D-23566 Lübeck, Germany (trumpets and trombones)

ANKERL: Haberlgasse 11, 1160 Vienna, Austria (Vienna horns)

B&S: Gewerbepark 13, D-08258 Markneukirchen, Germany

BACH: Box 310, Elkhart, IN 46515–0310 (trumpets and trombones)

BAUMANN: Kampenwandstrasse 83, D-8213 Aschau im Ch., Germany (rotary valve trumpets)

BENGE: United Musical Instruments, P.O. Box 727, Elkhart, IN 46515 (trumpets and trombones)

BERG: General Delivery, Dunster, B.C., Canada V0J 1J0 (horns)

BESSON (see Boosey & Hawkes)

BLACKBURN: 1593 Highway 30 West, Decatur, TN 37322 (trumpets, leadpipes)

BLÄTTLER: Dorfbachstrasse 21, CH-6430, Switzerland (Alphorns)

BLESSING: 1301 W. Beardsley Ave., Elkhart, IN 46514

BOHM & MEINL: Isardamm 133, 82538 Geretsried, Germany (rotary valve trumpets, tubas)

BOOSEY & HAWKES (BESSON):   (U.S.) 1925 Enterprise Ct., P.O. Box 130, Libertyville, IL 60048; (U.K.) Deansbrook Rd., Edgware, Middlesex, England HA8 9BB

BURRI: Morillonstrasse 11, 3007 Bern, Switzerland

CALICCHIO TRUMPETS: 6409 Willoughby Ave., Hollywood, CA 90038

CANADIAN BRASS: N56 W13585 Silver Spring Drive, Menomonee Falls, WI 53051

CALLET: 633 W. 130th St., New York, NY 10027 (trumpets)

ČERVENÝ: (U.S.) Geneva International Corp., 29 E. Hintz Rd., Wheeling, IL 60090 (tubas)

CONN: United Musical Instruments, P.O. Box 727, Elkhart, IN 46515

COUESNON: 37 Ave. d'Essomes, F-02400 Chateau Thierry, France

COURTOIS: P. Gaudet & Cie., rue de Nancy, 75010, Paris, France

DEG MUSIC PRODUCTS: Box 968, Lake Geneva, WI 53147

DE PRINS: Lammekensstraat 60, 2200 Borgerhout, Belgium

DER BLÄSERSPEZIALIST: Grossherzog-Friedrich-Strasse 56, D-6600 Saarbrücken 3, Germany (trumpets)

EGGER: Turnerstrasse 32, CH 4058 Basel, Switzerland

ENGEL: Koppstrasse 94, 1160 Vienna, Austria (Vienna horns)

FINKE: D-4973 Vlotho-Exter, Postfach 2006, Germany (horns, natural trumpets, sackbuts)

GANTER: Manzinger Weg 7, D-81214 Munich, Germany (rotary valve trumpets)

GETZEN CO.:   P.O. Box 440, Elkhorn, WI 53121

GLASSL: Adam-Opel Strasse 12, D-64569 Nauheim, Germany (trombones)

GRONITZ: Haydnstrasse 10, D-22761 Hamburg, Germany (tubas)

HAAG: CH-8280 Kreuzlingen, Kirchstrasse 15, Switzerland (trombones)

HAAGSTON: Summerstrasse 3, A-3350 Austria (rotary valve trumpets)

HECK: Mühlbachstrasse 6, D-97440 Essleben, Germany (trumpets)

---

[1] Most manufacturers produce a range of instruments. Where it is considered helpful, a firm's specialty has been noted.

HETMAN: Musikwerks, Inc., 18 Pettit Ave., South River, NJ 08882 (rotary valve trumpets, lubricants for brass instruments)

HIRSBRUNNER: Dorfgasse 4, CH-3454 Sumiswald, Switzerland; (dist.) Tuba World-Custom Music Co., 1930 Hilton Rd., Ferndale, MI 48220–1923 (tubas, euphoniums)

HOLTON: (LeBlanc) 7001 Leblanc Blvd., Kenosha, WI 53141

HOYER: Orpheus Music, 13814 Lookout Rd., San Antonio, TX 78233 (horns)

JBS: Norbert Böpple, Alter Postweg 27, D-71665 Vaihingen/Enz, Germany

JUPITER: P.O. Box 90249, Austin, TX 78709–0249

KALISON: Via Pelleg. Rossi 98, 1–20 161 Milan, Italy; (U.S.) Tuba Exchange, 1825 Chapel Hill Rd., Durham, NC 27707 (horns, tubas)

KANSTUL: 1332 S. Claudina St., Anaheim, CA 92805 (trumpets)

KING: United Musical Instruments, P.O. Box 727, Elkhart, IN 46515

KRÖGER: Saarstrasse 34, D-54290 Trier, Germany (trumpets)

KROMAT: Bahnhofstrasse 11, D-2733 Wilstedt (rotary valve trumpets and flugelhorns)

KÜHNL & HOYER: Neue Strasse 27, D-91459 Markt Erlbach, Germany (Slokar model trombones)

KÜRNER: A-4632 Pichl 44, Austria (rotary valve trumpets)

KURATH: (U.S.) Tuba World–Custom Music Co., 1930 Hilton Rd., Ferndale, MI 48220–1923 (tubas)

LÄTZSCH: Schmidtstrasse 24, Bremen 28, W. Germany (German trombones, sackbuts)

LAWLER: 118 Middle St. #3, Lake Mary, FL 32746 (trumpets)

LAWSON: P.O. Box 38, Boonsboro, MD 21713 (horns and leadpipes).

LEBLANC CORP.:   7001 Leblanc Blvd., Kenosha, WI 53141

LECHNER: Gaisberggasse 23a, 5500 Bischofshofen, Austria (rotary valve trumpets)

LEWIS ORCHESTRAL HORNS: 1770 W. Berteau Ave., Chicago, IL 60613

MARTIN (see LeBlanc)

RUDOLF MEINL: Blumenstrasse 21, D-8531, Diespeck/Aisch, Germany (tubas)

WENZEL MEINL: Seniweg 4, D-82538 Geretsried, Germany (tubas)

MEINL-WESTON (see Wenzel Meinl) (tubas)

MEISTER ANTON: 5000 Köln 1, Bonner Strasse 90, Germany

MELTON (see Wenzel Meinl) (tubas)

MIRAPHONE: D-84478 Waldkraiburg, Germany; (U.S.) Mirafone Corp., 25570 Rye Canyon Rd., Valencia, CA 01355 (tubas, euphoniums)

MONETTE: 6918 N.E. 79th Court, Portland, OR (trumpets)

MONKE: Körnerstrasse 48–50, D-50823 Köln (Ehrenfeld), Germany (rotary valve trumpets, sackbuts)

MÖNNICH, KARL: Klingenthaler Strasse 55, D-08265 Erlbach/Vogtland, Germany

MUHLER, HANS: 15 Union Ave., Freehold, NJ 07728 (trumpets and trombones)

OLDS: 1181 Rt. 22, Mountainside, NJ 07092

OTTO: D-84494 Neumarkt-St. Veit, Teisingerberg 15, Germany (horns)

PAXMAN: Unit B, Linton House, 164–180 Union St., London, England SE OLH (horns)

PFRETZSCHNER: Der Blechbläser, Freienwalder Strasse 25, Berlin, Germany (German trombones)

RAUCH: Prof. Kohts Vei 77, N-1320, Stabekk, Norway (horns)

SANDERS: (U.S.) Tuba World-Custom Music Co., 1930 Hilton Rd., Ferndale, MI 48220–1923 (tubas)

SCHERZER: Gewerbepark 13, D-08258 Markneukirchen, Germany (rotary valve trumpets)

SCHILKE: 4520 James Pl., Melrose Park, IL 60610–1007 (trumpets)

ENGLEBERT SCHMID: Kohlstattstrasse 8, D-87757 Kirchheim-Tiefenried, Germany (horns)

SELMER CO.:   Box 310, Elkhart, IN 46515–0310

SELMER: 18, rue de la Fontaine-au-Roi, F-75011 Paris, France

STERLING: (dist.) Tuba World–Custom Music Co., 1930 Hilton Rd., Ferndale, MI 48220–1923 (euphoniums)

STOMVI: Honiba, s.a., Antonio Mollé 10, 46920 Mislata, Valencia, Spain (trumpets)

STRAUB: Tettnanger Strasse 31, D-88239 Wangen-Primisweiler, Germany (rotary valve trumpets)

SYHRE: Cöthner Strasse 62a, D-04155 Leipzig, Germany

THEIN: Rembertiring 40, D-28203 Bremen, Germany (trumpets and trombones)

WIENER HORNMANUFAKTUR: Postgasse 13, A-1010 Wien, Austria (Vienna and Kravka horns)

WILLSON: CH-8890 Flums, Switzerland (euphoniums, tubas) (U.S.: DEG Music Products)

YAMAHA: Nippon Gakki Co., 10–1, Nakazawa-cho, Hamamatsu, 433, Japan

YAMAHA (U.S.):   Box 899, Grand Rapids, MI 49512–0899

YAMAHA (U.K.):   Yamaha-Kemble Music Ltd., Sherbourne Drive, Tilbrook, Milton Keynes MK7 8BL England

Historical Instruments

ALEXANDER (natural horns; see above)

EGGER: Turnerstrasse 32, CH-4058 Basel, Switzerland (natural trumpets, horns, sackbuts)

FINKE (natural trumpets, sackbuts; see above).

GLASSL: Adam-Opel Strasse 12, D-64569 Nauheim (sackbuts)

EWALD MEINL: Postfach 1342, D-8192 Geretsried 1, Germany (natural trumpets, horns, sackbuts)

MONKE (sackbuts; see above)

PAXMAN (natural horns; see above)

SERAPHINOFF: 9245 E. Woodview Dr., Bloomington, IN 47401–9143 (natural horns and historical horn mouthpieces)

SYHRE: Cöthner Strasse 62a, D-04155 Leipzig, Germany (natural trumpets and horns)

WEBB: Padbrook, Chaddington Lane, Bincknoll, Wooton Bassett, Wilts. SN4 8QR England (natural trumpets and horns)

Mouthpieces

ALEXANDER (horn mouthpieces; see above)

ANKERL (see above)

BACH (see above)

BENTERFA (mouthpieces made from wood, available from Stomvi; see above)

BRESLMAIR: A-2453 Sommerein, Austria

CURRY: 8665 Spearhead Way, Reno, NV 89506 (trumpet mouthpieces)

DECK: Orpheus Music, 13814 Lookout Rd., San Antonio, TX 78233 (tuba mouthpieces)

DILLON: 325 Fulton St., Woodbridge, NJ 07095 (tuba mouthpieces)

ELLIOTT: 13619 Layhill Rd. Silver Spring, MD 20906 (component mouthpieces for low brass)

GIARDINELLI: 7845 Maltlage Dr., Liverpool, NY 13090

HOUSER: 10 Clyston Circle, R.D. #2, Norristown, PA 19403

JBS: Norbert Böpple, Alter Postweg 27, D-71665 Vaihingen/Enz, Germany

JET-TONE: P.O. Box 1462, Elkhart, IN 46515

JOSEF KLIER (JK):   D-91456 Diespeck, Germany

LAWSON: P.O. Box 38, Boonsboro, MD 21713 (horn mouthpieces)

MARCINKIEWICZ: 126 Graham Place, Burbank, CA 91502

PAXMAN (see above; horn mouthpieces)

PERANTUCCI: Tuba World-Custom Music Co., 1930 Hilton Rd., Ferndale, MI 48220–1923 (tuba mouthpieces)

PURVIANCE (see Reeves)

REEVES: 711 N. Ridgewood Pl., Hollywood, CA 90038 (trumpet mouthpieces)

SANDERS: 952 124th Ave., Shelbyville, MI

SCHILKE (see above)

WERNER CHR. SCHMIDT: Zimmerlohstrasse 4, D-08258 Markneukirchen

SERAPHINOFF (historical horn mouthpieces; see above)

STOMVI (component mouthpieces; see above)

STORK: Rt. 2, Box 1818, Maple Hill Rd., Plainfield, VT 05667

TILZ: Pfaffenbühl 4, Postfach 1745, D-91413 Neustadt/Aisch, Germany

TRU-VU (transparent mouthpieces):   Ellis Music, 510–1333 Hornby St., Vancouver, BC V6Z 2C1, Canada (component mouthpieces)

WARBURTON: P.O. Box 5279, Orlando, FL 32855

WICK (see Boosey & Hawkes, above)

Brass Music

There are over 500 publishers who offer music for brass, many of them specializing in this area. A comprehensive list of publishers may be found in the *Brass Players' Guide,* available from Robert King Music Sales, 140 Main St., North Easton, MA 02356. In addition to the latter, the following firms can supply brass music of many publishers.

BROAD RIVER PRESS: P.O. Box 50329, Columbia, SC 29250

HICKEY'S MUSIC CENTER: 104 Adams St., Ithaca, NY 14850 (trombone music)

MAGNAMUSIC-BATON: 10370 Page Industrial Blvd., Saint Louis, MO 63132

THE MUSIC MART: 3301 Carlisle, N.E., Albuquerque, NM 87110

PURDY'S BRASS CONNECTION: P.O. Box 18862, Raleigh, NC 27619 (brass band music and recordings)

SHEET MUSIC SERVICE OF PORTLAND: 34 N.W. 8th Ave., Portland, OR 97209–3591; 800–452–1133

STANTON'S SHEET MUSIC: 100 E. Main St., Columbus, OH 43215

TAP MUSIC SALES: R.R. #1, Box 186, Newton, IA 50208; 800–554–0352 (brass recordings)

WARD MUSIC LTD.:   412 W. Hastings St., Vancouver, B.C. V6B 1L3

Periodicals

BRASS BULLETIN: CH-1630 Bulle, Switzerland

THE BRITISH BANDSMAN: The Old House, 64 London End, Beaconsfield, Bucks. HP9 2JD England

THE HORN CALL: Ellen Powley, Exec. Sect., 2220 N. 1400 E., Provo, UT 84604

THE HORN MAGAZINE: The British Horn Society, Freepost WC 4386, Epsom, Surrey KT19 OBR, England

THE INSTRUMENTALIST: 200 Northfield Rd., Northfield, IL 60093

INTERNATIONAL TROMBONE ASSOCIATION JOURNAL: Vern Kagarice, ed., Box 5336, Denton, TX 76203

INTERNATIONAL TRUMPET GUILD JOURNAL: Bryan Goff, ed., School of Music, Florida State University., Tallahassee, FL 32306–2098

T.U.B.A. JOURNAL: Steven Bryant, treas., Dept. of Music, University of Texas at Austin 78712–1208

Fingering/Position Charts

Trumpet / Cornet

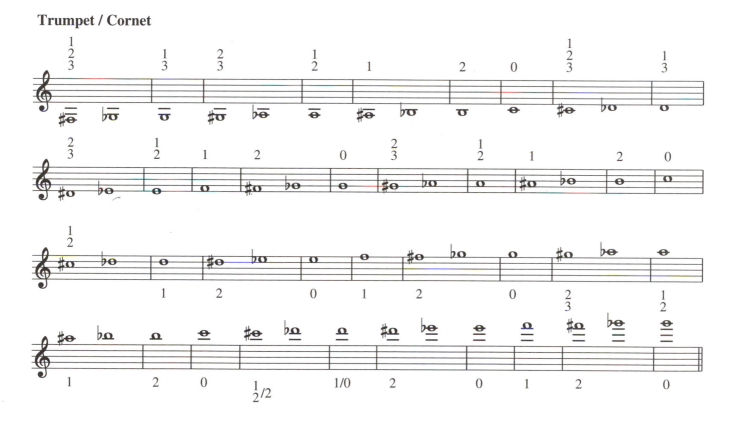

Single F horn

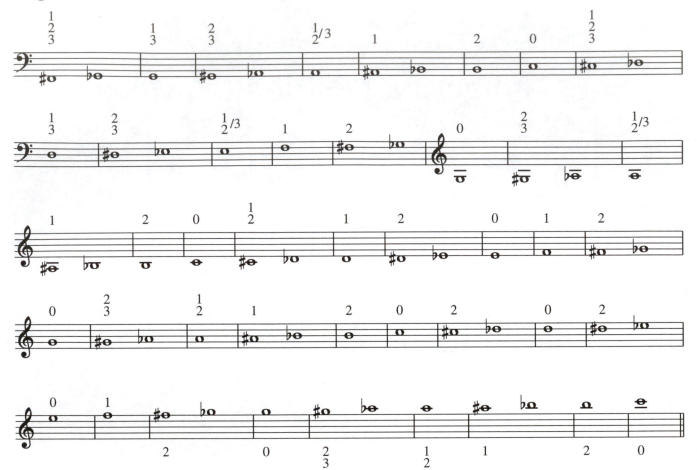

Single B♭ horn

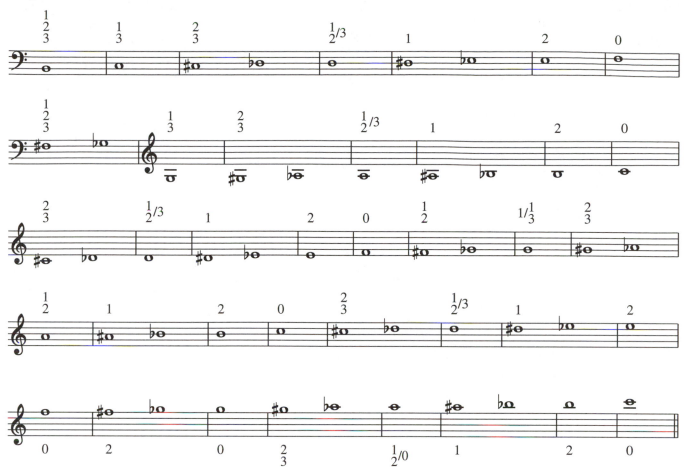

F/B♭ double horn
(pedal tones on B♭ side)

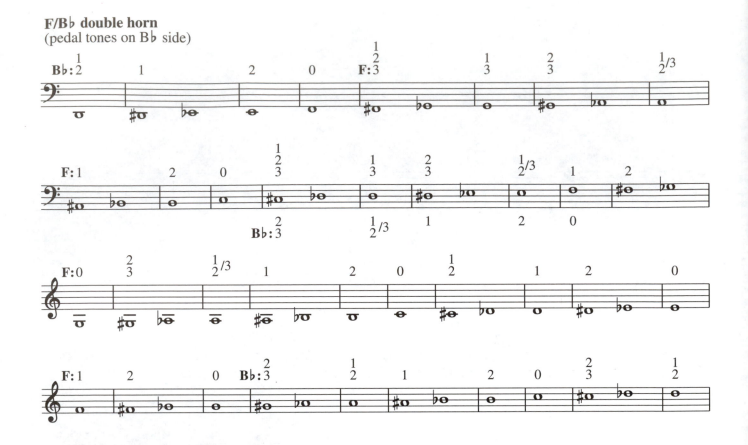

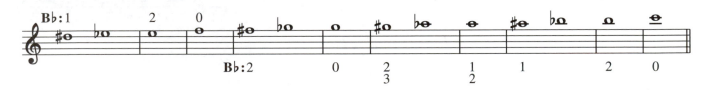

Trombone with F attachment

B♭ pedal tones

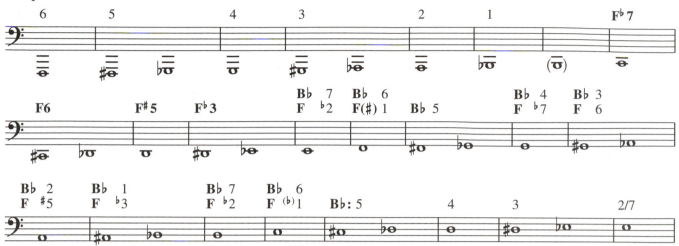

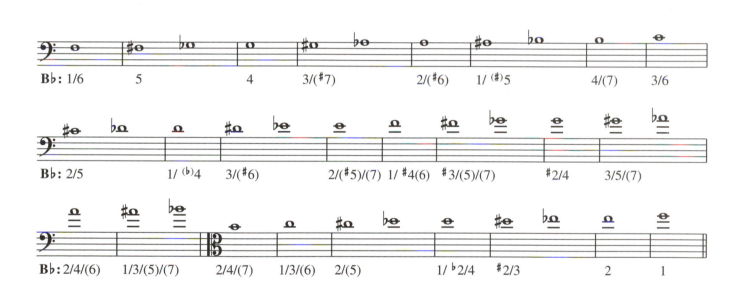

Euphonium ¹

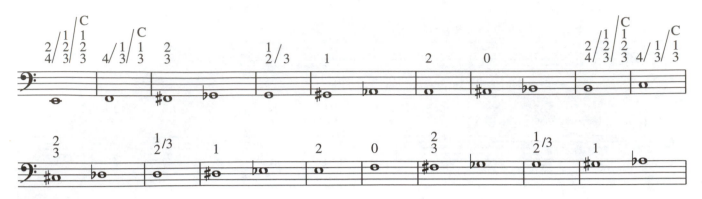

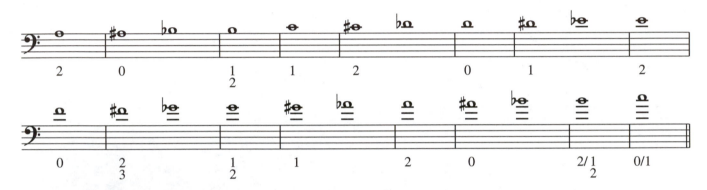

1 Where they differ, fingerings are shown in the following order: four valve uncompensated euphonium; three valve; four valve compensating euphonium.
The letter C indicates that the fourth compensating valve should be depressed.

To facilitate intonation, valve slides of the fingerings circled should be pulled outward.

ex. ①
2 = pull 1st valve slide outward.
4

When a valve slide is to be pushed inward, an arrow is added to the circle.

ex. 1
3 = push 4th valve slide inward.
④↑

Four - valve BB♭ tuba

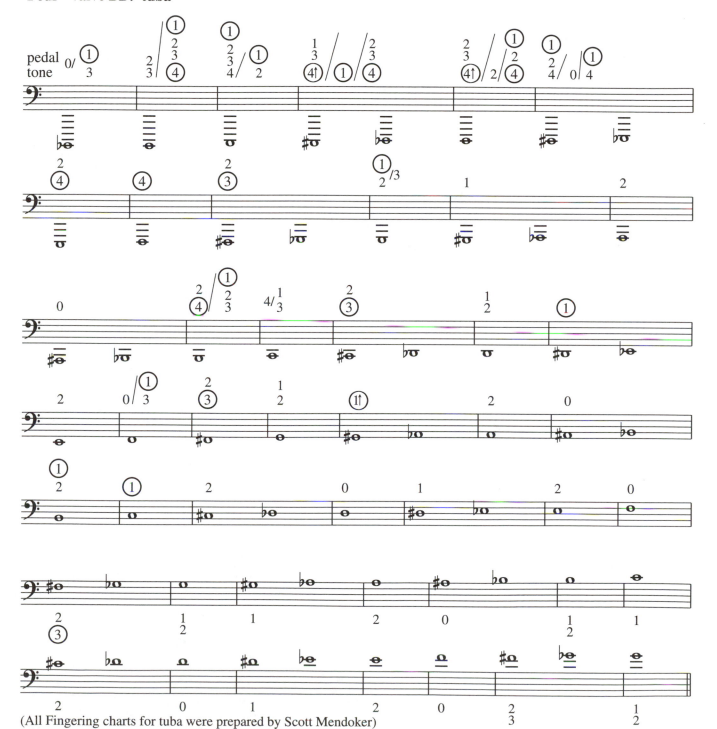

(All Fingering charts for tuba were prepared by Scott Mendoker)

Five - valve CC tuba   (5th valve lowers fundamental 5 - quarters of a tone: "flat whole step system")

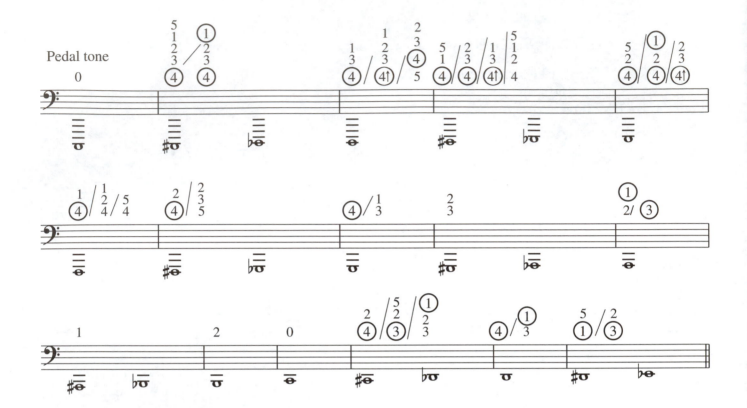

Five-valve CC tuba (5th valve lowers fundamental two whole steps: 2/3 system)

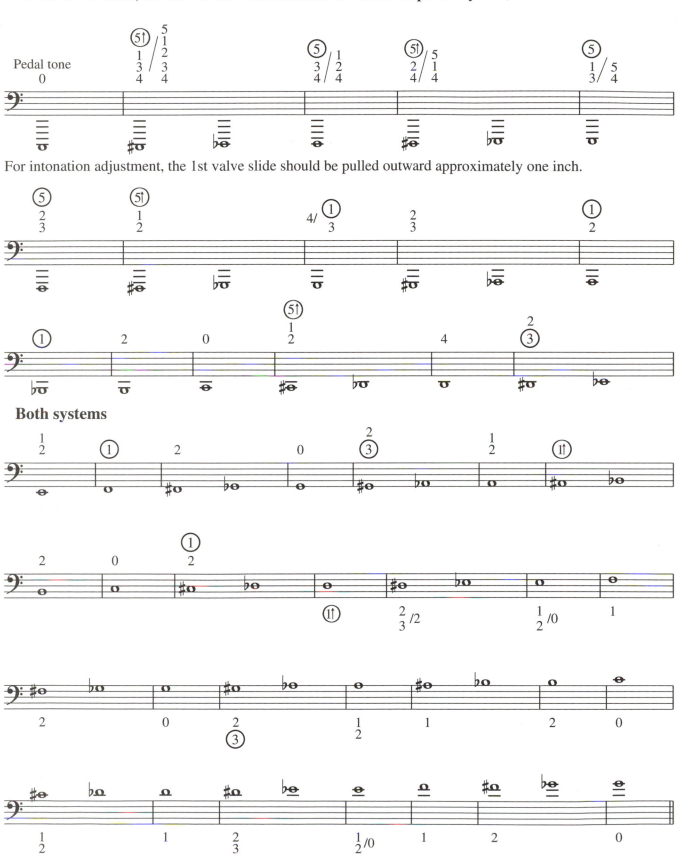

For intonation adjustment, the 1st valve slide should be pulled outward approximately one inch.

Both systems

Four-valve EE♭ tuba

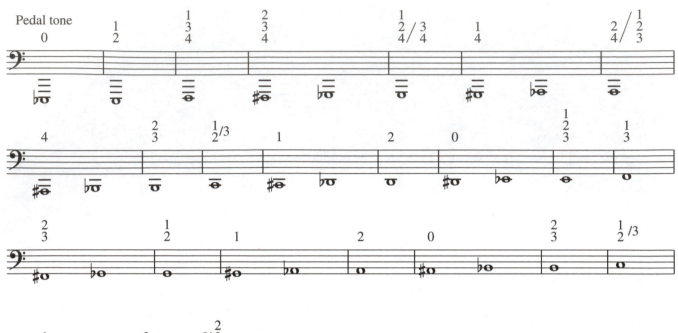

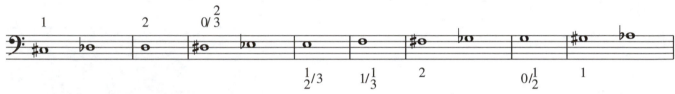

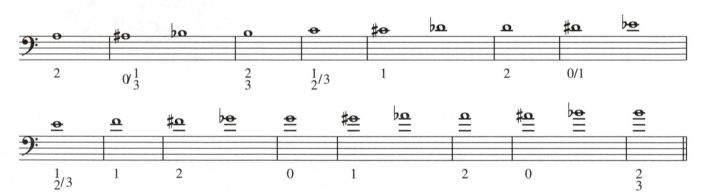

Five-valve F tuba / " 2/3 system"

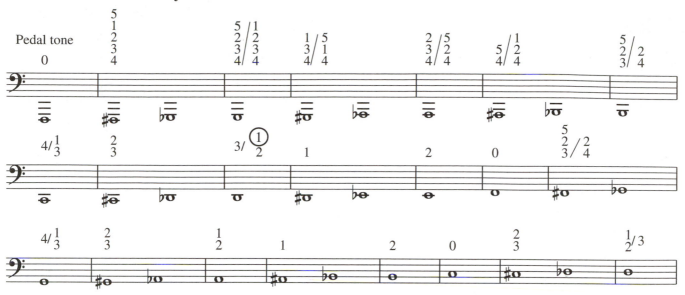

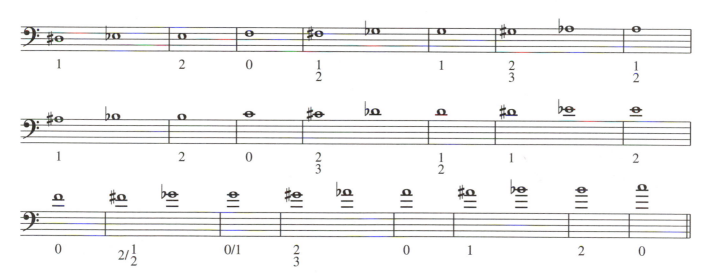

For intonation adjustment, the fifth valve slide should be pulled outward approximately 3 inches.

Five-valve F tuba (5th valve lowers fundamental 5 - quarters of a tone)

Harmonic Fingering Chart

Common fingerings are shown as whole notes.

Harmonic Fingering Chart

Common fingerings are shown as whole notes.

Harmonic Fingering Chart

Common fingerings are shown as whole notes.

Harmonic Fingering Chart

Common fingerings/positions are as shown as whole notes.

Trombone or 3-valve baritone

Harmonic Fingering Chart

Common fingerings are shown as whole notes.

Bibliography

Books

ALTENBURG, JOHANN ERNST. *Trumpeters' and Kettledrummers' Art.* Trans. by Edward H. Tarr. Nashville, Tenn.: The Brass Press, 1974.

ANDERSON, PAUL G. *Brass Solo and Study Material Music Guide.* Evanston, Ill.: The Instrumentalist Co., 1976.

ARLING, HARRY J. *Trombone Chamber Music: An Annotated Bibliography.* Nashville, Tenn.: The Brass Press, 1983.

BACH, VINCENT. *The Art of Trumpet Playing.* Elkhart, Ind.: Vincent Bach Corporation, 1969.

BACH, VINCENT. *Embouchure and Mouthpiece Manual.* Elkhart, Ind.: Vincent Bach Corporation, 1956.

BACKUS, JOHN. *The Acoustical Foundations of Music.* 2nd ed. New York: Norton, 1977.

BAINES, ANTHONY. *Brass Instruments: Their History and Development.* London: Faber & Faber, 1976.

BAKER, DAVID. *Contemporary Techniques for the Trombone.* 2 vols. New York: Charles Colin, 1974.

BARBOUR, J. MURRAY. *Trumpets, Horns, and Music.* East Lansing: Michigan State University Press, 1964.

BATE, PHILIP. *The Trumpet and Trombone: An Outline of Their History, Development, and Construction.* 2nd ed. London: Ernest Benn, Ltd., 1978. New York: Norton, 1978.

BELL, WILLIAM. *Encyclopedia of Literature for the Tuba.* New York: Charles Colin, 1967.

BELLAMAH, JOSEPH L. *Brass Facts.* San Antonio, Tex.: Southern Music Co., 1961.

BENADE, ARTHUR H. *Fundamentals of Musical Acoustics.* New York: Oxford University Press, 1976.

BENDINELLI, CESARE. *The Entire Art of Trumpet Playing, 1614.* Nashville: The Brass Press, 1975.

BEVAN, CLIFFORD. *The Tuba Family.* New York: Scribner's, 1978.

BOWMAN, BRIAN L. *Practical Hints on Playing the Baritone (Euphonium).* Melville, N.Y.: Belwin-Mills, 1983.

Brass Anthology. Evanston, Ill.: The Instrumentalist Co., 1984.

BROWN, MERRILL E. *Teaching the Successful High School Brass Section.* West Nyack, N.Y.: Parker Publishing Co., 1981.

BRÜCHLE, BERNHARD. *Horn Bibliographie.* (3 vols.) Wilhelmshaven: Heinrichshofen's Verlag, 1970.

BRÜCHLE, BERNHARD, and KURT JANETZKY. *Kulturgeschichte des Horns.* Tutzing: Hans Schneider, 1976.

BUSH, IRVING. *Artistic Trumpet Technique and Study.* Hollywood: Highland Music Co., 1962.

BUSHOUSE, DAVID. *Practical Hints on Playing the Horn.* Melville, N.Y.: Belwin-Mills, 1983.

CARSE, ADAM. *Musical Wind Instruments.* London: Macmillan, 1940. Reprint: Da Capo Press, 1965.

CLARKE, HERBERT L.   *How I Became a Cornetist.* Kenosha, Wis.: Leblanc Educational Publications, n.d.

COAR, BIRCHARD.   *A Critical Study of the Nineteenth-Century Horn Virtuosi in France.* DeKalb, Ill.: Coar, 1952.

COAR, BIRCHARD.   *The French Horn.* DeKalb, Ill.: Coar, 1947.

COUSINS, FARQUHARSON.   *On Playing the Horn.* London: Samski Press (Distributed by Paxman Musical Instruments), 1983.

CUMMINGS, BARTON.   *The Contemporary Tuba.* New London, Conn.: Whaling Music Publishers, 1984.

DAHLQVIST, REINE.   *The Keyed Trumpet and its Greatest Virtuoso, Anton Weidinger.* Nashville: The Brass Press, 1975.

DALE, DELBERT A.   *Trumpet Technique.* London: Oxford University Press, 1967.

D'ATH, NORMAN W.   *Cornet Playing.* London: Boosey & Hawkes, 1960.

DAVIDSON, LOUIS.   *Trumpet Techniques.* Rochester: Wind Music, Inc., 1970.

DEMPSTER, STUART.   *The Modern Trombone.* Berkeley: University of California Press, 1979.

DEVOL, JOHN.   *Brass Music for the Church.* Plainview, N.Y.: Harold Branch, 1974.

DRAPER, F. C.   *Notes on the Besson System of Automatic Compensation of Valved Brass Wind Instruments.* Edgware, England: Besson and Co., 1953.

EICHBORN, HERMANN.   *The Old Art of Clarino Playing on Trumpets.* Trans. by Bryan A. Simms. Denver, Colo.: Tromba Publications, 1976.

ELIASON, ROBERT E.   *Early American Brass Makers.* Nashville, Tenn.: The Brass Press, 1981.

ENDSLEY, GERALD.   *Comparative Mouthpiece Guide for Trumpet.* Denver, Colo.: Tromba Publications, 1980.

ENRICO, EUGENE.   *The Orchestra at San Petronio in the Baroque Era.* Washington, D. C.: Smithsonian Institution Press, 1976.

EVERETT, THOMAS G.   *Annotated Guide to Bass Trombone Literature.* Nashville, Tenn.: The Brass Press, 1978.

FANTINI, GIROLAMO.   *Modo per imparare a sonare di Tromba: A Modern Edition of Girolamo Fantini's Trumpet Method.* Boulder, Colo.: Empire Printing Co., 1977.

FARKAS, PHILIP.   *The Art of Brass Playing.* Rochester, N.Y.: Wind Music, 1962.

————.   *The Art of Horn Playing.* Evanston, Ill.: Summy-Birchard, 1956.

————.   *The Art of Musicianship.* Bloomington, Ind.: Musical Publications, 1976.

————.   *A Photographic Study of 40 Virtuoso Horn Players' Embouchures.* Rochester, N.Y.: Wind Music, 1970.

FINK, REGINALD H.   *The Trombonist's Handbook.* Athens, Ohio: Accura Music, 1977.

FISCHER, HENRY GEORGE.   *The Renaissance Sackbut and its Use Today.* New York: Metropolitan Museum of Art, 1984.

FITZPATRICK, HORACE.   *The Horn and Horn-Playing and the Austro-Bohemian Tradition 1680–1830.* London: Oxford University Press, 1970.

FOSTER, ROBERT E.   *Practical Hints on Playing the Trumpet/Cornet.* Melville, N.Y.: Belwin-Mills, 1983.

FOX, FRED.   *Essentials of Brass Playing.* Pittsburgh, Pa.: Volkwein Bros., 1974.

GREGORY, ROBIN.   *The Horn.* London: Faber & Faber, 1969.

GREGORY, ROBIN: *The Trombone.* New York: Faber & Faber, 1973.

GRIFFITHS, JOHN R.   *The Low Brass Guide.* Hackensack, N.J.: Jerona Music Corp., 1980.

HILL, DOUGLAS.   *Extended Techniques for the Horn.* Hialeah, Fla.: Columbia Pictures Publications, 1983.

HANSON, FAY.   *Brass Playing*. New York: Carl Fischer, Inc., 1975.

HERNON, MICHAEL.   *French Horn Discography*. New York: Greenwood Press, 1986.

JANETZKY, KURT, AND BERNHARD BRÜCHLE.   *The Horn*. Portland, Oreg.: Amadeus Press, 1988.

JOHNSON, KEITH.   *The Art of Trumpet Playing*. Ames: Iowa State University Press, 1981.

KAGARICE, VERN L.   *Annotated Guide to Trombone Solos with Band and Orchestra*. Lebanon, Ind.: Studio P/R, 1974.

KAGARICE, VERN L., et al.   *Solos for the Student Trombonist: An Annotated Bibliography*. Nashville, Tenn.: The Brass Press, 1979.

KLEINHAMMER, EDWARD.   *The Art of Trombone Playing*. Evanston, Ill.: Summy-Birchard Company, 1963.

KNAUB, DONALD.   *Trombone Teaching Techniques*. 2nd ed. Athens, Ohio: Accura Music, 1977.

LAWRENCE, IAN.   *Brass in Your School*. London: Oxford University Press, 1975.

LAWSON BRASS INSTRUMENTS.   *French Horn Mouthpieces: Material and Design*. Boonsboro, Md: Lawson, 1990.

LAWSON, WALTER A.   *Development of New Mouthpipes for the French Horn*. Boonsboro, Md.: Lawson, n.d.

LITTLE, DONALD C.   *Practical Hints on Playing the Tuba*. Melville, N.Y.: Belwin-Mills, 1984.

LOUDER, EARLE L.   *Euphonium Music Guide*. Evanston, Ill.: The Instrumentalist Co., 1978.

LOWREY, ALVIN.   *Trumpet Discography*. Denver: National Trumpet Symposium, n.d.

MACDONALD, DONNA.   *The Odyssey of the Philip Jones Brass Ensemble*. Moudon, Switzerland: Éditions BIM, 1986.

MASON, J. KENT.   *The Tuba Handbook*. Toronto: Sonante Publications, 1977.

MATHIE, GORDON.   *The Trumpet Teacher's Guide*. Cincinnati, Ohio: Queen City Brass Publications, 1984.

MECKNA, MICHAEL.   *Twentieth-Century Brass Soloists*. Westport, Conn.: Greenwood Press, 1994.

MENDE, EMILIE.   *Pictorial Family Tree of Brass Instruments in Europe Since the Early Middle Ages*. Moudon, Switzerland: Éditions BIM, 1978.

MEREWETHER, RICHARD.   *The horn, the horn. . . .* London: Paxman Musical Instruments, 1979.

MORLEY-PEGGE, REGINALD.   *The French Horn*. London: Ernest Benn, 1973.

MORRIS, R. WINSTON.   *Tuba Music Guide*. Evanston, Ill.: The Instrumentalist Co., 1973.

Musique pour Trompette.   2nd ed. Paris: Alphonse Leduc, n.d.

NAYLOR, TOM L.   *The Trumpet and Trombone in Graphic Arts, 1500–1800*. Nashville, Tenn.: The Brass Press, 1979.

PIZKA, HANS.   *Hornisten-Lexikon/Dictionary for Hornists 1986*. Kirchheim b. München: Hans Pizka Edition, 1986.

PETTITT, STEPHEN.   *Dennis Brain*. London: Robert Hale, 1976.

PHILLIPS, HARVEY, AND WILLIAM WINKLE.   *The Art of Tuba and Euphonium Playing*. Secaucus, N.J.: Summy-Birchard, 1992.

PORTER, MAURICE M.   *The Embouchure*. London: Boosey & Hawkes, 1967.

PRICHARD, PAUL, ed.   *The Business: The Essential Guide to Starting and Surviving as a Professional Hornplayer*. Surrey, England: Open Press Books, 1992.

RASMUSSEN, MARY.   *A Teacher's Guide to the Literature for Brass Instruments*. Durham, N.H.: Brass Quarterly, 1968.

ROSE, W. H.   *Studio Class Manual for Tuba and Euphonium*. Houston, Tex.: Iola Publications, 1980.

SCHULLER, GUNTHER.   *Horn Technique*. London: Oxford University Press, 1971.

SEVERSON, PAUL, AND MARK McDUNN.   *Brass Wind Artistry*. Athens, Ohio: Accura Music, 1983.

SHERMAN, ROGER.   *The Trumpeter's Handbook*. Athens, Ohio: Accura Music, 1979.

SKEI, ALLEN B.   *Woodwind, Brass, and Percussion Instruments of the Orchestra: A Bibliographic Guide.* New York: Garland Publishing, 1985.

SMITHERS, DON.   *The Music and History of the Baroque Trumpet Before 1721.* London: J.M. Dent, 1973.

Solos for the Student Trombonist. Nashville, Tenn.: The Brass Press, 1979.

STEWART, DEE.   *Arnold Jacobs: The Legacy of a Master.* Northfield, Ill.: The Instrumentalist Co., 1987.

STEWART, DEE.   *Philip Farkas: The Legacy of a Master.* Northfield, Ill.: The Instrumentalist Co., 1990.

TARR, EDWARD.   *The Trumpet.* Portland, Oreg.: Amadeus Press, 1988.

TAYLOR, ARTHUR R.   *Brass Bands.* London: Granada Publishing, Ltd., 1979.

THÉVET, LUCIEN.   *Méthode Complète de Cor.* Paris: Alphonse Leduc, 1960.

TUCKWELL, BARRY.   *Horn.* New York: Schirmer Books, 1983.

TUCKWELL, BARRY.   *Playing the Horn.* London: Oxford University Press, 1978.

VAUGHAN WILLIAMS, RALPH.   *The Making of Music.* Ithaca, N.Y.: Cornell University Press, 1955.

WATSON, J. PERRY.   *The Care and Feeding of a Community British Brass Band.* Farmingdale, New York: Boosey & Hawkes, n.d.

WATSON, J. PERRY.   *Starting a British Brass Band.* Grand Rapids, Mich.: Yamaha International Corporation, 1984.

WEAST, ROBERT.   *Keys to Natural Performance for Brass Players.* Des Moines, Iowa: The Brass World, 1979.

WEBSTER, GERALD.   *Piccolo Trumpet Method.* Nashville, Tenn.: The Brass Press, 1980.

WEKRE, FRØYDIS REE.   *Thoughts on Playing the Horn Well.* Oslo: Frøydis Ree Wekre, 1994.

WICK, DENIS.   *Trombone Technique.* London: Oxford University Press, 1975.

WIGNESS, C. ROBERT.   *The Soloistic Use of the Trombone in Eighteenth-Century Vienna.* Nashville, Tenn.: The Brass Press, 1978.

WILKINS, WAYNE.   *The Index of French Horn Music.* Magnolia, Ark.: Music Register, 1978.

WINTER, DENIS.   *Euphonium Music Guide.* New London, Conn.: Whaling Music Publishers, 1983.

YANCICH, MILAN.   *A Practical Guide to French Horn Playing.* Rochester, N.Y.: Wind Music, 1971.

Articles

AGRELL, JEFFREY.   "An Indexed Bibliography of Periodical Articles on the Horn," *The Horn Call,* 6, no. 2 (May 1976), pp. 51–54; 7, no. 1 (Nov. 1976), pp. 45–51; 7, no. 2 (May 1977), pp. 49–55.

ANDERSON, STEPHEN C.   "The Alto Trombone, Then and Now," *The Instrumentalist* (Nov. 1985), pp. 54–62.

BENADE, ARTHUR H.   "The Physics of Brasses" *Scientific American* (July 1973), pp. 24–35.

CAZALET, ANDRÉ.   "The Horn, the Brasses and France," *Brass Bulletin,* 81 (1993), pp. 48–55.

CICHOWICZ, VINCENT.   "Teaching the Concepts of Trumpet Playing," *The Instrumentalist* (Jan. 1996), pp. 27–31.

ČIŽEK, BOHUSLAV.   "Josef Kail (1795–1871)" (Part Two), *Brass Bulletin,* 74 (1991), pp. 24–29.

DROSTE, PAUL.   "Begged, Borrowed, and Stolen Solo Euphonium Literature," *The Instrumentalist* (May 1981), pp. 30–32.

EVERETT, THOMAS G.   "Solo Literature for the Bass Trombone," in *Brass Anthology.* Evanston, Ill.: The Instrumentalist Co., 1976, pp. 587–590.

HEYDE, HERBERT.   "Zur Frühgeschichte der Ventile und Ventilinstrumente in Deutschland (1814–1833)," *Brass Bulletin,* 24 (1978), pp. 9–33; 25 (1979), pp. 41–50; 26 (1979), pp. 69–82; 27 (1979), pp. 51–59. (Translations in English and French are included.)

LOUDER, EARLE L.   "Original Solo Literature and Study Books for Euphonium," *The Instrumentalist* (May 1981), pp. 29–30.

ROBERTS, B. LEE.   "Some Comments on the Physics of the Horn and Right Hand Technique," *The Horn Call*, 6, no. 2 (May 1976), pp. 41–45.

SMITHERS, DON, KLAUS WOGRAM, AND JOHN BOWSHER.   "Playing the Baroque Trumpet," *Scientific American* (April 1986), pp. 108–115.

THÉVET, LUCIEN.   "On the French School of Horn Playing," *Brass Bulletin,* 84 (1993), pp. 54–61.

TURRENTINE, EDGAR M.   "The Physiological Aspect of Brasswind Performance Technique: A Bibliographic Essay," *NACWPI Journal,* 26, no. 2 (Nov. 1977), pp. 3–5.

WERDEN, DAVID R.   "Euphonium Mouthpieces—A Teacher's Guide," *The Instrumentalist* (May 1981), pp. 23–26.

YEO, DOUGLAS.   "The Bass Trombone: Innovations on a Misunderstood Instrument," *The Instrumentalist* (Nov. 1985), pp. 22–28.

ZECHMEISTER, GERHARD.   "Die Entwicklung der Wiener Konzerttuba," *Brass Bulletin*, 75 (1991), pp. 44–47. (Translations in English and French are included.)

Dissertations

BECK, FREDERICK ALLAN.   "The Flugelhorn: Its History and Literature." D.M.A. thesis, University of Rochester, 1979. UM 79–21,124.

CARNOVALE, AUGUST N.   "A Comprehensive Performance Project in Trumpet Literature with an Essay on Published Music Composed Since ca. 1900 for Solo Trumpet Accompanied by Orchestra." D.M.A. thesis, University of Iowa, 1973. UM 74–16, 703.

CHESEBRO, GAYLE M.   "An Annotated List of Original Works for Horn Alone and for Horn with One Other Non-Keyboard Instrument." D.M.A. thesis, Indiana University, 1976.

HYATT, JACK H.   "The Soprano and Piccolo Trumpets: Their History, Literature, and a Tutor." D.M.A. thesis, Boston University, 1974. UM 74–20, 473.

KEAYS, JAMES HARVEY.   "An Investigation into the Origins of the Wagner Tuba." D.M.A. thesis, University of Illinois, 1977. UM 78–4044.

RANDOLPH, DAVID MARK.   "New Techniques in the Avant-Garde Repertoire for Solo Tuba." D.M.A. thesis, University of Rochester, 1978. UM 78–11,493.

SCHUMACHER, STANLEY E.   "An Analytical Study of Published Unaccompanied Solo Literature for Brass Instruments." Ph.D. dissertation, Ohio State University, 1976. UM 77–2497.

SENFF, THOMAS E.   "An Annotated Bibliography of the Unaccompanied Solo Repertoire for Trombone." D.M.A. thesis, University of Illinois, 1976. UM 76–16,919.

SMITH, DAVID.   "Trombone Technique in the Early Seventeenth Century." D.M.A. thesis, Stanford University, 1981.

SMITH, NICHOLAS EDWARD.   "The Horn Mute: An Acoustical and Historical Study." D.M.A. thesis, University of Rochester, 1980. UM 80–19,070.

SORENSON, RICHARD A.   "Tuba Pedagogy: A Study of Selected Method Books, 1840–1911." Ph.D. dissertation, University of Colorado, 1972. UM 73–1832.

TRUSHEIM, WILLIAM H..   "Mental Imagery and Musical Performance: An Inquiry into Imagery Use by Eminent Orchestral Brass Players." Ed.D. dissertation, Rutgers University, 1987.

WHALEY, DAVID R.   "The Microtonal Capability of the Horn." D.M.A. thesis, University of Illinois, 1975. UM 76–7010.

Index